## DATE DUE

| | | | |
|---|---|---|---|
| 6-19-96 | | | |
| | | | |
| | | | |
| | | | |
| | | | |
| | | | |
| | | | |
| | | | |
| | | | |
| | | | |
| | | | |
| | | | |
| | | | |

# TALKED TO DEATH

# TALKED *TO* DEATH

—

## *THE LIFE AND MURDER OF ALAN BERG*

—

Stephen Singular

BটB
BEECH TREE BOOKS
WILLIAM MORROW
*New York*

Library of Congress Cataloging-in-Publication Data

Singular, Stephen.
Talked to death.
1. Berg, Alan.   2. Radio broadcasters—United States—
Biography.   3. Fascism—United States.   I. Title.
PN1991.4.B4S56   1987   791.44'092'4 [B]      86-22250
ISBN 0-688-06154-0

Printed in the United States of America

First Edition

1 2 3 4 5 6 7 8 9 10

BOOK DESIGN BY RICHARD ORIOLO

*to my mother and father*

The radio is in the hands of such a lot of fools,
trying to anesthetize the way that you feel.

Elvis Costello, "Radio, Radio"

# CONTENTS

7

# Contents

*EPITAPH*

PART ONE

—

# GOING HOME

—

# 1

## *LYING IN WAIT*

---

Alan Berg was on the way home to feed the shaggy Airedale that shared his Denver townhouse. On the air Berg liked to say that Fred was the one steady love of his life, the creature he turned to when another relationship with a woman had failed or when someone approached him in a restaurant and said how much they disliked what he did for a living. Berg and the Airedale not only got along well, they also resembled one another. At six feet two and 150 pounds, Berg looked as if he were held together by wire instead of bones. He wore longish gray hair, a full whitish beard over his pockmarked face, and thick, eyebrow-level bangs. Many people believed that the surplus of hair was to cover his face, which he often made fun of on the radio. The bangs were hiding surgical scars. Berg had recently turned fifty but he looked both older and younger than his age. His movements were sudden, electric, adolescent in their energy. Lithium, a psychiatrist once told him, would make him calm. Berg's eyes were ancient, wary, with deep, wrinkled sockets. Something in his face drew one in so far it made one glance away.

He flicked cigarette ashes on his checkered sport coat, brushed them aside. Five minutes earlier he had dropped off his ex-wife, Judith Lee Berg, at a parking lot in Denver's fashionable Cherry Creek shopping center. She was in town from Chicago for her parents' fiftieth wedding anniversary. Since arriving on Thursday, she had seen Berg once, traded a number of phone calls with him, and on Sunday, the seventeenth of June, she had gone to his empty apartment and stuck a hand crayoned note ("I was here") into the crack in his front door. On the one occasion when they had met, he'd given her a necklace with a pendant of a woman's face in profile. The woman looked like Judith. The gift, Berg had said, was for emotional support during the upcoming weekend, with its anniversary festivities, its homecoming strain, and its demands on Judith to play the role of the dutiful daughter, something she had never particularly enjoyed. Her weekend in Denver, he had told her, could be rough.

Six years of divorce—the legal separation came in 1978—had done little to alter their relationship. It was still complicated and intense, a web of binding and volatile feelings. Some of their friends said the two of them got along better since the divorce. Others claimed they were utterly mismatched, always had been, two high-strung people who could never settle into anything like a working marriage. "I was born on March eighth, I'm a Pisces, and a very confused fish," Judith occasionally joked. "I love her," Berg often said of his ex-wife. "I love her as much as the day we married. But . . ." As a young woman Judith had been beautiful, dark-haired and dark-eyed and full-lipped, with an appearance of abundant health. That was thirty years ago, back when she was an aspiring dancer and actress in New York. Now she was thinner, more pared and vibrant, as if she were trying to imitate her husband. "I can't make love to Judy anymore," Berg told his friends. "We'd start a fire."

He was usually talking about marriage with someone, and the subject had come up between him and Judith this evening at dinner. They might want to consider remarrying—wasn't that the intelligent and right thing to do?—or perhaps he would marry his current girlfriend, a dental technician in Denver named Linda McVey. A thirty-eight-year-old blonde with long, curling hair and a sunburst smile, Linda was as quiet and shy as Judith was outgoing and verbally nimble. Hadn't the relationship with Judith failed after all these years? Wouldn't it make more sense to start a new life with this younger woman? In the past two months he had made a decision of sorts, when he updated a $100,000 life-insurance policy. He did what he had always done before, and made his ex-wife his beneficiary.

He and Judith had dined at the Jefferson 440 in Lakewood, a western suburb of Denver. Berg didn't care for the restaurant but its management had recently purchased advertising spots on his radio talk show and he felt obligated to stop by and chat with the owner, who never arrived. That annoyed Berg, left him moody and nervous. Besides having Judith in town and thinking about his future as a bachelor, he was involved in contractual discussions with KOA radio, his employer, and also concerned about the latest ratings, which would be published in three days. Had he beaten Peter Boyles, his morning talk-show rival at KNUS, or fallen behind in their head-to-head competition? Radio personalities, Berg knew from experience, were judged and fired according to their numbers. Even though he consistently had among the highest ratings in his market, he often anticipated the worst. What if the numbers were bad this time? How would management react to that? How would it affect his plan to ask KOA for more money?

Judith ordered sole, Berg a Reuben sandwich, which he picked at. Cigarettes and caffeine were the staples of his diet: three packs of filterless Pall Malls and fifty cups of coffee a day. Over the meal he mentioned his desire to collect all his tapes and papers in one place, perhaps a library, and they also talked about his program that morning. Berg had begun the show by quoting some recent comments of Pope John Paul II, delivered during a visit to Switzerland. Christian values, the pontiff had declared, were shaken when two people have sex only for "immediate and selfish pleasure, in the absence of definite commitment to the person of one's partner and the children born of the union." The notion of sex without pleasure intrigued Berg and he had decided, while having breakfast at Gyros Place, his favorite haunt on Colfax Avenue, to find a Catholic official in Denver who would enlarge upon the pope's remarks during this morning's program. Berg's producer, Susan Reimann, quickly began making calls but none of the local Catholic figureheads wanted to take up the challenge. Undaunted, Berg chose another tack: He opened the show by asking men in the listening audience to phone in and tell him if they were capable of having sex without pleasure.

"That's a physical impossibility," one man said.

"The pope don't know what he's talking about," stated a woman caller.

"Does it say anywhere in the Bible that you couldn't have pleasure while you're having sex?" Berg asked her.

"It depends on who you're with," the lady answered.

As the morning moved along, Berg criticized Father's Day, just past, because he felt that men didn't receive the pampering women did on Mother's Day. This stirred more protest, especially from female callers, but it was generally good-natured and humorous, Berg never displaying the side of himself that had provoked, fascinated, and enraged radio audiences in the Rocky Mountain West throughout the past decade. "What's happened to you?" a caller said to Berg during the show. "You've changed so much I can't believe it. I used to hear you on the radio and I'd turn you off . . . you're mellow."

"I'm the same guy I've always been," Berg said, a trifle defensively.

Later in the program Berg interviewed Colorado's governor, Richard Lamm, about an article the politician had written for *Play-*

*boy* magazine, and then, just before leaving the air, he spoke with Denver's U.S. representative, Patricia Schroeder, about the need for secrecy in handling government documents. When Berg said he was looking forward to seeing Schroeder at the Democratic National Convention in San Francisco in July, his voice betrayed his enthusiasm. The convention was only weeks away and KOA, the most powerful and prestigious radio station in the region (its nighttime signal was capable of reaching thirty-eight states), was sending him to California to cover the event. The assignment was a tremendous vote of confidence for Berg. In years past his behavior had often made his employers nervous, or downright afraid, even as his high ratings were making them money. His on-the-air antics had gotten him suspended from his job, fired, had brought bomb scares to the various stations where he worked and threats of personal violence to him. In 1979 a radio listener named Fred Wilkins had burst into the studio of KWBZ and told Berg that he was going to die. Berg reported to the audience that the intruder had pointed a gun at him, but Wilkins, who quickly fled and was then arrested and charged with felony menacing, claimed that Berg had only said that to raise his ratings. Wilkins, a local head of the Ku Klux Klan, was temporarily suspended from his job as a suburban fireman.

Berg himself now acknowledged that he had once been a wild man of the airwaves, blithely insulting people who called his show, cutting them off by pushing a button on the telephone, and sending forth his opinions, abrasiveness, and irreverence with little concern for its effect on the audience. From his perspective the results had been largely positive: In those days he had attained the highest ratings ever given a talk-show host in Denver. People seemed to need his outlandish performances, his monologues on the joys and dangers of oral sex, his merciless diatribes on the flaws of the Christian religion, his verbal riffs on why whites were afraid of blacks and how white women fantasized about sleeping with black men. "Sordidly pathetic" was how one local critic described Berg. His favorite program, which he presented each summer, was called *The Suntan Show*, and it had something to offend everyone. He delighted in putting forward the notion that whites spent so much time sunbathing because they secretly wanted to be black. Listeners always howled—with laughter or racial indignation. *The Suntan Show* would have been good material for a hipster comedian in a big city nightclub, but Berg's audience was AM-radio mainstream, overwhelmingly white, Christian, and middlebrow, comprised of housewives, shut-ins, working stiffs on the night shift, idle or lonely listeners, everyone within the sound of his nasal, insistent voice.

Over the years the Federal Communications Commission had received a regular flow of letters requesting that the agency take Berg off the air. They came most often from Colorado and adjacent states, except in those periods when he was on at night and his signal could reach farther and outrage more-distant listeners. Freedom of speech, the FCC would point out while answering these requests, was not illegal in the United States. As long as the First Amendment was intact and Berg avoided using obscenities, there was little the federal government could do to satisfy their complaints. Berg was almost never profane, at least not in his use of language. Obscenity was more likely to come from angry callers to his show. KGMC, the first station he had worked for, couldn't afford a tape-delay machine, which creates a seven-second gap between what the caller says and when it is broadcast. The device prevents a number of illegal words from hitting the air. Early listeners to his show were occasionally treated to an incensed caller telling the host to do something unnatural with himself. Yet for every person who loathed Berg's program, there was another who was enthralled with it. In the late 1970s a contest was held in Denver to determine who was the most liked and who was the most disliked media personality in town. Berg won both awards.

Those days of uncontrolled fury and belligerence were more or less behind him. He was now something different from the West's Last Angry Man. His program ideas were proof of that: the efforts to hook up, via his talk show, those who were out of work with prospective employers; his group therapy program, in which four callers were put on the air at once and encouraged to psychoanalyze each other simultaneously; his calling up the bosses of sheepish employees and seeking raises for them; his interviews with political figures and authors, although when writers came through Denver on book tours, he tore up the standard question sheet they provided for him and asked them about something other than their work; his lengthy discussions on countless social issues. He would still burn the ears of any caller—black or white, male or female, Jew or Gentile—who displayed the slightest vibrations of bigotry, but he was also more willing to listen now, more interested in exploring and expanding the possibilities of talk radio. For the past thirteen years he had sat behind a studio microphone and talked to strangers, absorbing their words, keeping them company, making them laugh, pushing them this way and that with his incessant staccato chatter, moving people to call him, to argue, to threaten, to talk back, to feel. And it was starting to gain him some real recognition. This past January he had been featured on CBS television's prize-winning program *60 Minutes*, and now he was going to the Democratic National Convention. At the age of fifty, in spite of his own terrible misgivings about his talent and his lifelong self-destructive habits, he was clearly making a name for himself in his chosen profession.

By the time he and Judith left the Jefferson 440, they were discussing the subject of tomorrow's show: gun control. Berg was a fierce supporter of controlling firearms and Judith not only shared his views but was well informed on the issue. On the ride back into Denver Berg told his ex-wife that if no one interesting called the show, he wanted her to phone KOA and ask some leading questions. They'd played this game on the air before and it usually worked; no one had ever guessed it was Judith calling. He felt better having a back-up support system like her; she was an asset in his radio career. That was another consideration in having her return to Denver to live—and in marrying her again.

As the black Volkswagen rolled toward downtown she told him not to worry, for she would be listening and would do whatever she could to help. Several blocks from his apartment Berg parked at a 7-Eleven store and bought dog food for Fred, bubble gum for Judith, and shaving cream for himself. He planned to stop by his Congress Park townhouse and feed the Airedale, then he and Judith would drive on to southeast Denver to visit some longtime friends. From the 7-Eleven he guided the car east toward Colfax Avenue,

17

a gathering of lights in the distance, the busiest street in Denver. On the avenue they passed an unruly combination of fast-food businesses, night people, prostitutes, cars full of cruising teenagers, and the Bluebird pornography theater at the corner of Colfax and Adams Street. It was a warm, late-spring evening, and as Berg turned right onto Adams only a faint breeze was stirring the maple leaves overhanging the narrow street, lined with cars on both sides. He said he was tired. It was only a few minutes after 9:00 but he had to get up at 7:00, as he did every working morning, and prepare himself for tomorrow's 9:00 A.M. show. Perhaps he should just go home and to bed.

They passed several large brick homes on Adams before he slowed the VW and came to a stop in front of number 1445, his townhouse looming on the right. The three-story structure, recessed from Adams by a wide, well-lit driveway, had white metal hand railings crawling up both sides of it and white circulation pipes, round and large and decorative, rising above the roof. The modern-looking building, constructed of wooden siding, jutted up at strange angles. Berg had looked for months to find the townhouse; for security reasons, he'd wanted to live on the top floor of his next apartment. A burning lightbulb threw shadows against the garage door, behind which were his two expensive and exotic cars. He rarely drove the Bricklin or the DeLorean. Berg didn't want to call attention to himself, at least not when he was off the air.

"Do you mind if I take you to your car and just come back home?" he said over the idling of the Volkswagen.

Judith reminded him that they were going to call his mother in Chicago this evening. Ruth Berg was seventy-five and her husband had died within the past eighteen months. She lived alone in a high-rise apartment in a neighborhood in Hyde Park, her front window giving onto Lake Michigan. Berg was always promising to stay in closer touch with her and with his sister, Norma, who also lived in Chicago.

"We can do that tomorrow," he said. "After the show. I don't want you to drive to Bobbe's house alone tonight. It's too dark and too late."

She laughed. "Alan, please. I'm not twenty-nine anymore. Take me to my car. I'll be fine."

The VW stayed in neutral as they discussed their options; like Judith, Berg wasn't known for his decision-making abilities. In one form or another, they'd spent the past thirty-three years trying to reach a conclusion about their relationship. If he didn't go with Judith this evening, he would worry about her making the drive by herself. If he went, he most likely wouldn't enjoy himself very much. If they both went into his apartment to feed Fred, the dog would become excited and create a ruckus in Berg's living room. The place was messy enough without that. Above all, Berg really was tired. He had spent last night with Linda McVey and tonight it might feel better to be alone. There was so much to think about: his future, Linda, Judith, KOA, gun control, Fred, his mother.

"I'll be fine by myself," she told him again.

He glanced at her, hesitated, put the car in gear, and slowly pulled away from his address. Driving toward the shopping center where her car was parked, Berg told her to get some sleep tonight, and told her again to call his show tomorrow or call right after the program ended and let him know how it had gone. Finally, as soon as she reached Bobbe Cook's this evening, she was to phone and let him know she had arrived safely, so he could relax and get some rest himself. At the Cherry Creek parking lot, Berg hugged and kissed her, then pointed the direction for her to exit toward Bobbe's. He got back into the VW and drove over the dark quiet streets to Congress Park, lighting another smoke. Pulling into his driveway and parking next to a white pickup, he turned off the engine, dragged on the cigarette, picked up the 7-Eleven bag, and stepped from the Volkswagen.

Round after round of gunfire hit him in the chest, cheeks, and neck, bullets spraying his torso and splintering the garage door behind him. He fell onto the pavement, face upward, his long upper body stretched out in a pool of blood, his right leg still inside the car, a hand gripping the paper bag, the cigarette still on fire.

Several minutes later, Susan Allen, one of the residents of 1445 Adams, called her boyfriend and said she was concerned. She had heard a peculiar sound, like a chain being rattled outside her apartment, or perhaps it was only kids setting off fireworks down the block; the Fourth of July was two weeks away. Would he mind coming over to take a look? Charles McDowell lived nearby; within minutes he had arrived at the driveway and found the body. His initial thought was to get the man some help, but, as he later recalled, "I realized he didn't need any help."

Nina Orton and Diane Brookshire were the first police officers to answer the call at 1445 Adams, soon followed by Patrick Phelan. The three of them cordoned off the area and assisted with the ambulance, which had pulled up in front of the townhouse at 9:39. Six minutes later Berg was pronounced dead. Newspaper, television, and radio reporters immediately came to the scene and began writing and broadcasting that the most notorious media figure in the history of the city and region had just been murdered.

Judith had made the trip to Bobbe Cook's without difficulty and called Berg as planned. His line was busy—a simultaneous call had triggered his answering machine—so she couldn't leave a message. Before she tried the number again, the phone rang in Bobbe's kitchen, a call from Lily Halpern, Judith's mother. Mrs. Halpern told Bobbe the news and Bobbe, after several moments' deliberation, relayed the words to her friend. The two women went into the living room, Judith sat on a chair and stared at the picture on the television screen—the image of her ex-husband lifeless on the driveway, his checkered sport coat next to the pond of blood. She saw the bag, imagined the dog food and shaving cream within, saw his huge opened hands. As she slid off the chair and into hysteria, Judith wondered if he had hurt his skull when he hit the pavement or if it hurt now. Within an hour she had been taken to a police station for questioning.

At KOA in downtown Denver, Ken Hamblin was conducting his own talk show when a news reporter, Rick Barber, walked into the studio at 10:10 P.M., sat down behind a microphone, and said, "It's been confirmed by the Denver Police Department that Alan Berg has been shot." He paused. "It has also been confirmed that Alan Berg is dead."

Hamblin stared at Barber, then gazed at the live microphone near his lips and began to cry. "I guess I'm not network material," he said into the mike, sobbing again. When he had regained his composure, he addressed both the audience and the killer, whom he was certain was listening. "I wish it were a damn hoax. I wish it was a damn publicity stunt, but it's not. . . . I can feel your presence out there. You're a loser. If Alan Berg was anything before you blew him away, you have made him an immortal. . . . Alan used to always say, 'They're out there, but you can't worry about them. You can never know where the nuts are going to come from, so you live day to day.' "

Some of Berg's friends, who had gathered at his driveway to stare at the empty Volkswagen and the patch of concrete where the body had lain, were asked to come downtown for police interviews. One of them, Al Zinn, an attorney in Denver, put through a call to Chicago to tell Berg's sister, Norma Sacks, what had happened. Norma and her husband, Martin, also resided in a high-rise near Lake Michigan, about a block from where Ruth Berg lived. The Sackses didn't know what to do. Should they call Mrs. Berg immediately or wait until morning or go over now and tell her in person? Would it be national news—something she might hear on a morning radio or TV program? Norma and Martin called a friend in New York to seek her advice. The murder wouldn't, the woman assured them, command national media attention, so they might as well wait until morning. The Sackses agreed. Five minutes later the woman phoned back to say that she had just heard the story on her radio—it was already breaking nationally—and they should tell Ruth Berg at once.

It was well after midnight when Norma called her mother and said that Martin had a medical emergency in his family and had to fly to New York City the first thing tomorrow. He was low on cash; could he walk over to borrow some money? She said yes, that would be fine, but thought it odd when Norma said she was coming with him. While waiting for them to arrive, Mrs. Berg flipped on a radio—she enjoyed talk-show programs—and tuned in WGN's Eddie Schwartz, a late-night host in Chicago. Briefly, she went into the kitchen of her small apartment, and when she returned to the bedroom Schwartz was telling the audience about the murder of Alan Berg. Ruth called her daughter, who was just leaving the apartment, and did something uncharacteristic: She yelled at her for not telling the truth. "It wasn't too pretty" was how Mrs. Berg described the rest of that night.

By morning the largest investigation in the history of the Denver Police Department was under way. Sixty officers were put on the case, and a new computer program was soon created in the department's data bank to hold the information the detectives were generating, the first time such a strategy had ever been necessary. Don Mulnix, the detective-division chief, came under instant criticism for assigning so many of his employees to work this one crime. Mulnix was prepared for such talk, maintaining that the killing was out of the ordinary and demanded more manpower and unusual procedures. "Clearly," he said, "whoever did this was sending a message to the public about Alan Berg, about his conduct, perhaps about his ethnic background." The murder appeared to have been done with extraordinary efficiency and viciousness—he was shot repeatedly at a range of five to eight feet—and the bullets used and the spent shell casings at the scene indicated a fairly rare automatic or semiautomatic weapon, rather than a more usual rifle, shotgun, or pistol. Perhaps a silencer had been attached to the firearm. The execution had all the signs of a political assassination, something that, to Chief Mulnix's knowledge, had never occurred before in the city of Denver.

By themselves these conditions would have made the murder important and complex enough to justify the "major case squad" Mulnix put together on Tuesday morning, the nineteenth of June. But there was one other factor that was going to make it an even larger and more complicated investigation. On Tuesday the chief was asked by a reporter if there were any suspects in the case. Mulnix shrugged and glanced at a nearby phone book. "There are at least two million suspects," he said. "Anybody within the sound of his voice might have had a motive for killing him."

# 2

## THE HEART OF A CITY

Normally, Ken Hamblin's talk show ended at midnight, but as June 18 passed into June 19, he didn't leave the studio. He sat in KOA's new offices in downtown Denver and took incoming calls from those who had just learned of the crime. They were angry calls, stunned calls, weeping calls, calls from people in shock, a spontaneous tribute to the slain man that went on after Hamblin gave way to Kathy Bradshaw and continued right through dawn. It was the beginning of a weeklong wake, conducted on the air and off; on Thursday Denver commuters drove home from work with their lights on dim and on Sunday afternoon a memorial service was held at Temple Emanuel synagogue, drawing nearly two thousand mourners. Corporate executives who had known Berg via the radio attended the service and so did the local bag ladies.

Denver's sudden and heartfelt reaction to the death could not have been predicted. For years Berg had called himself "the man you love to hate" and many people did indeed loathe him, or at best dismissed him as a rude nonentity. There was simply no accounting for whom he would charm or offend; his appeal or lack of it cut across racial, sexual, educational, political, religious, age, and class lines. Having a good sense of humor was no guarantee that one would approve of him. Many people who talked with reverence of the legendarily profane and abrasive comedian Lenny Bruce found Berg intolerable. He offended many people but most offended those who saw the world largely in terms of morality: good versus evil, liberal versus conservative, right versus wrong. Berg's radio personality and humor began where conventional morality stopped.

The depth of the response to his murder may also have been caused by the geographical location of his audience. Along with Phoenix, Arizona, Denver is the most radio-saturated city in the United States. Thirty-nine signals can be picked up locally, which is considerably more than in, say, New York or Los Angeles. Most big-city markets are penetrated by signals from surrounding areas. Denver—at least in the daytime, when radio waves travel shorter distances—sits alone at the far edge of the Great Plains, farm country and range spreading in three directions from downtown, the Rocky Mountains rising to the west. Driving east from Denver, one travels six hundred miles before reaching the first real urban center of Kansas City. To the south is Colorado Springs and Santa Fe, but it's more than four hundred miles to Albuquerque, New Mexico. To the west is Salt Lake City, well over five hundred miles across peaks and forest, canyon and desert. Cheyenne, Wyoming, a mere one hundred miles to the north, is a town of only fifty thousand people and in no sense a media rival of Denver. Flying into Denver from virtually any direction, one is struck by the openness of the countryside and how little mark human beings have made on the landscape, by how lonely and barren those spaces appear to be. The feeling of isolation contributes to the popularity of radio, especially at night. Eight-hour drives are commonplace when going from Montana to Utah, or Nevada to Colorado, or Wyoming to Kansas. Without a radio, the road can seem unbearably empty and long. The land dominates the West: its beauty, its harshness, its endless stretches that cannot really be exploited by agriculture or mining, and its frequent bad weather. People often appear transient here, secondary, an accident in the region. If radio in general is an attempt to link people over distances, to keep them in touch and communicating, then talk radio is even more so. The desire to connect, to find humor and meaning, becomes that much stronger when the people are fewer and the natural elements are great. Roughly 5 percent of the American population live in the Mountain Time Zone and radio keeps some of them from driving off the road.

"Good morning, Denver," Ken Hamblin said at nine o'clock sharp on Tuesday, the moment his dead colleague should have taken the air. "It's a bright sunny morning, the sky is blue and it's crisp. And life goes on. For Alan Berg, welcome to KOA. Turn your radio up, wipe your tears, and knock it off. If Berg were here, he'd be having the biggest laugh of all."

In spite of considerable conflict, Hamblin and Berg had lately become friends. Hamblin's show had once followed the older man's, and it had long annoyed Hamblin—who is black, outspoken, has a constant pained look in his eyes, and is a virulent nonsmoker—that Berg always left the studio in disarray, scattered with cigarette butts, ashes, and coffee stains. On occasion the two men had negotiated this point at the top of their lungs in the halls of KOA. After Berg told Hamblin that he was an angry young man and needed psychiatric help, and Hamblin had analyzed Berg, this odd couple learned to exist at the same radio station, and then to like one another. When the two of them appeared on the air together, Berg referred to the duo as "Sidney and the Schvartz." The black man usually laughed.

Throughout the morning, as Hamblin continued the tribute to his friend, Berg's Airedale, Fred, could be seen walking the halls of KOA. He looked lost, confused, and eerily like his dead master. When he came into view, some of the station's employees began to weep. A number of people called Hamblin and offered to adopt the dog—Berg had talked of him incessantly on the air—but all were refused. As Fred wandered through KOA, he encountered a lot of activity. The station's thirteenth-floor lobby was crowded with messengers delivering flowers, with police detectives strolling the halls and asking questions of radio personnel, with reporters interviewing the detectives. TV crews shot footage of the activity, cluttering the offices with cameras, lights, and electronic gear. Some of Berg's friends, professional acquaintances, and radio competitors had assembled at the station to cover his 9 A.M. to 1 P.M. slot, which Hamblin had dubbed *The Last Alan Berg Show* (the program on gun control had been dropped). *The Last Alan Berg Show* was filled with tapes of his voice from shows past, with speculation about who had killed him, with calls from across America expressing sympathy, calls from radio and TV stations in Canada and Australia. Psychics throughout the United States phoned to say who shot Alan Berg.

Talk-show hosts around the country, some of whom were as acidic as Berg, generally said the murder would not affect them at all. "Even if it turns out it was a listener [who killed him]," said Bob Grant of WMCA in New York, "I'd still want to go for the ratings. I don't like going into the ring with one hand tied behind my back. Privately, I wish [management] would turn me loose, because I could get the ratings, and I'm inclined to go for the ratings at virtually any expense."

"My objective is to get people to open up," said Steve Kane of WNWS in Miami, who had appeared on the recent *60 Minutes* program with Berg. "I deal a lot with provoking people's feelings —not just anger. But when I'm ripping somebody up, people are laughing."

"Berg was controversial for the sake of controversy," said Lou Crone, Kane's station manager and boss. "Kane believes in what he says. He doesn't just do it for effect. We're not going to ask him to change his style." He paused. "We are being a little more cautious. We lock the doors at night."

Don Imus, another radio personality in New York, indicated

that Alan Berg's act couldn't have been very successful or interesting; he was, after all, performing it in Denver. Among well-
known sharp-tongued talk-show hosts, only Gary D. Gilbert was
sobered by the killing. In early 1984, Gilbert, also featured on *60
Minutes*, had a four-year, $1 million contract with WPKX in Wash-
ington, D.C. At that time Gary D. was a true screamer, taunting
listeners with remarks like "Come on down here, you lily-livered,
yellow-bellied, egg-sucking dog, bed-wetter, pinko commie." After
Berg's execution Gilbert said that he might be more subdued on
the air in the future, adding that when his show was receiving its
greatest response, he got death threats every day.

All day Tuesday cars drove past Berg's townhouse, a parade of
curiosity and grief. Yellow roses were stuck in the bullet holes in
his garage door. Pink roses were strewn on the driveway. Attached
to the garage were two messages:
"Allan Berg We love ya May you rest in peace P.S. Lord take
care of him Love—"
"Dearest Alan, Thanks for helping me to grow—for being a
friend. Rest in peace."
A young blind man was led to the door, where he placed his
finger in one of the holes. "What a waste," he said. "You can have
all the intelligence in the world and have it wiped out in half a
second like that."
Reporters for *The Denver Post* and the *Rocky Mountain News* canvassed the city throughout Tuesday and uncovered a mixture of
emotions:
"When I first started listening to him, I thought, What a narrow-
minded creep the guy is. As time went by . . . I thought what a
narrow-minded creep I am. He's had a tremendous amount of
influence in my life."
"I wasn't surprised by his death, not at all. Not the way he
treated some of the people on the phone. He was more or less asking
for it."
"When he was on, I was always talking back to the radio, arguing
with him. I was never quiet, or alone."
"I think he really felt for people and their causes. I think a lot

of it was put on, when he used to get really irate and upset with people."

"Did you hear about the Alan Berg Happy Hour? Take a can of dog food to the bar and you get the first twelve shots free."

"He made me angry, but he made me look inside to see why. I was usually angry with myself."

"He was able to manipulate people into saying what they really wanted to say. That can be dangerous."

Soon after the news was broadcast Monday night, a man called *The Denver Post* and suggested that some fireworks, left over from Father's Day festivities at Mile High Stadium, be set off to celebrate Berg's demise.

While trying to make up its mind about Alan Berg, the town dwelled on the other questions: Who had killed him? Who could have hated him that much? Was it connected to his radio show or his personal life? The more the press dug up about his past, the wider was the range of theories:

Berg was once a lawyer for the Mafia, back in Chicago. I heard him say that on the air. The mob came to Denver and paid him off for something he'd done to them. . . . He hadn't practiced law for seventeen years. I read that in the papers. And his involvement with the underworld wasn't quite what he said it was. He made some of that stuff up. . . . It was drugs. Cocaine, I think. There were all kinds of narcotics in his apartment. . . . He had some disease. Those drugs were legal. . . . I heard he was a gambler. Jews like to gamble. He owed some debts he couldn't cover and got on the wrong side of the wrong people. It was probably all because of that drug habit. . . . It was a woman. He used to date this black lady, and her other boyfriend, who's also black, didn't appreciate that, especially after some of the remarks Berg made about her on the radio. . . . But he had a fight with a white woman in front of his house just a few days before. She must have taken all she could from him and said no more. . . . He offended black people with some of the things he talked about on the air. He said, "I like blacks. Everybody should own one." . . . That was a joke. Didn't you hear him talk about jazz and growing up around blacks in Chicago and how much he liked that? . . . That was a lie. He also told people that his mother was Irish and she was as Irish as Golda Meir. He had problems with being Jewish so he lied. . . . Colonel Khadafy of Libya killed him. Berg visited Israel in 1983—he talked about it all the time on the radio—and afterward he was more sympathetic to that country than in the past. Khadafy got wind of this and sent an assassin to Denver to shut him up. . . . That's insane. . . . It's not. Last year Khadafy was involved in a murder attempt on a student up at Colorado State University in Fort Collins. The student was speaking out on the campus about creating democracy in his homeland. An American soldier of fortune was hired to kill him but he just wounded the guy. They didn't wound Berg. . . . Maybe the Jews killed him. I heard him once on the radio interviewing Meir Kahane, the leader of the Jewish Defense League, and Berg ripped him apart. He turned Kahane's ideas upside down and showed him where he was wrong. He made him think. I couldn't stand Berg myself, but he did have guts. . . . It was a Christian. Religious fanatics were always calling Berg and telling him they were praying for his soul. One guy found his car in a parking lot and taped Bibles all over it. He probably did it. . . . I heard Berg call God once on his program. He got a busy signal. . . . Some nut killed him. One twisted person with a gun. Like the guy who shot John Lennon—Mark David Chapman. . . . Chapman was caught at the scene. Those guys usually stick around for the publicity. Berg's killer was more professional, more ruthless. He really knew what he was doing. . . . It was the Klan. Remember when Fred Wilkins ran into the studio and told Berg he was going to die? He finally came back and kept his promise. . . . It was Peter Boyles, the talk-show host at KNUS. He and Berg used to be buddies when they both worked at KOA but then they started competing with one another and Berg was winning in the ratings. Those figures just came out and he was ahead. It drove Boyles wild. . . . Peter Boyles was his best friend. That's what he's been saying in the papers and on the air all week long. Boyles is the main speaker at the memorial service on Sunday. He loved Alan Berg. . . . One deranged listener did it. One guy who hated Berg and held a grudge. That's all it takes to pull the trigger. . . .

On Tuesday morning, when Chief Mulnix first assembled his major-case squad, he called in detectives from the homicide bureau, lawyers from the district attorney's office, crime-lab specialists, the intelligence bureau, the metro unit, vice and drug-control experts, and in time several officers from the Colorado Bureau of Investigation. Without recovering the murder weapon itself, Chief Mulnix said, it was unlikely they would ever know for certain what had killed Berg. Since the bullets taken from the corpse hinted at the use of an illegal weapon—early reports indicated a .45-caliber fully automatic MAC-10 machine pistol—Mulnix contacted the Bureau of Alcohol, Tobacco and Firearms to look into who sold or owned such guns locally. The chief also hoped that the reward money—twenty thousand dollars from KOA and its former sister TV station KCNC—would help turn up an important lead. Following the initial meeting, some detectives began calling authorities in Chicago to look into Berg's past affiliation with the Mafia. Vice and drug officers thoroughly searched his apartment and car for narcotics, then checked out his gambling habits. Mulnix insisted that his staff collect all the available tapes of Berg's radio shows; some came from KOA and others were retrieved from the slain man's apartment. The station kept past shows for a month or two in case they had to be referred to for legal reasons. That was still a lot of tape.

"We had a sergeant on the night shift and we tortured him, if you will, by making him sit down and listen to all the shows we could find," explained the chief, a bespectacled man with a moustache and patient eyes. "He really didn't find anything significant. Most people never identify themselves on talk radio."

When the investigation began, the handwritten note discovered at Berg's front door—"I was here"—appeared to be a clue. Then Judith told the police she had left it. Linda McVey said that while Berg had never told her anything specific, she sensed that he had been receiving death threats very recently. Both of the women were so distraught they could barely function; nothing about either of them aroused any suspicion at the police station. For the rest of the week detectives canvassed Berg's neighborhood, fanning out in a circle that comprised a number of blocks, interviewing hundreds of people, knocking on some doors three or four times as they returned to ask, once again, if the inhabitants had noticed anything unusual about 9:30 the previous Monday night. One young man living next to 1445 Adams was listening to music when Berg was shot. Originally he told the police that he'd heard a woman scream "Stop!" or "No!" at that time, but later acknowledged that his stereo had been turned up high and the sounds were on the album. A young woman residing nearby recalled hearing gunfire at exactly the right time, but when asked why she hadn't phoned the police, no answer was forthcoming. Another woman said she'd seen a car speeding away from the scene but she didn't have a license number or a description of the vehicle. Before long the detectives were reaching a solid conclusion: Berg had been executed on a narrow illuminated street on a warm June evening, half a block from the most active strip of pavement in Denver, yet no one had seen a thing connected with his death. Or perhaps someone had. A third woman, who out of fear demanded anonymity, had driven up and down the 1400 block of Adams Street around nine o'clock Monday evening. Twice she went past a dark-colored sedan parked across from Berg's townhouse and both times she noticed two men sitting in the car. They were relatively young, wearing business suits— odd attire for that time and place, she thought—and were driving a full-sized automobile, which struck her as the kind of car rarely seen in the neighborhood. Each time she'd gone by, the men were talking and staring at number 1445, as if they were expecting some- one to come out of the building.

This was the best news Chief Mulnix received all week long. By Friday he had learned that Berg's Mafia connections were at the most of a minor nature and at the least flights of a wild imagination. Drugs found in the body by the Denver coroner and those found in Berg's apartment by detectives were strictly of the prescribed kind: Dilantin for epileptic seizures, phenobarbital for relaxation and sleep, and Serax as an antidepressant. At various times in his life Berg had been a baseball fan and a hockey aficionado but those who knew him well admitted that he had neither the gambling temperament nor the interest to bet on athletic events. They could also have said that while he had made a number of women angry enough to hit him, he wasn't drawn to homicidal females.

Every day people called the police and told them about an acquaintance who had wanted to kill Alan Berg, or about someone who owned a MAC-10 and was trigger-happy, or about someone who was overjoyed because the talk-show host was dead. The tips led nowhere. The day after the murder a man brought his brother to the station, where the latter told detectives that he had been out walking the night before and had seen the homicide, the assassin, and the getaway car. The vehicle was moving toward Colfax, the man said, when the murderer stuck a gun through the window and pointed it at him.

"He described the killer as a black male," Chief Mulnix said. "He had a license number and his story was very plausible."

The license plate belonged to a black man who worked at the *Rocky Mountain News*. Detectives brought him in, searched his home for the weapon, and gave him a polygraph test, which revealed him to be innocent. Within another day or two the police learned that the man who had fingered him was an alcoholic who had wandered past 1445 Adams soon after Berg was shot. The next morning, while riding across town with his brother and explaining how he'd witnessed the killing, he spotted a car with a black male driver and took down his license number. Eventually the accuser was sent to Denver General hospital and placed under psychiatric care.

Mulnix put together a long chart detailing Berg's movements during the last seventy-two hours of his life. More than once he unfurled the document, studied it, looked it up and down, before deciding that nothing in those three days appeared to have set in motion the events leading to the death. In time the roll was put away, other data on the homicide was placed in several large police file cabinets, and the computer program generated solely for the case began to grow at a less alarming rate. The investigation was slowing down. Sixty detectives had found little of substance: no eyewitnesses, no good leads, no other hard evidence. With the start of the second week the number of those still working eight hours a day on the case was falling fast. There wasn't anything left for them to do.

By that time, Berg had been taken home to Chicago and buried in the rain at a small private function at the Free Sons cemetery in Forest Park. His dead father was exhumed from another location and buried next to him. At the ceremony for the talk-show host, Rabbi Jules Furth said, "He was able to do with his mouth what others do with their fists. He was able to expose the phoniness and insanity and bias in others. . . . Alan beat it all. He beat alcoholism. He beat brain surgery. He hit rock bottom. And he came back. . . ."

In Denver the memorial service came and went, the speculation about the killer continued, and then, because the police had uncovered little of interest, the talk about Berg began to fade. One heard that Ken Hamblin was now carrying a gun to work and Peter Boyles was thinking of wearing a bulletproof vest, but that was about all. Berg's death had been shocking enough, but the notion that someone could kill him so easily and so perfectly and get away with it so well was an added jolt. People didn't seem to want to think much about that. By mid-July what one heard mostly around town was that the crime never would be solved and the police had wasted an incredible amount of time and money on the case. Chief Mulnix had only one thing resembling a lead and it was essentially just another source of frustration. Forty-eight hours after the investigation began, Dan Molloy, a veteran intelligence detective, had mentioned a name he'd been thinking about since the murder: David Lane, a forty-five-year-old suburbanite, a title researcher in the real estate field and an avid golfer.

Part of Molloy's job in the Intelligence Bureau was to keep an eye on right-wing activists in the metropolitan area. A few years earlier Lane had been stopped by police in Denver for handing out literature decrying "race-mixing," but this was a misdemeanor, a trivial offense. Detective Molloy had known of Lane's affiliation with the Colorado Ku Klux Klan back in the 1970s and the officer had stayed casually aware of him ever since. Although he'd watched Lane's movements in and around Denver in late 1983 and early 1984, he regarded him with little more than passing interest. When it came to radical politics, there were doers and there were thinkers, and there was nothing illegal about holding unpopular or inflammatory thoughts. Molloy viewed Lane as primarily a thinker, a man who preferred to talk and write about social change. In March 1984, when the detective was informed that Lane had left the state for the Northwest and most likely wouldn't be coming back, it didn't have much effect on him. He didn't even feel relieved. Guys like David Lane conducted their revolutions in libraries.

All the same Alan Berg had been shot to death in his driveway and Molloy knew that Lane had on several occasions argued with the talk-show host on the radio. And during the first week of the investigation an anonymous caller had told a police officer to take a long hard look at Mr. Lane. When this information was conveyed to Molloy he decided to follow through. He found Lane's ex-wife, Carol, in Golden, just west of town, but she and her former husband had split up some time ago and Carol didn't know where he was. Molloy also located one of his friends, Warren McKinzie, who had once shared an apartment with Lane, but McKinzie had lost track of him too. Molloy found Fred Wilkins, the man who had told Berg he was going to die in 1979, but he wasn't much help either (Wilkins himself was never seriously considered a suspect). Wilkins and Lane had once had a dispute over leadership in the local Ku Klux Klan and Wilkins had thrown him out of the organization. That was about five years ago. He had no idea what had become of Lane since then. Molloy looked up a few other people who had been acquainted with Lane, and one said, "Dave used to lie on his bed and seethe at Berg. He hated the guy, absolutely hated him, but couldn't shut his radio program off. He was compelled to lie there and listen until it was over." None of Lane's former Denver associates knew of his whereabouts. Molloy received another tip that Lane kept firearms in a storage locker in the suburb of Aurora. Detectives searched it and found nothing.

By midsummer only two detectives were left on the case and both were spending time on other things. Their interest revived briefly in July when the *Rocky Mountain News* received a letter purporting to be from David Lane, denying his involvement in the Berg matter and the earlier bombing of a synagogue in Boise, Idaho. Police experts studied the signature on the note, postmarked Denver, and concluded that it was probably authentic. The author castigated the local media for not interviewing him to see where he had been on the night of June 18, 1984, and added that he "wasn't even in the city of Denver at the time the late Mr. Berg met his demise. . . . It appears that the Denver media hopes that by character assassination, they can persuade me to paint a target on my chest and march into police or federal gunfire." After receiving this missive, Police Captain Douglas White issued a challenge for Lane to come forward and clear his name. When that didn't happen, White said, "We're beginning to look at his absence with some suspicion."

In the days immediately following the murder, Detective Molloy had mentioned Lane's name at the police station and even gone so far as to say that he was "a suspect . . . a prime suspect." What he didn't tell his superiors was that he had had intelligence reports the previous January, from one of his anonymous informants, that Lane had followed Berg around Denver, stalking him at least twice. Little was made of this information at the time. Lane couldn't kill anyone, the detective reasoned, and he had no evidence to believe otherwise. Also, Molloy's own feelings about the talk-show host may have affected his actions, if only unconsciously.

"I was not an Alan Berg fan," he said some time after the killing. "It sounds kind of cold and callous, but I did not feel too sorry about the guy getting shot, other than the fact that he had a right to live like anybody else. I didn't have any inclination to listen to him. If I happened to turn it on by mistake, I just kept on going on the dial. He turned me off. They say that was just his personality on the radio and he wasn't that way in real life, but I still had no inclination to go up and get his autograph."

As the summer came to an end, Denver detectives continued

searching for Lane but without results. Their purview did not extend beyond the metropolitan area, and they were confident that Lane was not in their midst. They had done their job, exhausted the options. Chief Mulnix was disappointed and had become somewhat defensive about the Berg homicide. The local media was constantly badgering him for answers: What had they learned that day? Were they about to name a suspect? Where was David Lane? Was he a solid lead? Didn't they have one yet? Not much. . . . No. . . . We don't know. . . . Not really. . . . No. He advised the reporters to be patient.

"We understood from the beginning that it would be a long-term investigation," he once said, "and we felt certain that one person alone hadn't done it. People would eventually talk about it and take credit for it. And they would tell people who would tell other people who would tell us."

By early autumn no one had told them much of anything. The only recent news they had was bad: The woman who had claimed seeing the getaway car leave Adams Street had since died in an automobile accident. As September became October the Denver police could do little but wait, wait and hope for a break or a confession or someone turning in the killer in order to collect the twenty-thousand-dollar reward. They waited but nothing turned up, not in Denver anyway. When the break finally did come the local detectives were pleased but could take no credit for it, since they were no longer working on the case alone. The Alan Berg murder had emerged as one piece of a vast, entangled fantastic drama, one part of a nationwide investigation. The Secret Service was involved, and the IRS, and the FBI, and law-enforcement agencies in sixty cities and eighteen states. The manhunt stretched from one end of the United States to the other, a diagonal cutting jaggedly from the Northwest to the Southeast. The activities of the Denver Police Department and the ten thousand bits of information they had gathered on the Berg execution were minuscule compared to the work of the feds. By the end of 1984 the investigation was not merely widespread and intense. It was the largest such battle against domestic terrorism in the history of the FBI.

# PART TWO

—

# FINDING A JOB

—

# 3

---

# *A FATHER'S EFFORT,*
# *A SON'S LAMENT*

---

Three photographs spread out side by side: The story must be in them or in the spaces between them. The first is Alan Berg with his 1947 graduating class at Chicago's O'Keeffe grammar school. He is thirteen years old and wearing a sweater with a moose embroidered on the front. The black-and-white picture conceals his bright-red hair and freckles but does reveal a pleasant-looking smooth-cheeked smile and eyes that appear shy, happy, and innocent. He looks like the boy who won a medal for a piano recital. The youngster has a well-made face, which seems both intelligent and certain to develop into the visage of a handsome man. For the moment it is unquestionably sweet.

---

The next photo was taken in his mid-twenties, near his marriage to Judith. The face has lost some of its prospects for being handsome. It is too long and thick-lipped and the individual features overwhelm the frame. There is an awkwardness in how everything falls together but it is still a pleasant awkwardness, a friendly one. He looks young for his age; his innocence remains intact. Berg is clean-shaven (most people in Denver never actually saw his face; by the time his picture had begun to appear in newspapers or on TV, his jaws, cheeks, and forehead were covered with hair). The second image is not a face one would find particularly memorable, or at least not when captured by a static photograph. Berg's face changed when he talked, came alive in unpredictable ways. The longer he spoke, the better-looking he became to a listener. At twenty-four or -five he appears gawky and familiar, like countless other young adults in the 1950s.

The third picture is stunning. He doesn't look twice as old as in the previous photograph, which he is, but three times older, or four. It is the very face of age. Where did the pockmarks on his cheeks come from? Why are his lips crusty? What created those weary, uncomfortable eyes? He looks in pain, or is he laughing? He looks haunted, as if he had seen an apparition. One moment the face is ugly, gaunt, frightened, angry, and the next almost handsome or at least captivating. His eyes can see through one or only through himself. They see something disturbing. The future? Something he knows about us? Or only about himself? A terrible quality shines forth from those eyes, vulnerable and knowing and fixed. Berg's career was made possible by electricity; some juice must have entered his face and left it in shock.

Clouds are spare, the breeze chops the water but doesn't relieve the July heat. Looking north one sees the Chicago skyline in a haze, east is Lake Michigan, and to the south are its beaches. West of the park bench is Hyde Park, considered by many of its residents to be the most successfully integrated neighborhood in the United States. It is well mixed racially and surrounded on every side, except the eastern waterfront, by a black ghetto. Hyde Park is not merely integrated and thriving, it also contains the University of Chicago, giving the neighborhood a highbrow tone to go along with its big-city funk. It is the kind of place urban sociologists, who are usually looking for a vital blend of street life, ethnic variety, and intellectual ferment, drool over. Local people are proud of the neighborhood; they talk of it as a dynamic urban culture that works. The place has a rhythm, a grit of its own. Urban blues came out of the South Side of Chicago, and Hyde Park retains some of that feel. It combines the city and the down-home, sidewalk hostility and solid values. Alan Berg spent part of his youth here and never stopped coming back to the neighborhood to visit. He left home and stayed away—then defended everything he'd left behind.

"We don't go there anymore," says Ruth Berg, smoking a cigarette and gazing toward the window of her Hyde Park apartment. Outside the wind howls over Lake Michigan and heat makes the air thick, stultifying, like dirty milk.

"If it wasn't so bad," says Norma Sacks, above the wind, "we would drive you there and show you. But we don't want to risk our lives."

Both women, mother and daughter, are referring to their old South Side neighborhood where Berg spent the first years of his life. It's black now, off limits to Jews and white Gentiles alike. A sadness tinges the women's voices when they talk of not being able to visit their past, as remote as their ancestors'.

Joseph Berg's people were Russian Jews who moved to London to escape the anti-Semitism of the mother country. The first nine years of his life were spent in England before the family sailed, in 1906, for America and the city of Chicago. Joseph's father had once been a shoe manufacturer, turning out fine ladies' dancing slippers. In Chicago the family lived in a West Side Jewish neighborhood —but were not religious—and the boy's father worked in a shoe-repair shop. When Joseph came of age, he decided to attend dental school, supporting himself with two jobs and graduating at twenty-one. He set up a practice in a southeastern section of Chicago, and moved his family into his office building. A few years later he transferred his business to the Beverly Hills area of Chicago, and

41

a few years after that he was ready to take a bride.

Ruth Berg's father emigrated to the United States from Germany, while her mother was a native of St. Louis. The parents, both Jewish, separated less than a month after she was born. Ruth and her sister stayed in St. Louis, her brother and father left the city for good. Four years later, in 1913, the two girls and their mother moved to Chicago and took up residence in a large house on the West Side. A grandfather and half a dozen uncles and aunts raised the girls, whose mother died when Ruth was eight. The sisters had no formal religious training, although Ruth did attend a Christian Science Sunday School for several years. She was a bright youngster, interested in taking business courses, but her education ended at fourteen when she went to work in a bank. In time she met Joseph Berg at a party; when vows were exchanged, the groom was an established dentist of twenty-seven, the bride a mere nineteen.

Norma arrived in March 1928 and Alan in January 1934. During the pregnancy with her son, Ruth Berg was running a number of clothing shops on the South Side, selling dresses for $2.88. The combined strain of childbirth and managing her stores caused her to have a nervous breakdown. "It was just a matter of overwork," she says. "I came out of it very well. Never incapacitated. I called Alan once on his birthday; he was on the air and I picked up the show from Denver. He interviewed me on the radio and wanted to know all about how it was when he was born. My answer was that it was painful. He loved that."

The baby boy had a chubby face, bright red hair, and peach-colored cheeks, so his family called him "Peachy Puss." The Bergs employed a white maid, Irene, an imposing-looking figure who took responsibility for raising him after Ruth had recovered and returned to work. She stayed on until he was five.

"He was a very quiet baby, very manageable," says Ruth, a handsome white-haired woman with narrow, intelligent eyes. A hint of permanent sadness lingers around her mouth, as if she is determined to persevere but is finding it hard. From time to time she stares at his baby picture, propped against the foot of the television in her apartment, and barely shakes her head. "He was a very happy little boy, with a nice normal household where he was greatly loved. A lot of relatives paid attention to him. It wasn't at all psychotic." The last word makes her laugh; she knows people have applied it to her son.

From an early age he had a temper. He would buy his mother a birthday or Christmas present well in advance of the date and when he'd get angry he'd bring it out and jump up and down on it in front of her. Then he'd take it back and wrap it up again. "He was innovative even then," Ruth says.

Berg spent his young adolescence in a South Shore neighborhood, before the family moved to Hyde Park in the 1950s. The nickname Peachy Puss had evolved to "Fumy Plumey" (both the hair and the outbursts were red). If he was volatile he was also enterprising. At eight he began delivering groceries and followed this with a job selling magazines. At twelve he wanted to become a shoe salesman but the first day he went to work at the footwear store the boss made him clean the bathroom. "Very disillusioning," his mother says. "But he stayed there a few years." His hobbies were golf, stamp collecting, photography, and performing magic tricks, and his childhood was free from physical illness. "No signs of epilepsy whatsoever," Ruth says.

If there was nothing awry with him medically, the boy was developing a lifelong fund of bitter resentment toward his father, whom he would one day call "an inexcusable dentist." Dr. Berg looked something like Spencer Tracy—his face had a similar shape but was less craggy—and when the youngster went to Tracy's movies he imagined that the actor on the screen was his father and Dr. Berg was a fraud. Berg had observed his father, while practicing dentistry in Beverly Hills, trying to pass himself off as a Gentile, since most of his patrons had Christian backgrounds. Then he would come home from work and rail at the non-Jewish world. If the boy expressed an interest in jazz or other forms of black music, Dr. Berg would say, "That's a lot of applesauce." Alan was the only Jewish male in his neighborhood who did not get Bar Mitzvahed, although he was invited to the homes of other thirteen-year-old boys to watch them take part in this ceremony and receive presents.

"My father was a hypocrite and a notorious bigot against anything that wasn't Jewish," Berg said when he was forty-eight. "As a kid I would say, 'How can you go to temple on the weekend and hold yourself out to be a Gentile during the week?' He never hit me but he would wail back."

Ruth Berg lights another cigarette and gazes at her apartment window. "Joe didn't look Jewish," she says with some hesitation. "When he opened his office in Beverly Hills, Jews were very unwelcome there so he just didn't tell anybody, for business reasons."

Norma inhales smoke, and as it escapes it forms a cloud around her features. Her eyes are stained red from crying, she wears shortish gray hair, large glasses with even larger frames, a necklace with a beige egg at its nadir. The egg has hatched and a baby bird sticks its head above the lip of the shell. Norma glances uncomfortably around her mother's apartment, the walls of which are covered with books and pictures (Alan and Linda McVey are present) but mostly with animal figures and primarily foxes—foxes on cups, foxes on canvas, foxes knitted on the couch.

"Now, Ma," Norma says, "can I talk straight?"

"Certainly."

"My father looked Swedish. He was a very naïve man. He lived in a world he set up and the limits were very small. He outraged us all. I've got to say this," and she glances at her mother.

"I said the same thing."

"He was good but he did not recognize the whole world out there."

"The three of us, myself and Norma and Alan, had this understanding and sense of humor, but my husband didn't have that. It left him a little on the outside."

"Alan always felt that my father didn't care enough about him," Norma says. "My father was very proud of making money, very chauvinistic about being Jewish, but he really wasn't that involved in being Jewish, as none of us are. My father was very prejudiced about black people. That affected Alan. Hypocrisy," and again she glances at her mother. "Is that right?"

"More or less."

"I was very angry at my father too. We could never go out with anybody who wasn't Jewish. We once had a Seder and my father made a joke about our Gentile aunt being there and I got very upset."

"That's nothing disgraceful that he made a joke," Ruth says.

"He was really a good person with his family, giving and everything. I can't say too much without feeling disloyal." She pauses and looks at the older woman fully now, before going on. "I never thought he appreciated my mother as much as he should have and Alan felt the same way. Okay, I said it out loud."

Norma lights another cigarette, wincing as she does. "That was my father. He wanted to do everything right for us he could but he just didn't know how to do it. He didn't come from anything. Any money or any parental direction or any religion. My mother came from no parents, raised by the aunts and the family that was there. And a brilliant father who never spoke to his children and left them a dollar when he died. When you think of these two people, my mother and father, getting together and raising children—they didn't have anybody behind them to make it good. They did this on their own and they were just wonderful and we had a home and nice dinners on the table and good schools, but this thing with my father made us both a little crazy. Am I doing anything bad now?" she says to her mother.

"No. Children always see these situations in a different light than adults do."

"I feel very guilty because it was so good for us. When we were young there was a family, not just us two chickens. We'd go to dinner on Sunday." She begins to cry. "Daddy would not accept anything except in his little circumscribed world. Nothing else could enter."

"Most people in his generation were like that," Ruth says.

The women stare at each other, both of them smoking again.

Norma starts to pose a question but is cut off.

"Don't ask me," Ruth says. "Talk."

"You lived with him."

"I was probably more tolerant of a lot of things than you and Alan were."

"Too tolerant. My mother did a lot of terrific things and my father was complacent about that."

"Most men are. They don't turn handsprings because their wives do certain things. You don't say thank-you to a wife. It's a thankless job. Right?" and she looks across the room, smiling at her remaining child, her eyes moving once again around the apartment, over the images of foxes and the baby picture near the TV.

# 4

---

# *THE WHITE SEED*
# *OF HATE*

---

One approaches the compound on a road wending through the Coeur d'Alene National Forest in northern Idaho. At the entrance are a chainlink fence, a shed, and a semaphore, raised to let visitors in. On the shed in red-and-blue letters, against a light background, are the words WHITES ONLY and beyond the shed are a guard tower, a clapboard house, a school, a printing press, a church with a white cross on its top, a rifle range, a protective covering of trees, and guards with German shepherds and Doberman pinschers. The headquarters of Aryan Nations, twenty acres of forest and land five miles to the east of Hayden Lake, Idaho, has been referred to as the Heavenly Reich.

In the mid-nineteenth century a small English sect, following a doctrine that would eventually be known as Anglo-Israelism, became confused by a quotation from the Bible's Old Testament. "Be fruitful and multiply," God had said to Jacob in the Book of Genesis. "A nation and a company of nations shall be of thee." In the Bible, Jacob was the grandson of Abraham, Abraham was the father of the Israelites, and the Israelites were the Chosen People of God. Based upon the nineteenth-century evidence—the nation of Israel did not exist, let alone "a company of nations"—the members of the sect might have reached the conclusion that God's prophecy had gone unfulfilled. Instead they decided that the Chosen People were not the Israelites (or modern-day Jews) but certain groups of Gentiles; more specifically, they were the Anglo-Saxons and Scandinavians who had, according to the sect, escaped from the Middle East in ancient times and traveled north to the far reaches of Europe. These "lost tribes of Israel" had indeed formed a company of nations: England, Ireland, Scotland, Deutschland (Germany), Sweden, Norway, and, finally, the United States of America, which was the long-prophesied Promised Land. Jews, the sect believed, were homeless, cursed impostors, who had come from the illicit coupling of the biblical Eve with Satan. Their offspring was Cain, who slew Abel in the Old Testament and thereby became the first murderer, the first killer of God's true Chosen People, the Gentile race.

Not many people accepted Anglo-Israelism and the doctrine fell into disrepair. It was more or less forgotten until the early twentieth century, when it was rediscovered by an American, Gerald L. K. Smith, the founder of the Christian Nationalist Crusade. The Crusade sided with Hitler and Mussolini in World War II but was not discouraged when the Axis powers lost. One year after the war ended, 1946, a follower of Gerald Smith named Wesley Swift started the Anglo-Saxon Christian Congregation in the city of Los Angeles. When Swift died in 1970, two new leaders of Anglo-Israelism (now known as the Identity Christian movement) had emerged in Southern California. One was Colonel William Potter Gale and the other was Reverend Richard Girnt Butler. Colonel Gale had been on

General Douglas MacArthur's wartime staff and directed anti-Japanese operations in the Philippine Islands. That duty helped prepare him for a later one, in the 1960s, when he put together a paramilitary group of his own, the California Rangers. He also established a Ministry of Christ Church in Mariposa, California, a gold-rush village near Yosemite National Park. Gale, a handsome man with a broad, pleasing smile and a crew cut, ran for governor of California, wrote manuals on guerrilla warfare, delivered anti-Semitic sermons from his church and over radio stations, and strenuously promoted the idea that Jews and Christians were engaged in a racial and religious war, a holy struggle for the soul of America.

A student of aeronautical engineering at Los Angeles City College, Richard Butler had been an air force flight-engineer instructor during World War II. According to Aryan Nations literature, he went on to become a senior engineer at Lockheed's Palmdale, California, plant, and then the owner of a manufacturing firm for airplane parts. He turned the last venture into a considerable bank account. In the early 1960s he met Wesley Swift and within a few years he had helped him establish the Christian Defense League, another right-wing paramilitary outfit. With Swift's death, Gale and Butler each saw himself as the logical successor to the man's ideas and power. Butler took over Swift's congregation, now called the Church of Jesus Christ Christian, and briefly tried to join forces with Gale's Ministry of Christ Church and another Identity sect, The National Emancipation of the White Seed. Too many prophets ruin a vision. The White Seed foundered, Pastor Gale continued to show the way in Mariposa, and Butler left the state.

In 1973 Butler began moving his religion, politics, and handful of believers to Hayden Lake, Idaho. It was a natural place for a group of Aryan soldiers, Nordic in their blood. Some folks called the area God's country, others said it was a white man's paradise. Kootenai County held 1,200 square miles and a population of about sixty thousand, with only fifty Jews and twenty blacks, exactly the percentages Butler was looking for in his effort to create a white Christian homeland in which black people would be regarded as subhuman. Not only was Kootenai County racially homogeneous, it had some of the most impressive woods, finest sailing, best back-packing territory, and most productive fishing spots in the North-west. Thousands of summer tourists visited Hayden Lake and Coeur d'Alene Lake to escape harsher climates or heavily populated towns. The magnificent stretch of country provided a special feeling of freedom, of escape.

Something more than beauty and freedom permeates the Idaho forest. Nostalgia is also present, a deep primal sense of nostalgia, the kind that gets below logic and reason and pushes them aside. Two thirds of modern Idaho is national forest and while some of this land is occasionally logged, most of it is beyond the reach of human dominance. That generates myths, desires, dreams: the no-tion of man struggling against the elements, the need and nostalgia for heroism, male heroism, frontier heroism, the heroism of con-quering the woods and whatever may be hiding within them, of protecting good citizens from the evils closing in. The image of the white gunslinging western hero is embedded in the American memory.

Few gun-toting outlaws or quick-draw sheriffs live in the western United States anymore. For a number of decades in the Northwest, these two archetypal male heroes were replaced by another romantic figure: the logger who felled huge trees and domesticated the woods, turning it into lumber, homes, and a thriving industry. Lately that occupation has soured. Decreasing timber sales, increasing logging competition from Canada or the southeastern United States, and overproduction have cost the Northwest fifty thousand jobs. It's difficult to prop up one's mystique in the face of such hard economic news. New myths and fantasies come into vogue.

Richard Butler's fantasy, conceived in Southern California in the early 1970s, began to take shape a few years later in the northern woods. He had the money, the land was available, and there was no one to prevent him from practicing his private set of beliefs on his own twenty acres. The West is full of sects: Sikhs in New Mexico, Buddhists in Colorado, Mormons in Utah, and scores of smaller groups conducting their own spiritual searches across the landscape. Butler had the will to create his vision. One could see that in his hard, lined, proud, tanned face. There was something unusual in the eyes of this heavyset, rugged man: a dullness or a blankness, a stare that some people have called the blindness of insight. His political and religious beliefs may have stood contrary to most every force of modern history, yet he was unswerving, certain he would prevail. And he would do so with a tiny band of followers, perhaps fifty or a hundred or two hundred at the most. That's heroism on a grand scale.

Inside the compound he built Aryan Hall, a diminutive brown church in which he delivered sermons denouncing Jews, blacks, homosexuals, and communists, all of whom were invading the white Christian world and diluting its purity. In the pews the men dressed in blue poplin jackets, white shirts, and blue ties, while the women donned blue or white blouses and skirts. On their shoulders the men wore the Aryan Nations insignia, an emblem with two crosses, a shield, a double-edged sword, and a crown. From time to time they raised their arms in the Nazi salute made popular by Adolf Hitler before World War II. "Hail Victory!" they cried to one another for reassurance. "As long as the alien tyranny evil occupies our land," preached Butler, "hate is our law and revenge our duty."

At night crosses were burned on the grounds, illuminating the trees and the Aryan warriors who stood in the firelight, guns in hand. The compound's printing press sent forth tracts on Aryan Nations law: "The thoughts of Aryan woman are dominated by the desire to enter family life. Aryan woman brings true love and affection and a happy, well-run home to refresh and inspire her man. The world of contented womanhood is made of family: husband, children and home. It is a far greater love and service to be the mother of healthy Aryan children than to be a clever woman lawyer."

For years Aryan Nations literature was mailed to white inmates in prisons throughout America in order to recruit them to the cause. After leaving jail, some of the ex-cons came north. In the summertime, Butler invited to the compound members of other Identity Christian or white-oriented groups—the Ku Klux Klan, the Christian Defense League, the Posse Comitatus (a loose alliance of farmers, tax protesters, and vigilantes). Butler called the annual gathering the Aryan Nations World Congress and occasionally he persuaded a European Nazi to attend. The emphasis at these congresses, which attracted hundreds of followers from around the United States, was on weapons instruction, religious indoctrination, and burnings of the cross. Speakers at the event invariably talked about preparation for the race war to come, while the visitors' children might sit in on classes at the Aryan Nations school, designed to teach youngsters the four Rs: readin', 'ritin', 'rithmetic, and race. The state of Idaho required no accreditation for this "Christian Academy" so kids within its walls learned about white Christian separatism and supremacy without the intrusion of other ideas. If they failed to absorb the message in school during the week, Butler repeated it in church on Sunday.

White people, he told adults and children alike, are the "light bearers of the world. That's the Law Order of God. . . . It's a natural law order that races don't mix. You can see it in nature. Robins are robins, salmon are salmon, and tuna are tuna."

# 5

## *MEETING HIS MATCH*

Kenny Shraiberg's family had a summer home outside of Chicago, where the youngster and Alan Berg used to go on weekends. Although he was Berg's best childhood friend, he can't recall seeing the boy, who was terribly self-conscious about being skinny, without a shirt on. "He never went to the beach," says Shraiberg. "As I grew up I went to the beach and participated in sports, which he really didn't do."

One afternoon when Berg was fifteen, he and his friend drove Dr. Berg's gray Buick to Chicago Heights, a suburb near the South Side. They turned right at Stella's Cleaners, as they had been told to do, and began looking for an old house at the end of the street, finding only a sprawling residential district like so many others. They tossed a coin to see who would ask a nearby cab driver for directions. "Alan lost," says Shraiberg, "but didn't have the courage to ask him, so the deed fell upon myself."

The boys gave the cabbie five dollars and the hack guided them to another Stella's Cleaners, where they found the old shack they were searching for. In separate rooms, they lost their virginity with white prostitutes. That night when they met their friends Alan began to boast about their feat.

"If Alan had a bad reaction, he didn't let on," says Shraiberg, who runs a lawn-and-garden-fertilizer manufacturing business in Indiana. "It was the greatest, right? I never told him about it and he never told me."

At seventeen Berg went to college at the University of Colorado in Boulder. The campus had a Jewish fraternity, Phi Sigma Delta, with a large Chicago contingent that included several of his friends. One of them, Jay Levinson, had come to the school because he wanted to ski in the Rockies. Another had asthma and found the mile-high climate beneficial. Years later Levinson said that Berg decided to join them in Colorado mainly to get away from his father.

Berg and Levinson were roommates in Boulder, where the former soon acquired another nickname, "Thermo," short for thermometer, because of his red hair, penchant for dressing all in white— shirt, shoes, pants, sport coat—and his temper. Others called him "Bergie." His Adam's apple was prominent and more than one observer compared him to Ichabod Crane. He was known as something of a dandy: with his custom-made pocketless shirts, tailored to fit his endless neck and arms, his good manners when he chose to use them, and his ability to dance in a ballroom. Unlike many college boys, Berg sipped an occasional beer but had no desire for hard liquor.

In later years he claimed that during college he was joined in matrimony with an older woman, a nurse, whom he had met in a Boulder tavern. "She said she wouldn't sleep with me unless I married her," he said. "So I did." At night, he contended, he would sneak away from Phi Sigma Delta, dash across town to his wife's apartment for a tryst, and run back home before dawn. Berg said the marriage, which has no court documents to support it, was annulled after thirty days.

"I was his roommate for a year in college," says Stan Gardenschwartz, a Denver stockbroker, "and I'm a light sleeper. I would have known if he was doing that."

"He absolutely could not sit still," says Nick Siegel, an ex-fraternity brother who runs a printing business in Denver. "His mouth would be going and I'd tell him to shut up. He would keep talking and I would paddle him; in those days paddling was legitimate. He'd be quiet for a while and then start talking again. We'd have tell-offs, where you'd put pledges in a room and tell them what's wrong with them. I clearly remember telling him that he was a clown."

There were sides of Berg they knew nothing about. Everyone at the fraternity was aware he was the son of a successful Chicago dentist, but not that on weekends the young man slipped into Denver and sold shoes for extra cash, perhaps as much as a hundred dollars a Saturday. By all accounts he was "a helluva shoe salesman." When presented with a difficult problem—for example, a woman who wanted a pair of loafers but not in a size that Berg had in stock—he would simply talk her into buying the same style one or two sizes larger. His fraternity brothers also didn't know he was troubled or curious enough to spend part of his earnings on a Denver psychiatrist. It isn't clear what he was looking for in therapy. His doctor isn't available for comment and Berg never talked publicly about the sessions. Perhaps the young psychology major merely wanted to know what took place during an analytic encounter.

The fraternity members liked him, and most did not find Berg unusual, although there were exceptions. "Alan was the first of the angry young men," says Jay Levinson. "He was angry all the time. I guess the anger was because he was down on himself. All he ever talked about was his weight. His sense of humor and of anger were there from grammar school on."

His college friends didn't seem particularly to notice that Berg was developing a passion for jazz, a deep inquisitiveness about black people, or a strong identification with Holden Caulfield, the protagonist of J. D. Salinger's *Catcher in the Rye*, who sees the adult world as a collection of phonies, a hypocritical charade. Berg had a vague air of dissastisfaction, an unhappiness forming at the edges of his personality. Two opposing characters—the clownish teenager and the serious, questioning young man—were both surfacing within him in Boulder. In high school he had admitted to a friend that he liked listening to classical music and watching ballet. The boy asked him: "Are you queer?"

"I wondered if maybe I was," Berg once said. "Not in the sexual sense but that I was a queer person. I didn't feel I belonged anywhere and that feeling has never changed."

If, in the early 1950s, he saw himself as a rebel without a cause, a bright restless teenager who was looking for something he couldn't begin to name or define, he was about to meet someone who would mirror his feelings—not just then, but for the remainder of his life.

Denver's East High School is on Colfax Avenue, a few blocks from the scene of the murder. Its grandeur appears somewhat out of place today, next to the drifters, whores, and street life that dominate nearby stretches of the boulevard. At the southern entrance to the school is an elaborate half-circle flower garden and two huge pedestals with pioneers standing atop of them and gazing west. A six-lane tree-lined road leads to the school building itself, a touch of Paris right in the middle of a city that often talks of trying to overcome its image as a cow town. The road past the school ends at the edge of City Park, with a large round fountain in which an ancient goddess is being sprayed by water jets. Built in 1924, East High School is made of red brick, trimmed with white lace, and has a commanding tower with a cupola overlooking the whole structure. On each of the cupola's four sides is a verdigris clock, announcing the time of day to a good portion of Denver. The school was meant to be grand, like the east side itself.

Denver's west side is older, more immigrant and ethnic, essentially the working-class part of town. If you were poor and Jewish,

Irish, or Italian and arriving in Denver at the turn of the century (or Hispanic and arriving today), you would have settled on the western edge of the city. Many Jews originally came to Denver for its climate. The National Jewish Hospital on Colfax Avenue had gained a reputation for treating tuberculosis, asthma, and other respiratory diseases. The community was considered reasonably tolerant from a religious and ethnic point of view, even though the Ku Klux Klan had flourished in Denver in the 1920s before fading with the Depression and World War II. When people on the town's west side were ready to step up socially, they moved to the east side and sent their children to the stately, four-story high school on Colfax, which would look right at home in Virginia.

Alan Berg first saw Judy Halpern beneath the clock tower at East High School one evening in 1951. He was seventeen and she was two years younger, a dancer at East performing that night in an all-school show. Berg's fraternity friends, many of whom had grown up in Denver and knew Judy, had brought Berg to the school to meet her. She had thick dark hair, dramatic eyebrows, a womanly smile, and lively brown eyes—not entirely dissimilar in appearance to a movie idol of the 1950s, Annette Funicello. Judy liked sports cars and opera, she wrote poems and hid literary magazines under her bed. The daughter of a successful pawnbroker, she had her first piano recital at four and by fifteen she had traveled extensively and attended the best summer schools for promising young dancers and musicians. Like Berg, she was a combination of worldliness and innocence, of a quick piercing intelligence and emotional fragility, of the need to cut a figure in society and to escape it. Apart from the fact that the two of them looked very different, their inner similarities were remarkable. They were a psychic fit, but whether that fit was for good or ill was something their friends and families would be debating thirty years later.

"He was tall, gangly, had flaming red hair, a crew cut, and was wearing white bucks and blue denims," Judith says of their first meeting. She's in the living room of her parents' spacious two-story house on Denver's east side, a residence containing beveled glass in the front windows, original works of known contemporary painters, and many images of cats. The taste is expensive. This room is furnished with a piano and the one behind it, shot through with sunshine from a skylight, is replete with a bar and stools. Upstairs is the bedroom where Judith once hid highbrow magazines and where Berg found them when he came to visit.

Her parents, Bernard and Lily Halpern, were prominent in the Urban League, in Judaic activities, interfaith activities, in Zionism, in many cultural things taking place in Colorado and beyond. They were pillars of the east side's Temple Emanuel. In the late 1940s and early 1950s, when black musicians or actors or dancers came to Denver, they could not—or would not—stay at downtown hotels. So they boarded with local friends and acquaintances, including the Halperns. Duke Ellington and Oscar Peterson played piano in their living room. For a gathering of admirers, Paul Robeson, in his deep astounding voice, recited the lead from *Othello*. Ray Brown tuned his bass in one corner and Pearl Bailey sang in another. Jascha Heifetz played violin for the lucky few.

"When a Jascha Heifetz came to town," explains Judith, "your basic synagogue was going to have a dinner for him at three hundred dollars a plate, and the money would go to the state of Israel. My parents were always involved with groups that were hiding guns for Israel and waiting for the new state to be born."

The second time she saw Alan Berg he had exchanged his blue jeans for a three-piece suit and began talking to her about dinner dancing.

"I was taken with him from the start, like when someone takes a hook and puts it in your heart," she says. "He was not a happy kid. Norma was eighteen when she got married and right off the bat Alan found her [ex-]husband in bed with another woman. He was very distraught. Norma was pregnant and Alan was only thirteen. How do you deal with that? You begin to question too much and you don't have the answers. You meet someone who is also questioning and think you might find the answers there. So you just go along with that. It was like an adventure."

Berg's interior adventure was matched by what he found at the Halpern residence. The skinny, well-dressed, argumentative young man who thought of himself as a sophisticate from Chicago suddenly walked into this maelstrom of artistic and political activity. The Halperns, or at least Lily, something of a Denver legend in community affairs and for years the chairman of the state's Democratic party, represented many things that Berg's own parents did not: involvement with national and international personalities, a global political awareness, a sense of liberal Democratic purpose with a distinctly Jewish bent. Berg was smitten by it, more or less. He and Judith were drawn to her parents' guests and frenzied social life but didn't know whether to take them seriously. They liked meeting famous people and hearing major ideas thrown against the wall, but didn't feel comfortable among the celebrities. Was it real or was it all show business? Did one belong in that solid liberal tradition or was it as snobbish and hidebound and narrow-minded as the conservatives the guests were always criticizing?

"Alan was never taken by status," Judith says. "If you brought him a celebrity, he'd say, 'Show me what you can do to deserve your name.' He and I would go upstairs and listen to the radio and make fun of the people downstairs and he'd say, 'How can that guy be a famous writer? He can't even talk.' "

Decades later, when he was on the radio, Berg would often be characterized as a liberal. Had he truly been a person of liberal Democratic sympathies, he might have slid easily into life at the Halperns and found a home, a niche among people who supported labor unions, Zionism, and intellectual high culture. He was considerably more complicated than that, and in time felt as estranged from that culture as he did from the golf-playing Republicans at the restricted country club on the other side of town. From the beginning of their relationship, Berg and Judith questioned their Jewishness—what it meant or was supposed to mean. Their misgivings and dissatisfaction with the answers they came up with were another bond.

Berg's views on black people were similarly complicated, and cannot easily be reduced to an adjective. He did not have a trace of conventional bigotry, yet his relationship with blacks was love-hate. In Chicago Judith was once severely beaten by a gang of black youths. Berg was ready to kill. Speaking in public in the 1980s, he said uncommon things for a white man who had long been thoroughly supportive of the civil rights movement: "They [black people in his youth] had a looseness, almost a rhythmic perception of life. To me life became very rhythmic. There was an earthiness about black people then, a special kind of happiness that you don't see anymore. Blacks have become so whitened in their style of behavior that they've lost what they were by trying to merge with all of society. There was a great beauty in growing up in an ethnic neighborhood then. There was a delicatessen on the corner, a black guy's rib place nearby, an Irishman's this or that. I was beaten up by black people, but I always saw it as one person I wasn't getting along with, not a black-white thing. There was a lot of anger there, but it was different from the inner-city anger you see today. We didn't hate each other."

On the radio he was lightning quick to criticize blacks when he felt they were using the issue of racism to cover up their own shortcomings or flaws. In other words, he treated them the same way he treated everyone else, and was intensely aware of the real and ongoing problems that surround the whole subject of race:

White woman caller: "Do you associate black people with monkeys?"

Berg: "To be very honest, yes. Let me explain why. We were brought up in the era of Little Black Sambo and other things. Culturally, the white man is taught that the black is very much the evolution of the monkey. I think there is a little of that in most white people and they aren't honest enough to admit it."

WWC: "But do you believe that way?"

Berg: "No. I think I've long since surpassed any thinking in that realm. If I do think that way, I'm in a lot of trouble [at the time of this on-air conversation, in the mid-1970s, he was dating a black woman]. The point is that the black gorilla—King Kong—is a black sexual symbol for white men. I think most whites, growing up— their attitude is that the black man is a beast of sorts. It is very connected to associations with the chimpanzee and the gorilla. I think I'm a victim of that myself. It also represents power that we're frightened by. The gorilla is a threat to us because it's a powerful being. We transfer that to the black man and say, 'That's a threat, that's powerful.' If we really got into the nitty-gritty of how many people associate blacks with monkeys and gorillas, you'd be shocked."

WWC: "That's a shame."

Berg: "Of course it's a shame. But that's part of what we learned in white society. . . . Look at the jargon. People say, 'That guy looks just like a monkey.' Where does that come from?"

WWC: "That's true."

Berg: "Of course it is. To say that isn't part of our thinking—it certainly is."

WWC: "I wonder what they call white people?"

Berg: "Hyenas."

After two years at the University of Colorado, Berg transferred to the University of Denver, where he began to study law and to play musical schools: the University of Denver to the University of Miami (his parents spent time in Florida in the winter) to the De Paul University law school in Chicago to nearby Northwestern and then back to De Paul. He graduated from there in 1957, at twenty-two, one of the youngest people to pass the bar in the history of Illinois. Following Judith's graduation from East High School, she attended Pine Manor Junior College in Chestnut Hill, Massachusetts, for two years, then studied dance for a year at Manhattan's Juilliard school of music before returning home to the University of Denver to get an undergraduate degree in linguistics and education. She had visited Berg no matter where he went, and he did the same for her. While in college the young woman traveled to Europe, was in summer-stock productions around the country, and continued to dance. Berg felt she would pursue a career in one of the performing arts and had always supported her ambitions.

"When I came back from New York," she says, "I think he realized that I wasn't going to spend my life on a stage. I began to show more interest in teaching than performing and we decided we could settle down together. With everyone else I'd gone out with, I knew what my life would have been like, but not with Alan.

If I don't marry him, I thought to myself, I'll always wonder what I'd be missing."

He proposed in the Palmer House hotel in Chicago and they were married in 1958 in Denver's Temple Emanuel. Lily Halpern hoped that her daughter and son-in-law would return from their honeymoon to Denver and live close by. Alan could practice law in Colorado and Judith would be near her parents and old friends. The Halperns would even provide money to help the young couple get started. The newlyweds felt otherwise. After the wedding excursion to San Francisco, they planned to move to Chicago and start marriage with the sixty dollars they had between them. Neither of them had any intention of ever returning to the bride's hometown.

"My mother," says Judith, "was so upset that she called us every day on our honeymoon."

# 6

---

# *THE TURNING POINT*

---

By the late 1970s Aryan Nations and other forces on America's radical right were beginning to change. In the past their emphasis had largely been on rhetoric—defiant words or words tinged with violence—but words nonetheless, with little or no action to back them up. The professed goals of the far right—the Ku Klux Klan, for example—had long focused on separation of the races, on certain white people not wanting to live equally or commingle with blacks or other minorities. The issue of whether blacks, Jews, or other nonwhites had a right to exist was not in question.

In 1978 William Pierce, whose pseudonym is Andrew Macdonald, published a fantasy novel, *The Turner Diaries*. An Atlanta native and former professor of physics at Oregon State University, Pierce had once been a follower of George Lincoln Rockwell, the founder of the American Nazi Party who was assassinated in 1967. Pierce went on to form the Washington, D.C.-based neo-Hitlerian organization, the National Alliance. The novel opens in 1991 and is written as the diary of Earl Turner, a thirty-five-year-old white racist revolutionary who had been trained as an electrical engineer. Turner records how a band of white supremacists form an underground paramilitary movement, known as The Organization, and institute a murderous campaign to overthrow the American government and purify the land of "mongrel" races. Innumerable Jews, blacks, and white women are killed along the way. Turner's descriptions of violence are jaunty: "Well, early this morning the responsible conservative lost both legs and suffered severe internal injuries when a bomb wired to the ignition of his car exploded. The Jewish spokesman was even less fortunate. Someone walked up to him while he was waiting for an elevator in the lobby of his office building, pulled a hatchet from under his coat, cleaved the good Jew's head from crown to shoulder blades, then disappeared in the rush-hour crowd. The Organization immediately claimed responsibility for both acts."

The Organization sees the FBI as one of its greatest enemies; it contends that through the use of computers and other means the federal government (or "The System," as the revolutionaries call it) is trying to turn America into a "police state." When the organization bombs FBI headquarters in Washington, seven hundred people are killed. Then they escalate the warfare by bombing the U.S. Capitol building.

It is appropriate that Pierce's novel appeared in 1978, exactly a decade after 1968, which saw the height of leftist radical activity in the United States, the riots in Chicago during the Democratic National Convention, and the subsequent election of Richard Nixon. While the nation began its long gradual movement toward the right, a curious thing happened to the rhetoric that had flourished on the left in the 1960s. The extreme right adopted it. William Pierce, under the guise of Earl Turner, rails against authority, the government, the FBI, the System, liberals and conservatives, against big business, big institutions, bigness in general. With one notable difference he sounded like countless radicals, black and white, of the sixties. Where the latter often used the rhetoric to encourage racial tolerance or equality or to protest the war in Vietnam or to spread the ideas of socialism, Pierce had another purpose. He used it to promote racial fear and hatred, to deny that the Holocaust (the systematic elimination of European Jewry and others in World War II) had occurred, and to raise questions that were increasingly on the minds of young, white working-class American males in the late 1970s. What if a minority person takes your job? What if black men begin dating and marrying white women? What if a female competes with you at your place of employment and does better than you do (Pierce refers to the women's liberation movement as "mass psychosis")? What if your children are being taught by homosexuals? What if you are deeply afraid to walk city streets at night? What if you watched the hippies of the 1960s decry wealth, materialism, and patriotism and are now watching them become affluent, materialistic, and powerful in American society, while you are still an undereducated worker trying to cope with an upward surge of inflation? What if you were sent to Vietnam to fight a war the government decided not to win? And you were scarred in the body or the mind? And now you must compete against Southeast Asians for employment, because the United States let them into the country in large numbers—and they work cheap? What if you feel your nation slipping away—lost?

William Pierce's answer to such questions is simple: Kill the enemy. Earl Turner kills young black men and young white women with a crowbar and gun. He kicks young white "degenerates" in the testicles. He is always ready for a race war.

The Organization has a particular hatred for the American news media, which the group believes is manipulated by liberal Jews. In spite of this, Organization members can't resist watching the results of their bombings and executions on TV, and then complaining that "the controlled media intend to convince the public that what we are doing is terrible. . . . I remember a long string of Marxist acts of terror twenty years ago, during the Vietnam War. A number of government buildings were burned or dynamited and several innocent bystanders were killed, but the press always portrayed such things as idealistic acts of 'protest.'

"There was a gang of armed, revolutionary Negroes who called themselves 'Black Panthers.' Every time they had a shootout with the police, the press and TV people had their tearful interviews with the families of the Black gang members who got killed—not with the cops' widows. . . . One day we will have a truly American press in this country, but a lot of editors' throats will have to be cut first."

The Organization goes on to terrorize the offices of the *Washington Post*, without much success, but all of these acts are merely preparation for the infamous "Day of the Rope." When it arrives, white women who have slept with black men are hanged, along with politicians, lawyers, teachers, judges, newscasters, newspaper reporters and editors, bureaucrats, and preachers. Many of the victims wear "I betrayed my race" placards around their necks. Sixty thousand people die on this day. Eventually the Organization drops nuclear weapons on its enemies. More than sixty million people will perish for the cause.

To finance these activities the Organization conducts robberies and nationwide counterfeiting operations. The group assassinates political figures and carries on guerrilla warfare against nuclear power facilities and transportation systems. William Pierce knows a good deal about military engineering and bomb building; through the mouthpiece of Earl Turner he details how such things are done. At one point Turner is taken into the innermost circle of the Organization—the Order—where he receives the Sign, takes the Oath, and decides that he will never be able to look at other people or his own life as he did before. He is ready to die for the Order and finally will when he drops a nuclear warhead on the Pentagon. In the end the white supremacists defeat their foes; all blacks, Jews, and other minorities are obliterated and a Caucasian government is put into power not only in America but worldwide, as the earth is set on course again, purified and made good in the eyes of the author. The vision of Adolf Hitler, whom Pierce calls The Great One, has triumphed at last.

The "heroes" of the novel—and Turner desperately wants to be a hero—are white men who despise what has happened to their country in recent decades, who feel threatened by the emergence of women and minorities as political forces, and who want to destroy that which is different from themselves. In the end the book's politics have no consistency: On one page Turner sounds like a Soviet head of state criticizing the moral bankruptcy of America (the drugs, pornography, and materialism), while on the next he sounds like a spokesman for the ultraright. What underlines the whole book is the feeling that something is *spiritually* wrong with our time; he rages like any number of modern intellectuals, including Alan Berg, against the loss of things vital and good in the life of their nation, against the conversion of "a society of free men into a herd of cattle."

William Pierce's strategy for revolution is blunt: "If the White nations of the world had not allowed themselves to become subject to the Jew, to Jewish ideas, to the Jewish spirit, this war would not be necessary. . . . No matter how long it takes us and no matter to what lengths we must go, we'll demand a final settlement of the account between our two races. If the Organization survives this contest, no Jew will—anywhere. We'll go to the uttermost ends of the earth to hunt down the last of Satan's spawn."

Just before Turner is sent off on his Pentagon-bombing-suicide mission he meets with other members of the Order, whom he greatly admires: "These were *real men*, *White* men, men who were now *one* with me in spirit and consciousness as well as in blood. . . . I know, as certainly as it is possible for a man to know anything, that the Order will not fail me if I do not fail it. The Order has a life which is more than the sum of the lives of its members. . . ."

# 7

## *THE RAGE OF INNOCENCE*

In the late 1950s, Berg began his career in Chicago as a law clerk, making twenty-five dollars a week. He was bright, ambitious, underpaid, and frustrated. At night he returned to his Hyde Park apartment and told Judith that it wasn't working, he should be doing something else for a living, that even with her salary as a teacher of gifted children they would never get ahead. Berg eventually talked a lawyer friend into letting him come to his office and sit at a desk in the hall, in the hope of attracting clients. He didn't. One day, while walking past a neighborhood police station, he spoke to a cop on the street and they fell into conversation. The officer knew a bail bondsman who worked next door and asked if Berg wanted to meet him. The bondsman, Henry

Nathan, took an instant liking to the fledgling attorney and explained to him how the legal system functioned in Chicago. For a kickback fee, bondsmen told their clients which lawyer to seek out and what a fine job he would do for them. Berg soon went into business with Nathan and his career was suddenly in motion.

His childhood friend Kenny Shraiberg had an uncle who was also a bail bondsman in Chicago, a big operator in the Loop. Lou Volin, recalls Shraiberg, "made bail for Mafia-type characters. He had a partner who was a contact to the gangsters." Shraiberg knew that Berg was recently out of law school and struggling, so he asked his uncle if he would offer the young man advice. He gave Volin Berg's name and phone number.

"I didn't see much of Alan after that," says Shraiberg. "But I did see my uncle and he said that Alan was an expert at what he was doing."

Berg handled cases for shoplifters, prostitutes, gamblers, athletes with paternity suits. He defended rapists, mafiosi, or those who claimed they were. Sometimes, after winning in court, his clients gave him cash or hockey tickets or other free passes to events around town. He and Judith bought an MG and were then given as payment a Jaguar 38 sedan. It was black with red leather seats and a pulldown bar. Judith named it The Big Dog.

"It was like a house," she says, "with mahogany doors."

Berg's skills in the courtroom made him, in the words of his colleagues, "a comer." Julius Echeles, a portly, bewhiskered criminal lawyer in Chicago, was twenty years Berg's senior and shared an adjoining office space with him in the early 1960s. Echeles made his law library available and Berg took advantage of it.

"He was superb in court," says Echeles, who wears red suspenders, speaks in a clipped voice, and looks like an aging ribald sailor. "He had a charismatic relationship with juries and judges took to him. He had a striking and pleasant appearance and never rubbed anyone the wrong way. In criminal law you want a response from a person or jury that is in your favor and you use psychological persuasion to get it. Alan was fundamentally great at recognizing the psychological possibilities before him and how to use them."

Echeles's words notwithstanding, Berg did offend a few people in the courtroom in 1964 when he defended a model, Toni Lee Shelley, on an indecent-exposure charge. She earned it by appearing on a Chicago beach in a topless bathing suit. In the course of pleading Ms. Shelley's case, Berg called the female breast "one of God's most beautiful creations" and challenged those who would call it obscene. The jury's idea of beauty didn't stretch that far and they assessed the model a one-hundred-dollar fine.

The money behind his law practice was fast, the people paying it were faster, and Berg was soon trying to keep pace with everyone else. This didn't come naturally to him or Judith. One evening he told his wife that he had heard something terrible in court that afternoon. A woman had used a word (Berg spelled it out slowly: "S-H-I-T") that had made him so angry he'd wanted to slap her face. Judith was equally shocked. "I thought I was progressive," she says, "but bad language bothered me." On another occasion he mentioned some prostitutes he'd been defending, and how one of them had talked about "turning a trick." When Judith asked him what the expression meant, he confessed that he didn't know. He was hoping that his wife could fill him in. A teacher at Judith's school, an older man, sent a dozen roses to her apartment one afternoon, a gift for her, the note said. She was flattered by the gesture and when her husband came home from work, she expected him to be too. He blew into a rage.

"We were babies," Judith says, smiling at the memory. "Two little kids bumbling along, wondering if what we were doing was right. Being married was different then. People got married younger and before your wedding you had spent your whole life with certain morals. You could only kiss on the third date or you were a whore. Then all of a sudden you walk down an aisle and you're supposed to be open and free and it's all sex and supposed to be perfect. Have you ever wondered why so many of those marriages ended in divorce? Maybe that's a lot of pressure on a person. And you're supposed to make a lot of money. And that's more pressure. Alan attended the virginal campuses of the 1950s and a few years later he's a lawyer who's defending pimps and prostitutes, and he's learning that the pillar of the community is really a pimp with forty girls working for him in a motel. All of this is real confusing, especially if you're already not a together, mature man. You're still a kid and it's frightening."

Like her ex-husband, Judith Berg radiates intensity and talks roundly, in a stream of consciousness, her words beginning and ending nowhere in particular. She flows, making jokes, touching on a horde of ideas, insightful, inventive, tuning in another person with amazing speed, so she knows how to be interesting and provocative. She once had a therapist who told her to keep coming to her office, not because she needed better mental health, but because she was so entertaining. Also like Berg, she has presence, the ability to make you see and hear things not necessarily there. Both of them might have been superior actors. Each made the other resonate in a way no one else could. They were so finely attuned to each other's moods and misery, each other's need for electricity and crisis, they made a perfect match—perfect, if one is attracted to high-voltage romance.

"Alan told me about going to a whorehouse when he was younger," she says. "He was so upset by it. All he could think about was, 'My mother is so beautiful and my sister is so great and they're nice pure women and . . .' It was innocence. Absolutely innocent. This attitude about women was important to him. This feeling about what women should be but what you know human nature isn't and hasn't been and won't be. I think that idealization left an impact he could never cope with."

Berg's annual income climbed to $25,000, to $50,000, perhaps as high as $100,000 (later in life he told people that the only time his father ever walked up and shook his hand was after learning that the young attorney was making a hundred grand a year). In return for the kickbacks he was throwing the bondsmen, they were sending him more business than he could handle. A few years earlier he had entered the legal profession with firm ideas and ideals; justice was real and attainable and he was going to use his training to ferret it out, to defend the innocent, to make a contribution to society. By the early 1960s he was not only defending people he knew were guilty and thought should be punished, he had also discovered that he was very good at his job. At night in their apartment, he created defenses for clients who had raped or murdered and then recited them to Judith, convincing her that his logic was airtight and his client hadn't done things both of them knew he had. Berg was a verbal magician, a performer, when he went into the courtroom or just talking to his wife. He could argue any point of view with brilliance and conviction. His gifts pleased him, because they worked so well and made him a great deal of money, but they also made him ashamed.

In the small hours of the morning he left their bed and went into another room to sit, smoke, and think about what he did for a living. Judith often found him in the dark, weeping.

"He knew the rhetoric, he knew the law, and he liked how he presented himself in court," she says. "He really hated himself for what he did but *how* he did it he liked."

Berg had long been a restless sleeper—he shook, the veins stuck out on his temples, and according to Judith, he looked like a man in battle running for his life. He often awoke feeling strange, wrong. In the morning he experienced momentary blackouts or briefly lost control of his tongue when he tried to speak. Judith noticed the signs, unsure of what they meant but certain that she had to find out and offer help. On her own she went to doctors and questioned them, she read to learn more, and gradually she understood that he was experiencing petit mal seizures, a mild form of epilepsy. In time, as he became busier at work and more successful, the seizures got worse, changing from petit to grand mal. He blacked out completely or thrashed around on the floor, first at night but then in the daytime, in public, in the courtroom.

"You completely lose control," says Judith. "You fling yourself and smash everything in space. You have the most strength anyone ever has. You could break a wall or bite a chair in two."

You also lose control of bodily functions. He had seizures during intimate moments with his wife. Once he was sitting in front of a mirror in Chicago and saw his face begin to contort, his mouth twist and his cheeks twitch as the fit took hold. He was mortified.

Grand mal seizures are often followed by a comalike trance, from which victims of the illness wonder if they will recover. Berg came through all the seizures and comas, came through fighting and determined to triumph over the problem, ready to go back into the courtroom. But later, when he was away from his work and at home listening to jazz or sitting in silence, he recalled the last seizure and fell into a consuming depression. Epilepsy was a weakness, he believed, an ingrained, mysterious, awful weakness that was visiting itself upon him for reasons beyond his comprehension. Like a curse. Or maybe he did understand the reason why; maybe one is selected for the disease because one is physically weak or doing things morally questionable or there is simply something wrong inside that will never go away. The seizures are only the outer manifestation of the inner monster.

Judith tried to ignore Berg's illness and his worrying about it, tried to comfort him, tried to tell him that it didn't matter or portend anything bad for their marriage. She never used the words "handicapped" or "disabled" in reference to the condition, and she attempted to dispel the air of embarrassment that came with the aftermath of a grand mal seizure. Doctors put him on medication —the dosages got stronger with time—but the pills didn't stop the epilepsy or the problems left in its wake.

"I can't imagine how he would go through those seizures and then pick himself up and cope and go back to court," Judith says. "But finally, he just couldn't handle it. I don't know why I handled it. But if something's natural, what can you do? You can't hate someone for that. The fact that I understood a lot of stuff—maybe he resented that. The fact that I didn't shame him. You try to give someone encouragement that this affliction is not degrading and demeaning. But how do you do that? It planted the seeds for a lot of future problems. Maybe he used to think, How come this woman doesn't leave me? I can't answer that."

They went to a number of physicians and heard many different explanations and theories. One doctor made a suggestion that was concise and easy to act on. Berg was simply high-strung, full of anxiety, and that caused stress, which drove the neurological disorder and ended in seizures. He needed to relax after work and get away from his professional environment. He was not only wound exceptionally tight, he was also becoming more angry at himself and the world. The doctor knew just how to ease the pressure that so often caused headaches in the young man's overheated mind.

One evening Berg was sitting in a restaurant in Chicago waiting for his wife to join him. Arriving, Judith noticed something unusual in front of her husband and asked what it was.

"I don't know," he said. "But it has an olive in it and it's good."

Neither she nor Berg had ever been a drinker so Judith didn't give the martini much thought, not until he began swallowing them regularly, quickly acquiring the taste. After drinking one he indeed felt a little calmer; with two or three he felt even more calm and in control. His friends believed otherwise. They thought Berg became intoxicated remarkably fast and was then difficult, if not impossible, to be around. Within months of sipping his first martini, he had a new illness to go along with the epilepsy—alcoholism. Years later he told colorful stories about his escapades in Chicago as a drunk: being arrested a number of times for driving while inebriated and buying his way out of every arrest (he knew friends in high places who owed him one); parking his Porsche in Lake Michigan; picking a fight with Chicago Bears linebacker Dick Butkus, widely considered to be the toughest pro-football player of his time.

Some of these stories were apocryphal but the reality had color enough. In 1964 Berg began sharing an office with another, older attorney, Frank Oliver, known both as a highly skilled criminal defense lawyer, who would go on to represent Vietnam-era draft dodgers and free-speech advocates, and as a man with a taste for a cold drink. Oliver was quite taken by Berg's courtroom manner, by his potential and sense of humor.

In no time Oliver and the young attorney were friends and boozing companions, although Berg was clearly out of his league in the second capacity.

"He did not handle drinking at all well," recalls Oliver. "He underwent a most bizarre personality change, a real Jekyll and

Hyde. When he was not drinking he was very sweet, kindly. The most charming thing about him was his incessant wit. He and I had almost a love affair because we enjoyed each other so much. Every day late in the afternoon, he came into the office and his way of looking at the world tickled me and vice versa, and we were practically rolling on the floor."

Late afternoons became evenings of drink.

"His face would undergo a change, and an ugly personality transformation accompanied that," says Oliver. "He kind of lost the charm and gentleness. Alan was fundamentally very sensitive and caring of other's people feelings, but not when he was drunk."

In addition to epilepsy and drinking too much, he was trying to come to terms with a troublesome lifelong companion—boredom. While juggling his crowded legal schedule, he constantly thought up new schemes, diversions from the law. He and Judith promoted a few jazz concerts at Orchestra Hall, for a while they ran a Chicago movie theater, Berg opened a toy store, Granny Goodfox, for his mother and sister to manage. He became friendly with Judy Roberts, a jazz singer and pianist who performed in The Midas Touch, a nightclub across the street from Granny Goodfox.

"Alan was a man who tried to appear to be happily married," Frank Oliver says, "but I was not very persuaded. I think he felt that it was socially correct to give that impression."

Berg was drawn to late-night entertainment: He knew the jazz pianist Oscar Peterson and had provided informal legal counsel for Lenny Bruce, who from time to time was being charged in Chicago with using obscenity on stage. When Berg met Jackie Mason, the comic, Mason, like many other people, was charmed by the young man and found him funny. He decided to launch Berg as a stand-up comedian, but when he arranged for a tryout, the novice froze in front of a live audience, terrified of having a seizure during the show. This failure, along with the martinis and the ongoing boredom, put him in a bad funk.

He went back to the law, trying hard to fit into it and his domestic arrangement. He and Judith lived in Chicago's new Marina City towers, two circular apartment buildings rising above the lakefront and housing fashionable tenants. On the thirty-third floor, the Bergs entertained musicians, actors, sports figures, politicians, and people visiting Chicago who had once passed through Judith's parents' home in Denver. They rarely missed a Black Hawks' ice-hockey game. They went to private parties where Frank Sinatra sang. The action was constant. They were too busy to eat. Berg's legal reputation was growing, as was his spending money, which he dispensed with fast: a trip to London for his parents, a new car more exotic than the last, gifts (clothes usually) for Judith and himself. When Berg went shopping with friends, especially those from out of town, he liked to pull out a roll of bills and spend them with conspicuous nonchalance. He told observers that he didn't believe in credit cards; they were crass. Life was a whirlwind for the young couple, a roller coaster of intense social interaction and moments of private despair, particularly after a grand mal seizure or before he entered the courtroom to deliver a defense in which he did not believe. Even on nights when the epilepsy paid no visit, he awoke the next morning and asked his wife: What happened? Did something go wrong? Why do I feel this bad? He was a changing man, shedding his naïveté, leaving behind many of those who had known him in the past. Kenny Shraiberg saw his old friend a few times during those years and was always surprised. One evening they went out for drinks and Berg became so intoxicated and unmanageable that Shraiberg left him sitting alone on the front stoop of an apartment complex to fend for himself.

"Next morning he called me and everything was fine," Shraiberg says. "At that point he was talking a lot about women. He'd say, 'Kenny, you can get girls but I can't.' All the woman chasing he did was because of his feelings of inadequacy."

Shraiberg pauses, thoughtful, a perplexed sadness crossing his face. "You deal with prostitutes and lower-echelon Mafia people and some of it rubs off. It can get to the point that if you needed someone to do you a cruddy favor, you could ask them and say, 'Hey, look what I did for you.' That feeling of power led him down the path he ended up taking. He was just a nice kid but probably not the nicest adult in the world."

Judith watched the deterioration, hesitant about what to do. She knew her husband was miserable—when he wasn't ecstatic over a new idea or project—and she was trying to answer a very basic question: Were his unhappiness and the seizures and the drinking a result of things that were troubling in his law practice and marriage and social surroundings? Or was it deeper, a condition that was never going to leave? Was he simply an uncomfortable person, a disturbing presence—too questioning, too nervous and intense to adjust and fit in anywhere? Wasn't he dissatisfied with almost everything, including the idea of satisfaction itself? Hadn't he often told his wife that there was no hope for the satisfied mind? What could be duller than a complacent human being? Didn't things exist to be probed, examined, picked at until the truth was finally revealed?

Judith couldn't argue with any of his ideas or questions; she shared them herself. But where were they leading? What if they took you only up a blind alley of angry drunkenness? She was aware that something had to be done and she would have to initiate it, and eventually she did. Late in 1966 she made arrangements to return to Denver, with the notion that she would start the process of relocating to her hometown and Berg would follow. At the least it would be a change from their patterns in Chicago, and perhaps just what he needed.

"It was good for us, we were making money on our own, we were so close," she says of the first years of their marriage. "And then the epilepsy came as a shock. He had an elegant way of doing things—of dressing, of speaking, of handling himself—and he was brilliant and then this. It destroyed him, but it didn't have to. That's the thing. It was in his mind. Because it didn't destroy what we had. It should have but it didn't. His sickness served him well. It let him be sicker than he was. Do you understand?"

She's crying, and halts the words long enough to collect herself. "There was so much that Alan denied. And never wanted to acknowledge about being a handicapped person. I went along with that and didn't do as much as I might have. But that statement puts me in the savior category, and who knows? Sometimes, I wonder if loving somebody is more destructive than not."

# 8

## _REMEMBERING DAVID LANE_

Fred Wilkins is a ten-year veteran of a suburban Denver fire department and a native of Birmingham, Alabama. In his late thirties, the fireman is soft-spoken and good-looking, with muscular arms and an air of commitment—hard determination—in his speech, even in his smile. He has rather long hair and a Southern accent, but not a deep one. Half a decade ago he decided to give up his local leadership of the Ku Klux Klan and became a husband and a father instead.

"The Klan tries to preach racial pride," he says. "Racial pride is loving your race. Everyone else today—blacks and Mexicans—loves their race but when the white man does that he's called a bigot. Racial pride is something everybody should have. If you define a racist as someone who loves his race, then I am one. But I'm not against other races."

He shifts his weight, sitting on a bed upstairs at the Lakewood Fire Department. Nearby is a hole in the floor and inside it is the pole firemen slide down when the alarm rings. Wilkins looks prepared for emergencies. His maternal grandfather and grandmother were associated with the Klan in the South until a few years ago. Wilkins carries his grandfather's membership card with him everywhere. The fireman's parents had no truck with the organization because "my daddy was in World War II and the Klan wasn't big then." In the early 1970s Wilkins came to Colorado and noticed that there wasn't much right-wing activity in the area. As a patriotic gesture he became a member of the small local Klan chapter on July 4, 1976. In Alabama he had once seen a newspaper ad seeking people who might want to become members of the KKK, so he ran a similar advertisement in Denver's *Rocky Mountain News*.

"The shit hit the fan," he says. "Blown out of proportion. 'The KKK Invades Denver, Colorado'—that kind of bullshit. They took it real seriously but we got supporters from the ad.

"David Lane was in the Klan for a while, but I kicked him out. He refused to take orders. He would hand out Nazi literature and Klan literature at the same time. I told him not to, that the Klan had a bad enough image without that. The name 'Nazi' turns a lot of people off, so I never wanted anything to do with that. It's a stigma the Nazis will never overcome."

After Wilkins and Lane parted company in the late 1970s, Lane, a tall, rather handsome man with gentle eyes and a frowning mouth, spent several years looking for a new leader and political home. In 1981, when the National Association for the Advancement of Colored People held its annual convention in Denver, he decided to act on his own. The police had been informed of this and on June 28 they dispatched several cars to his apartment in suburban Aurora; when Lane departed home that evening the patrolmen were on his tail. They followed him for several blocks, but when the officers feared losing him they pulled him to the side of the road and searched his trunk. Inside was a rusty knife and sacks full of literature calling for death to people who cause or allow the races to mix. Lane wasn't arrested but the combination of being stopped by police and seeing no united right-wing movement in the Denver area left him considering new options.

One alternative was known as the United Klans of America, headed by Charles Howarth of Colorado Springs, who found recruits in eastern Colorado among farmers falling on hard times. The area was turning into something of a right-wing outpost. In bordering Kansas, the Posse Comitatus, which believes that the federal income tax is illegal and recognizes no authority higher than county officials, was becoming increasingly visible. And in 1983 William Potter Gale began delivering sermons on the evil in Jews, broadcast over radio station KTTL of Dodge City.

In 1982 Charles Howarth, along with Posse member Wesley White, was arrested and charged with transporting a pickup-load of TNT, which was to be used to destroy a federal courthouse in Denver. The defendants were intent on punishing judges in the courthouse who had given tough sentences to right-wing tax protesters. Both men were convicted and sent to jail. Without Howarth to lead the United Klans of America, David Lane was again at loose ends. His local prospects were not good but he did have another alternative. The Reverend Richard Butler's Aryan Nations compound in northern Idaho wasn't that far from Colorado; perhaps the answer lay there.

Fred Wilkins shifts on the bed again, as though expecting a fire alarm. Like David Lane, his involvement with the local Klan did not extend much past the late 1970s. After a highly publicized confrontation with Alan Berg in 1979, Wilkins decided that he didn't want the instant and long-term notoriety such an event can bring.

"Berg talked about the Klan a lot on the radio, putting the bad mouth on us continually," Wilkins says. "He knew about me. I was the leader. My name was in the paper. No one else would accept the position 'cause they were afraid of job security. I had a civil-service job and said what the hell.

"One day I heard Berg ridiculing us on the radio and it bothered me. I called a sponsor of his show and told him who I was and he listened to the tape we'd made of Berg and then canceled his ad on Alan's show. On the air Alan said to me, 'Come on down here,' so I did. I went into the studio and pointed my finger at him and said, 'I'm Fred Wilkins and you're gonna die.' I said that to scare him. It was my way of saying, 'Leave my ass alone on the radio.' "

He shakes his head. "When Berg was killed, my reaction was surprise. A guy like that's gonna have a lot of enemies, just as I do. People that know my reputation but not me. That was Alan's gig—to get people riled up. If you get ten thousand people mad at you, you might have one idiot in the crowd that would do something about it."

Wilkins was also surprised that police questioned him about David Lane.

"When they mentioned him to me, it set me back. I said, 'Oh, God, I forgot all about this guy.' David and I never had a conversation about Alan Berg."

# 9

## *TOTAL FAILURE*

A decade earlier Berg and his young bride had left Denver for Chicago and his career as a bright and promising lawyer. They were an enthusiastic, lively couple, moving confidently toward the future. Back then Lily Halpern had beseeched her daughter to come live in Denver near her parents. In the late 1960s Judith did return to her hometown to live, returned with her alcoholic husband, an ex-attorney who was afraid to go back to the pressures of the law, an epileptic whose illness made him reject the idea of fatherhood, a lost, unemployed drunk. The Halperns were less than delighted.

Berg entered St. Joseph's hospital to dry out, and to avoid seeing people in Denver who would remember the jovial, wisecracking redhead of his college days. Even his hair was losing its color. Judith moved in with her parents. Every day she went to St. Joseph's to visit her husband, check on his progress, and discuss their next step. He was depressed, not because of the withdrawal from alcohol but because he had failed in the legal profession, failed as a stand-up comic, failed as a husband, winding up in the psychiatric ward of a hospital—while other men were out making money and providing for their kin. He said he was sorry. He put his head in her lap and cried. Judith wasn't critical; she tried to understand; she said she understood. Weeks went by and Berg's spirits gradually began to rise. He had no desire for another drink (he never took one the rest of his life, and helped enroll any number of problem boozers in Alcoholics Anonymous), and slowly he began to feel stronger, more certain he could leave the hospital and function in the working world. But what would he do? Where does a talkative, angry, funny man whose head is bursting with ideas and observations look for a job, once he has turned his back on the courtroom and the stage? Perhaps he should return to the law; surely there was less pressure and less corruption in Denver than in Chicago. Maybe he could handle it here. He and Judith talked it over but their conclusion was finally no. He needed something easier, at least for a while, something that would let him more gently connect with life on the other side of the hospital walls.

One day he called her from St. Joseph's and told her to come immediately, he was escaping the psych ward for good. That morning he had read an ad in the paper about a shoe store called Fontius in the Cherry Creek shopping center, which was looking for a salesman. As a boy he'd sold shoes in Chicago. He'd worked for a shoe parlor during college. It was something he was good at, especially in women's footwear. He could persuade them to buy anything.

"That's great," Judith told him, pleased that he wanted to find employment but worried about its effect on him.

"No, it's not great," he said. "But it's a start."

Judith drove him from the hospital to Fontius, where he talked himself into the position in a matter of minutes. The store wanted him to begin immediately—Berg had orders to return to St. Joseph's. He also had a hospital identification tag on his wrist and was under strict admonitions not to remove it. Judith went to a nearby Walgreen's and bought Scotch tape, Berg shoved the tag up to his elbow, taped it in place, covered it with his shirtsleeve, and went to work. While he pitched shoes Judith went to her parents' house and phoned Berg's doctor with the news. The physician was upset—it was against hospital rules to remove a patient as Judith had done and not bring him back. Did Berg have his pills with him? How would he cope with the strain of the job? Didn't patient? The doctor insisted that she call Berg and make certain he had his medication and was taking it. When she refused, the physician asked if she was arguing with him.

"I was arguing with him and I was right," she says. "Calling Alan and asking about his pills was another way to remind him that he was sick and to embarrass him. This was not the time for that."

Every morning he walked the ten blocks from the Halpern residence to his job in Cherry Creek, gaining strength and the feeling that he was recovering from his ills in Chicago. The epilepsy was still there, petit and grand mal seizures, but the drinking was gone and he was working again and bringing home a paycheck, albeit a small one. Something new would come along; things would change; they always had. When he ran into old friends from college neither they nor he dwelled on his job at Fontius. Most of his classmates had families and successful careers in business or stockbrokering or other lucrative pursuits. Instead of discussing the present, Berg regaled listeners with tales of being a defense attorney in Chicago, making big money and pleading the cases of mafiosi. Those things may not have been easy to live through, or with, they may have turned him into a despairing alcoholic, but they now made for spellbinding stories and deflected the reality of being a shoe salesman in Cherry Creek. And if the tales were only partially true, what did it matter? They entertained people and that was what he wanted to do: be interesting, be amusing, convince other people that he was leading a fascinating life. He liked to talk about himself, but was it himself he was really talking about? Or was it another character, like an invented man in a novel? Who was Alan Berg anyway? A good Jewish husband and provider, who had once sent his parents to England on vacation so his father could see where he had emigrated from? Or was he a boozer who liked to chase women? Wasn't he someone who loved jazz and good poetry and believed in truth and justice and equality more than anything else? Or wasn't he, finally, a wicked man with an unholy disease? Between shoe sales, he had a lot of time to think about such questions. He was beginning to wonder if the answer to all of them was yes.

One noon hour, he was the only employee in the store and waiting on a black woman customer when a white woman came in. He knew the second woman; she was older, Jewish, a force in Denver social circles and the owner of many pairs of expensive shoes. Once or twice, standing by herself, she tried to get Berg's attention, but he was occupied with finding a pair of heels for the black woman. Exasperated, she waved at the salesman and he dismissed her with a terse remark, adding that he would be with her as soon as he finished with his customer. An hour later, after she had complained to the store's manager, Berg called his wife from a pay phone in Cherry Creek and told her to come pick him up.

"I knew it was bad," says Judith. "Either a seizure or he took a drink or something serious. When he said, 'I've been fired,' the words were like happiness compared to the other possibilities."

They rode around town that afternoon, Berg venting his anger at the management of Fontius, calling them bastards and bigots. When his ire toward them began to fade, he started in on himself. He was a total failure. The man who had passed the Illinois bar at twenty-two now couldn't hold a job as a shoe salesman and bring home a few dollars a week. This was the bottom, worse than sitting in that hospital and being treated like a drunk. He was nothing— nothing! They should never have returned to Denver. Why hadn't she married someone who could make her life tolerable? Why hadn't she divorced him years ago? There was no reason for him to live. None.

Judith was so upset by his ranting that she drove around the block once, then did it again, then started again, going in circles and trying to counter his words, telling him that he wasn't a failure and the firing was for the best. That made him angrier. He finally asked where the hell she was driving—the question startled her into clutching the steering wheel and pointing the car downtown.

"Let's go there and get you another job," she said.

He sneered, lit a cigarette, and returned to the issue of racism in shoe stores.

On Sixteenth Street, in Denver's business district, Judith came to Stout Street and paused at a red light. Berg noticed a new department store being built on the corner; at his wife's behest he got out of the car and wandered over to the construction site. He saw Dick Auer, a friend of the Bergs who owned several clothing shops in Denver and planned to open another at this location. They began to talk. Judith sat in the car and watched them, fretting, trying to imagine what it was like for her husband to interact with successful people who had once been his peers. Perhaps she had been wrong to bring him downtown, where people were busy and thriving, so quickly after he had been fired. When he returned to the car he was employed as a clothing salesman.

They rented a townhouse in Cherry Creek for two hundred dollars a month, moved into their new address, got a basset hound named Esquire, and Berg's mind became fervid with ideas. He had long been interested in design and decor and now he wanted to start a business of his own: something in custom-made apparel. He was so taken with the prospect he couldn't sleep at night, lying awake in the living room, smoking, listening to music, and thinking about his store. It would be unlike anything Denver had ever seen. He would show these rubes how to dress, he would teach them something about style. Through all his previous adventures, Berg had never lost his taste for expensive, perfectly fitted clothes, and over the years he had accumulated scores of suits, shirts, sport coats, and hundreds of pairs of shoes—he would study his wardrobe and create his own designs. That was his real calling, wasn't it?

The world of fashion. He would be the finest haberdasher in the history of the town.

Very early one morning Judith awoke in bed and was alone. When she went into the living room her husband wasn't there or in the kitchen or anywhere else in the townhouse. She found a note and quickly stuffed it into her pocket, got in the car, and drove downtown, searching the deserted 3 A.M. streets for a tall, thin man smoking a cigarette. She cruised the avenues, twisting her neck, but seeing no one who resembled Ichabod Crane, so she kept driving. He was standing on a dark corner staring at a building, pointing up with his long vivid hands. When she pulled alongside him and spoke his name, he didn't take his eyes off the structure or say hello.

"Isn't that a perfect spot for The Shirt Broker?" he wanted to know.

# 10

---

# *"THE SWORD IS OUT"*

---

By the early 1980s the political
and social changes taking place across the United States were all
pointing in the same direction. At the center—or mainstream—of
that change was the landslide presidential election of Ronald Reagan
in the first year of the new decade. His politics, like many people's,
may have been hard to define or accurately label, but he clearly
represented conservatism, Republicanism, patriotism, and traditional values that were in reasonably close alignment with the beliefs
of the emerging Fundamentalist Christian right.

A year before Reagan's first election, the Reverend Jerry Falwell
of the Thomas Road Baptist Church in Lynchburg, Virginia, began

---

the lobbying and political-action group the Moral Majority, which campaigned for the acceptance of practicing the Christian religion in public schools, and campaigned against abortion, pornography, homosexuality, and other forms of "immorality." Several years after Reagan's election, Falwell's lobby claimed 6.5 million members. By the mid-eighties, 1,000 of America's 9,642 radio stations and 200 local TV stations had become affiliated with evangelical or Fundamentalist Christianity (in Denver alone, three such stations were competing with *The Alan Berg Show*). At mid-decade various Fundamentalist preachers around the nation were not only constantly delivering their Christian message via television, they were also involved in a battle for ratings that resembled a soap-opera derby. According to 1985 figures released by the Nielsen ratings service, these were the Top 10: 16.3 million of the country's 80 million TV households tuned in the Reverend Pat Robertson's evangelical program *The 700 Club* at least once a month. Jimmy Swaggart's weekly show reached 9.3 million homes; Robert Schuller's 7.6 million; Jim Bakker's and Oral Roberts's 5.8 million; Jerry Falwell's 5.6 million; Kenneth Copeland's 4.9 million; Jimmy Swaggart's daily Bible-study show 4.5 million; Richard DeHaan's *Day of Discovery* 4 million; and Rex Humbard's 3.7 million. Based on this research, the Christian Broadcasting Network of Virginia Beach, Virginia, estimated that more than one half of all Americans with a TV set watched at least one of the sixty nationally syndicated religious programs every month.

In the fifties, sixties, and seventies, liberal Protestant church leaders and Catholic priests had marched for civil rights or against wars or nuclear armaments. In the eighties Fundamentalists decided it was their turn to have the spotlight and to use their political clout. They succeeded through organizing, through efficient fundraising—every Sunday evening during his TV program, Reverend Falwell had sixty-two telephone operators standing by to take donations—and through the belief that their religious convictions were absolutely right. They perceived a vast spiritual void in the country and had the answers to fill it. Throughout the nation Fundamentalists opened and ran ten thousand day schools for small children and thousands more grade schools; they followed a curriculum known as Accelerated Christian Education, which tries to parallel the teachings of the Bible and avoids what is generally regarded as a liberal humanist education.

The Reverend Pat Robertson talked often about running for president in 1988. But even without a Fundamentalist preacher in the White House, the religious right had a plan for increasing their influence under President Reagan. The American Coalition for Traditional Values, a conglomerate of evangelical Christian groups, lobbied hard in Washington to establish a quota system in line with their views. Since at least 25 percent of the American population was Fundamentalist, they argued, then at least 25 percent of the government's employees should share that faith.

While the country's mainstream conservative forces were becoming more powerful and active, the radical right was drifting toward violence. In the early 1980s membership in the Ku Klux Klan began to fall, from a high of nearly 12,000 in 1981 to 6,500 in 1984. Large Klan rallies were tapering off and the national leadership was becoming fragmented. Financial support was sliding—things got so bad that the United Klans of America Imperial Wizard, Robert Shelton, had to take a job selling cars in Tuscaloosa, Alabama. Yet while the Klan's numbers may have been dwindling, those who stayed in the organization were committed to a harsher set of ideas than in the past; and instead of welcoming the conservative shift in the country, they tended to loathe it, for it drew members from their ranks toward more conventional center-right politics. It left them isolated on the fringe, without a liberal in the White House to rail against.

In 1979 Ku Klux Klan members in Greensboro, North Carolina, opened fire on white left-wing demonstrators, killing five of them. In 1981 Henry Francis Hays, Exalted Cyclops of the UKA's Mobile Klavern, beat and hung a black teenager. At the trial it was revealed that the victim was killed "in order to show Klan strength in Alabama."

Don Black, Grand Wizard of the Knights of the KKK, had once

denounced neo-Nazis and their sympathizers as anti-American. With the 1980s the stigma of Nazi Germany was beginning to fade into history (as punk-rock musicians were turning the trappings of Nazi culture, the swastikas and salutes, into an extremity of chic). During the summer of 1982, Don Black went to Hayden Lake, Idaho, to attend Reverend Richard Butler's Aryan Nations World Congress. Right-wing activists from around the United States, Canada, and West Germany came to the conference and wore Nazi-like uniforms, went to political and religious indoctrination seminars, and heard speeches about an impending race war in America. They received weapons instruction and lessons in cross burning. Gunfire and paeans to Hitler filled the Idaho air.

Don Black was eventually imprisoned for his role in an aborted scheme to invade and take over the tiny Caribbean island of Dominica. Tom Metzger, once a leader of the Klan in Southern California, split from the group to form the White American Resistance—WAR. He began hosting a cable-TV show, *Race and Reason*, the message of which was to treat those who stand in one's way just as the "boys in Greensboro" had treated the leftist demonstrators in 1979. In 1981 several Klansmen, led by Louis Beam, a Vietnam veteran and former Grand Dragon of the Knights of the KKK, attacked Vietnamese refugees who were operating fishing boats off the coast of Texas. Several boats were burned but no charges were filed in the matter. Beam was convicted of using government property in Fort Worth, Texas, for paramilitary exercises without a permit. In 1983 he wrote a book called *Essays of a Klansman*, in which he outlined how Aryan "Warriors" could earn decimal points by assassinating Jews or blacks or federal officials or by committing other criminal acts; when the points equaled the number one, you had earned your place in the "Heavenly Reich." Beam would lay plans to host a cable-TV show in Dallas and for a nationwide computer network for those who subscribed to the beliefs of Aryan Nations.

In 1983 the Human Rights Commission in Idaho reported that statewide cases of racial harassment had increased by 550 percent in the past three years. Swastikas and the words JEW SWINE appeared on the exterior of a Hayden Lake restaurant owned by a sixty-two-year-old resident named Sid Rosen. Connie Fort, a local white woman who was married to a black man, received hate mail and death threats from an area neo-Nazi, Keith Gilbert. The situation in Idaho was serious enough to move the state legislature to pass a law declaring the harassment of anyone for racial or religious reasons—or burning a cross on private property—a felony with a five-year prison sentence. In 1984 Idaho passed another law making it illegal for white-supremacist literature to enter state penitentiaries and for followers of white supremacy to conduct the "religious services" that accompany their philosophy. "I feel there is substantial concern for the safety of life, liberty and property of minority inmates if this group were allowed to meet," wrote Al Murphy, the state's corrections director, in explaining his support of the statute. Despite these laws and warnings by local authorities that northern Idaho was an explosive waiting to be detonated, Aryan Nations continued to function and thrive, just as it had in the past. Freedom of religion was intact in the Northwest woods.

Beyond Idaho, radical-right organizations were growing in numbers and influence, with a membership in the thousands and sympathizers in the tens of thousands. As of 1984 the federal government had identified seventy-five separate groups that were more or less committed to the ultimate goal of those at the annual Hayden Lake summer congress: a white Christian America with roughly 100 million citizens, all of Aryan extraction. The nation would be ruled by the divine will of God as revealed in the Scriptures and interpreted by Aryan preachers and acted upon by Aryan Warriors. The message of William Pierce's *Turner Diaries* was starting to reach, and make sense to, an expanding number of people.

In 1981 Joseph Paul Franklin was convicted of a sniper attack that killed two black youths who were jogging in Salt Lake City. Earlier he had shot and killed a young interracial couple in Madison, Wisconsin. Franklin was sentenced to two life terms. In 1982 Frank Spisak of Cleveland, Ohio, shot two black men dead and then lay in wait for a Jewish professor whom he knew would be passing by. As the man approached, Spisak took a .22 pistol from a hollowed-out copy of Hitler's *Mein Kampf* and fired point-blank, killing him. At his trial, when Spisak learned that the victim was neither a professor nor Jewish, he apologized to the jury for executing the wrong man. His goal, he said, had been to kill Jews and blacks, "as many as I could before I got caught. One thousand, one million, the more the better." The thirty-three-year-old concluded his courtroom speech with "Heil Hitler!" and a Nazi salute.

In February of 1983, when U.S. marshals came for Gordon Kahl, a longtime member of the Posse Comitatus, he offered resistance. The marshals and local police from Medina, North Dakota, were there to arrest Kahl for violating probation after his conviction on a false-tax-return charge. Kahl and his son opened fire with automatic weapons, the father killing two of the marshals but losing his boy in the exchange of bullets. After escaping and fleeing to the Ozark mountains, Kahl engaged in another gun battle with authorities. One lawman was killed but so was the fugitive.

In Arkansas, near where Kahl had died, the Covenant, Sword and Arm of the Lord had a 224-acre compound where converts were taught that famine, race-rioting, and economic collapse were imminent in the United States, and were instructed in paramilitary and survivalist strategies. The compound contained a stockpile of rifles, grenades, computer equipment, a small bomb factory, and a good supply of cyanide. In 1983 the spiritual leader of CSA, Jim Ellison, was indicted on an arson charge in the burning of a Bloomington, Indiana, synagogue. At that summer's Aryan Nations congress, he told the gathering: "I'm sorry I wasn't with Gordon Kahl when they found him. I just wish I'd been there. . . . I'm here to tell you that the sword is out of the sheath and it's ready to strike. For every one of our people they killed, we ought to kill one hundred of theirs."

The early 1980s were mere prelude, a time for scattered acts by individual men; time for Reverend Butler to be arrested for traveling to Los Angeles and taking part in a cross-burning ceremony in the San Fernando Valley; time for the extreme right to began talking about the "propaganda of the deed," an old anarchist phrase meaning terrorism; time for David Lane, speaking on behalf of Aryan

Nations in an interview on National Public Radio, to say that "no step is too radical to take to ensure the survival of our Aryan race. All of Western civilization and all of civilization through eternity depends on the survival of our race."

Did the plan for survival include violence?

"We have a strategy, which I cannot tell you about, that is being undertaken all around the world," he said. "If I answered that question I would reveal to you what is going on and I can't."

Then, for no apparent reason, he broke into laughter.

# 11

---

# *A NATURAL*

---

By the late 1960s Berg was making a success of The Shirt Broker in Denver's Albany hotel. He was a good designer and sold his product with verve. But while wearing the latest fashions, driving a sports car, and earning money again held his interest for a few years, they weren't enough to fill the recurrent void. He had escaped the legal profession in Chicago and beaten alcoholism, but where had it taken him? He didn't want to be a haberdasher for the rest of his life. What could he do with this infernal pounding in his head, this river of words and thoughts that were always there and straining to get out? They created a painful throb that nicotine and caffeine dulled only temporarily.

---

He considered returning to the law—he could pass the Colorado bar and go into practice in Denver—but was that what he really wanted? He was nearing forty and he didn't know what he wanted to do.

When the boredom and constraint of The Shirt Broker became too much he opened another branch of the store. His mind was swift and explosive, he was superb at conceptualizing new ideas, but running a business on a daily basis was another matter: the handling of invoices, the order forms, and the paying of bills meant endless detail work, follow-through, and a steady sense of responsibility. He soon hired a young man, Dick Agren, to run one branch of The Shirt Broker so he could concentrate on other things.

What he enjoyed most about the business was meeting new people, getting to know them. His shop closed at 10 P.M. and after work he and a new friend often went to a cheap all-night White Spot restaurant in downtown Denver, where Berg talked about what was on his mind: politics, jazz, women, men, religion, divorce, Jews, blacks, Vietnam, Gentiles, President Nixon, city affairs, infidelity, American culture, marriage, unhappiness, women's liberation, homosexuality, drinking, drugs, everything. He was an avalanche of words. He loved words; he didn't seem to have any fear of them at all. They filled up the air and kept people from noticing that he was (in his opinion) an ugly man. His words could make people laugh or cry or get women into bed or bring him new friendships or make time disappear. Words were like breath itself, keeping one alive. He had always wanted to be a jazz musician— to stand before people and improvise moving, intricate solos—but the only instrument he had ever learned to play was his voice. Talking fast and talking nonstop relieved some of that pressure in his head. And allowed him to be entertaining, in a safe way. A live audience of several hundred strangers sitting before him and waiting for him to perform was terrifying, but just one person, a friend, was nothing to fear. If, while talking, he had a petit mal seizure and his mouth contorted or his tongue lost coordination, he'd discovered how to avert his face for a moment and drive his words onward, until his tongue was under control. Then he would slip his hand into his pocket for a pill and deftly slide it between his lips. He loved these White Spot restaurants late at night, with only the waitresses and a few loners or drifters present. He could carry on here as long as someone would listen. He was drifting too, but toward what no one could have known. Many of the acquaintances who went with him to the White Spot were charmed by this "new" Alan Berg, even more frenetic, loquacious, and intense than in the past. A few of his older friends from college found him too self-absorbed for their taste. They didn't like being an audience.

One day at The Shirt Broker he met a tall, striking black woman, Audrey Oliver, and was intrigued. Before long he had envisioned a plan for he and Audrey to form a partnership, using her sex and race to help secure a loan from the Small Business Administration, and to open The Boot Broker, a shoe store to complement his other enterprises. Although he was still living with Judith, he hoped that romance—and selling footwear—would flourish with Audrey.

To Judith's dismay, both The Boot Broker and the love affair came into being; the store functioned well enough but the romance was wildly tempestuous, generating many anecdotes. Berg's favorite, which he later talked about on the radio, concerned the time Audrey broke his nose with a shoe stool.

"I can't describe their relationship," says Dick Agren, who eventually left The Shirt Broker to work for a similar business in Los Angeles. He is a handsome, well-dressed man who claims that Berg taught him everything he knows about clothing. "I can't do the relationship justice. I saw it—a lot of it occurred in public, but . . . If you took the most bizarre, far-out soap opera and doubled it, that's what you had. . . . I don't know if she actually broke his nose that day, but she certainly bloodied it. When I came in, she had him down on the floor. But there was a lot of caring between them. He gave her a business opportunity, helped her through a difficult divorce, and was always there for her. But they fought— a look or a word would set it off. When it happened at two P.M., that was the end of the work day. Every time, just when I thought the relationship was over, it would come back again. Alan once told me that if he could take a pill to handle his libido, he would. He said that after a particularly exasperating day."

In The Shirt Broker, Berg also met Laurence Gross, who hosted a radio talk show on KGMC, a small daytime-only station in the suburb of Englewood. Gross not only liked visiting the store to buy shirts but was enthralled with the tall, skinny fashion plate who owned the shop. Berg seemed able to talk spontaneously on any subject, talk with humor and insight and a point of view that caught Gross's fancy. He suggested that Berg come on the air with him some afternoon, just to promote his business. Berg protested: What would he find to say? What if he had a seizure on the air? What if he froze as he had when trying to be a stand-up comic? Eventually Gross and Judith persuaded him that he had nothing to fear, so he agreed to go on. The first time Berg sat behind a microphone at KGMC was on an autumn Sunday afternoon, in 1971, a media time slot competing with a radio and TV broadcast of a Denver Broncos football game. In the metropolitan area, following the Broncos was, and remains, a local religion. For years the games have attracted most of the available Denver audience. Gross asked Berg to be on the air at this time in part because he knew there would be little pressure on the guest. No one would be listening.

"We started talking about downtown development in Larimer Square but that lasted about two minutes," Gross once recalled. "Alan turned the subject to the law and then he was into birth control, the Panama Canal, plea bargaining. It was nonstop. He was so fast. All of the sudden the phones lit up. I said to myself, 'The guy's absolutely incredible. A natural.' "

Gross invited him back on several occasions. Then one weekend the host had to go to California to attend to personal matters. He approached Bob McWilliams, KGMC's owner, and wondered if it would be all right for Berg to run the show by himself.

"I was sort of desperate," says McWilliams, in his late sixties and suffering from a serious respiratory ailment known as fibrosis of the lung. He speaks with some difficulty and in order to breathe must carry a small tankful of oxygen with him at all times. "I was going skiing that weekend and didn't want to stay home and do the show myself. Laurence brought Berg in. I'd never seen him in my life. Strange individual. Sort of gaunt, scarecrowishlike. He didn't have a beard at that time, or I probably wouldn't have hired him. I was one of those narrow-minded old curmudgeons who didn't go for that. He had a gift of gab and repartee that was good. I could tell. Fast on the uptake. Pretty good voice for it. I said, 'Well, let's give it a try.' He came on that Sunday. I was in Breckenridge, where reception isn't very good. I listened and it was readily evident that he knew how to excite controversy, develop ideas and elicit response. He didn't set the world on fire that afternoon. In fact he didn't set the world on fire for the first year. But he was competent and developing."

Listening to Berg's early appearances on the radio leaves several impressions. First, he completely overshadowed Laurence Gross. The host, like most talk-show personalities in 1971, seemed committed to polite dialogue. If things started to veer toward color or controversy he quickly moved them in another direction. And his Denver audience matched him in good manners and genuine friendliness. Virtually every caller began his on-the-air session with, "Hello, Laurence, how are you feeling today?" "Fine, thanks." "Well, that's good." At KGMC radio rudeness was not out of line; it was nonexistent.

Technically, Berg did everything wrong: He inhaled cigarettes in such a manner that a listener heard him sucking the smoke, and he exhaled the same way; he talked too fast and slurred some phrases; his voice wasn't polished or measured as were most professional radio voices; his words grew louder and faded away because he was incapable of keeping his mouth at a set distance from the microphone; when he became excited, he sounded as if he were spitting; the rustling of his sport coat might have been thunder.

He never did overcome most of these problems, and in time studio engineers decided the only way to solve them was to hang the mike from the ceiling where he couldn't spill coffee on it or bat it away. He was a disaster with radio commercials—he could not memorize anything or read the same copy the same way twice in a row; could not complete a thirty-second ad in half a minute, because something in the commercial would strike his fancy and launch him into extraneous anecdotes and he would ramble until he ran out of breath. When he became better known, TV producers tried to employ him for ads in that medium but after twenty takes they usually threw up their hands and sent him home. These were minor troubles. If Berg became angry during his show, he would leave the studio or the building and other radio personnel would have to find him and coax him back onto the air. Part of his job in the early days was reading the talk-show call-in rules to those listening—how often one could call, how not to mention one's last name on the show, and other matters of etiquette. While attempting this, Berg might confess to having several failed romances with lesbians or do five-minute riffs on how much he loved his dog.

If he managed to get around to outlining the rules to a caller, he usually told the person to break them: "I've got to explain this— it's part of my job—didn't you call yesterday? You don't know? What do you mean you don't know? What's the matter with you? Don't you understand we have rules on this show and you have to follow them? Here are the rules—are you Jewish? If you're Jewish you can't call today. I'm a lawyer—I should be able to understand these rules—they're not that complex. Can you imagine thinking these up—what if that was your job? Did you call yesterday? Why not? I don't care if people call every day—it wouldn't bother me —this is a lonely position—but we have these rules. Are you Polish? Poles can't call on Tuesday or from the southern part of town. Now here are the rules—where are you calling from?—are you in a phone booth?—this is the craziest thing—will you call me to-morrow? Please. Why don't you answer me? Do you want to hear the rules or not? . . ."

Technical difficulties and his manic digressions notwithstanding, from his first appearances on Gross's show he displayed qualities that were captivating and cannot be taught. He intuited the inti-macy of radio. He spoke to the private emotions of an individual. He made a virtue of his excess; somehow that mad energy was uplifting. He went from one subject to the next without a pause. His voice had an edge of tension, of possibility, as if it might take you someplace you had never been before, somewhere exciting and perhaps even dangerous. Sharing the program with Laurence Gross, Berg so utterly dominated the show and attracted so many new callers—especially women, who consistently found him "a very remarkable person"—that at one point Gross, in mock anguish, began to shout, "What about me? What about me?"

"The first moment he walked into my studio," Gross has said, "he knew exactly what he was doing."

What was most arresting about Berg was that he created the notion that one was listening to a very honest man. And that in turn set off an odd sensation. After hearing him talk on live radio for several minutes, one realized that the conventional media had dulled the senses; one had little expectation of hearing someone say what they really thought or felt. They would be polite and, most often, predictable. Berg was neither of these, even when being soft-spoken and gentle, and he consistently kept one off balance.

"At first," he said, referring to his past on an early show with Gross, "my drinking was fun and relaxation. Then it became pure escape, a way of avoiding all the ugliness in myself and my profession. Arguing a trial in front of a judge and jury, and having these epileptic problems—I found this to be the greatest failure of my life. Alcohol became a way of ensuring myself when this happened. For me the key to stopping drinking was a total loss of dignity, a feeling of ugliness I was showing to everyone. Finally when I got low enough and saw myself crumbling as a human being, in terms of losing speech and the ability to walk, there comes a moment when everyone abandons you. My very own mother had indulged me, which is the worst thing you can do. But when she abandoned me too, the only choice was death or getting back on my feet. When you are no longer an alcoholic, that is not a miracle cure. You are still depressed and unhappy, you can just handle it now. . . . Being an ex-alcoholic is something to be extraordinarily proud of."

When a woman called and started in on the evils of drink, Berg told her that imbibing alcohol can be very beneficial for certain people. When another woman phoned to congratulate him for leaving the bottle, and then began to condemn the use of marijuana, he politely but firmly argued with her about the drug, telling her not to equate his tobacco-and-alcohol abuse with smoking pot (by all accounts, he never took drugs for recreation). The woman on the phone seemed confused by his remarks. How could an ex-alcoholic defend the use of illegal drugs? Was he trying to be funny? Before the conversation could develop, Gross broke in, got the woman off the air, and went to a commercial. More calls came in, mostly from women. It appeared they were unaccustomed to a man who was so open and comfortable talking about his problems. Several of the women wanted to know if he would be back on Gross's program to speak with them again.

Berg's "honesty" on the radio, which was present at his first show and his last, was not a simple thing. For much of his adult life he fabricated stories about himself; some were exaggerations of reality, some were outright lies (he had a first wife, his mother was Irish, he drove a cab in college and delivered johns to houses of prostitution . . .). Yet on the radio he *seemed* honest, in a way that many talk-show hosts never do. He was emotionally truthful—he told you what he felt at the moment he was feeling it—if not always literally telling the truth. Listeners sensed this and responded in ways other people could not make them respond. They opened up, exposing certain positive emotions or their own inner ugliness. Berg's kind of truthfulness worked well on the radio. It works equally well for great actors or politicians or anyone interested in finding people's viscera and making them twitch.

When Gross decided to move to San Diego, McWilliams gave Berg his job. Before taking this position and becoming the morning talk-show host on KGMC, Berg told his wife innumerable times that he would not succeed as a regular on the radio, it was too much pressure, he didn't have enough to say, he would have a seizure during a broadcast and be humiliated, or lose his program. To allay his fears, Judith often came to the station with him and sat in or near the studio during his show. In time, when he was able to overcome his trepidation about being on the air and didn't have to be talked into going to work, there were other difficulties. Frequently he was late to KGMC—his car would break down; his basset hound, Esquire, would run away and Berg would search for the dog until it was found; he couldn't find the right tie to go with the rest of his outfit and wouldn't leave home until he did. Employees at KGMC had never seen a life so erratic or a man so impeccably dressed. When he did manage to get to work on time he had problems with cigarettes. His smoking annoyed some listeners, his habit of littering the studio with butts and ashes disturbed certain fellow workers, and his penchant for unconsciously dropping live cigarettes into trash cans and starting fires was a source of concern to management. When Berg began talking with a caller, he appeared to have no control over what else he might be doing. His trash fires became as routine as his lateness. Yet he was functioning. With the constant support of Judith, with the indulgence of his boss and colleagues, with the encouragement of callers to his show, he gradually began to feel more comfortable sitting behind a microphone and talking to the world.

"This was safe for Alan," Judith says. "This was possible."

"I never knew what he would do next," says Bob McWilliams. "He had a tendency to go in for the bizarre and what I call the tasteless stuff. You know he'd invite anybody onto his show. There was a gal here who was a star of a porno movie—forget her name—but he wanted to bring her on the air. I'm not sure I let him do that. But he did ask. I had to step on him once in a while because he was sort of wild and exuberant. Once he understood that I meant business, I didn't have any trouble with him."

McWilliams coughs. "I always thought that he thought I was strictly a square and a deadhead, which was all right. I operated my station when the FCC [Federal Communications Commission] was very much on your neck. As I understand it now, the FCC rarely gets involved in programming anymore. We had protests to them about Berg. There were bomb threats. The Englewood Fire Department was out there at the station two or three times. Oh hell, I'd come to work and I couldn't get in. The doors were locked. Employees would say that the police had just been there. I didn't reprimand Alan because he'd expressed an opinion and got some nut out there excited. That, after all, was freedom of the press. It wasn't my job to curtail him.

"Although he was the last guy in the world to admit it, I think Alan studied pretty carefully the techniques of the radio business, accepting this and rejecting that. There was method in his madness. He learned the subjects that touched the buttons and he pushed them regularly. He'd say to the audience, 'I want to talk about this,' and they wouldn't sometimes. But he'd get them back on it, which is the mark of a good talk man. Talk radio is so successful because of the sense of community people get out of it. We live in an era that is so impersonal, so mechanical, so remote that people love to get on the country party line and talk with Aunt Jessie and raise a little bit of hell. It's a throwback to the old country store, and sitting on the porch and whittling and yakking about this and that. It's partly the desire to listen in on a long-distance call. Or anything that's human. People just sort of like it. They figure it'll tune them in to what's happening."

In later years on the radio Berg would become something quite different from what he was in the early 1970s. Then, under Bob McWilliams, he was more or less straight and it was his straightness that was appealing. He would evolve into a screamer, rude, cutting off callers, bludgeoning people from his microphone. In many ways he was more interesting when he began than after he became popular and notorious, and in time he would circle back toward his point of departure on the radio. It had taken him decades to find a home for his voice, his mind, and his passionate need to make a connection with other human beings. It would take the best part of another decade to understand the gift. By then, it was too late.

# 12

## "WHITE WOMEN GIVE UP ON WHITE MEN"

Warren McKinzie is eating a steak with enthusiasm, pausing to swat at a fly near his head. He misses and returns to his plate with gusto. In his late thirties, McKinzie has long dark sideburns, a moustache, and is wearing a black cap. His eyes are greenish blue, questioning, revealing some shyness. It is 5 P.M. and he has just gotten out of bed to come to one of his favorite Denver restaurants. He works a government job, graveyard shift, and enjoys a steak for breakfast. Country music plays in the background and waitresses frequently pass by the table on their way to serve other customers or to ask McKinzie if he wants anything. The cadence of his speech alters slightly when he looks at a pretty woman.

"I've known Dave Lane for five, six years. I was once his best friend. I'm still his friend. I want you to know that."

He glances around the restaurant to see if anyone is listening.

"I went to Dave's house in Aurora one time for a naturalization ceremony for the KKK. They were letting people into the Klan. Fred Wilkins called me and asked me to go there as a witness. This was in 1978, the fall. I'd met Fred at a McDonald's on East Colfax. I didn't have a job and I was down and out. I had a twenty-dollar bill in my pocket. He said we'd file a lawsuit against the fire department for discriminating against hiring white people. He said all you have to do is join the KKK and we'll do this for you. He took fifteen of my twenty dollars for an initiation fee and signed me up on the spot. I'd gone to places for a job and they said, 'We can't hire you. You're not black or a woman.' So I listened to Fred. What did I have to lose? I was living in a condemned building. Some Jew owned it. I didn't have a car, or anything. Eating at McDonald's was a big night out for me. Fred had high ideals but didn't carry them out. The Klan didn't help me get a job. I got work myself. So I had no involvement with them or any other group after that. I only went to two meetings at Fred's apartment in Lakewood. Pretty boring.

"One old lady used to come in and sit there in her white robe, and one night she said, 'Why don't we all go bowling?' It was funny as hell. I thought, Boy, this is really a terrorist organization. On the other hand I saw letters that came into the KKK from women and kids at Denver high schools who felt they were being harassed by blacks. So there was potential for a Klan movement in Colorado. And a few people at those meetings weren't little old ladies who wanted to go bowling.

"Dave and I hit it off personally. He was a really likable guy. A good sense of humor. We laughed and joked and talked about girls. He always tried to find something good in them. I'd say, 'Her nose is too big' and he'd say, 'Yeah, but she has pretty eyes.' I wish I was more that way, and not so critical. He loved women. White women were just beautiful to him. It was almost a spiritual thing. His marriage wasn't very good. He and his wife didn't openly fight but it was cold. No communication. They were married ten, twelve years. No kids. Both were miserable. They cared for each other but couldn't live together.

"His wife made good money at the phone company. But she wasn't all that sympathetic to his political ideas. I think that was the thing that blew them apart. Dave was so intense. No one was more intense than he was. He saw himself as an old-fashioned patriot, like George Washington or Thomas Jefferson, defending all the good decent things in America. He wants to bring back old-fashioned morals, values. I admire him for taking a stand. Maybe I don't have the courage to."

McKinzie carves the steak efficiently and chews it with pleasure. He is soft-spoken and his eyes are constantly moving, scanning the room.

"Dave took me to the Aryan Nations place up in Idaho in the winter of '81. I was impressed with the people at Hayden Lake. It was a real strong family atmosphere, not a bunch of people talking about violence. They had Sunday brunch, with little kids running around, and they were happy people, just enjoying themselves and taking pride in being white. They were glad their kids were blue-eyed and blond. Nonwhites preach racial pride. White people don't. They need to learn to love themselves more. They're lost. They need to learn they have a soul, like black people. Dave doesn't hate blacks. He just doesn't believe in race-mixing. He believes in racial separation. He wants white people to have a spiritual pride in themselves, to see what a beautiful thing it is to be white. He has a certain reverence for God but you wouldn't know that unless you knew him well.

"At Hayden Lake it was a religious atmosphere and I enjoyed myself. We were there for three days and when we came back he said, 'You're still hung up on the Mormons, aren't you?' I'm a Mormon but not a religious one. He didn't fight this in me but he did resent it. He'd say, 'I know a Mormon girl and she's the biggest slut in Denver.' Mormons aren't that far away from the Aryan Nations beliefs. They just don't talk about it. I drop into church once a year. I'm still a Mormon in my heart but I can't get along with the Mormon people, but I still believe in it."

He swats at another fly and smiles at the waitresses, several times commenting on how much Lane would appreciate them.

"Dave was once a boxer and could handle his fists. He was quick, and fit. He could throw a football a long way. He didn't drink much, never smoked. He was about six feet two and he could run fast. One time we went to a country-and-western bar and a woman came up to Dave. She was tall and went for him, asked him to come home and hot-tub with her. She was half Jew and admitted it. David thought the whole thing was pretty funny. When we left the bar he said, 'If she only knew who she was inviting over.' But he was polite to her, not an asshole about it. Women sort of fell for him. Once we were driving down the street and we saw a black kid looking at some white girls. Dave rolled down the window and said, 'You like that white pussy, Buckwheat?' The kid jumped. He was scared. I thought Dave might get out and fight, but he didn't.

"He used to work in real estate but quit that. He lived very frugally, could make twenty dollars go farther than anyone I ever saw. If he wanted to pick up a woman, he didn't wave money in her face but used his personality. We'd go into a McDonald's and he'd get a cheeseburger and a small Coke. Nothing else. He didn't want to be a pot-bellied middle-aged man. He hustled money on golf courses. He'd bet on shots and holes but he had sore hands. After hitting the ball all day the vibration of the club began to hurt his hands, so he couldn't play that much. He used to play in tournaments and could knock the hell out of the ball. When he'd hit a drive three hundred yards, he'd stand there and say, 'Not bad for a goy boy.' He'd also buy and sell a few guns to make money but he wasn't a gun nut. He carried a handgun in his glove compartment but didn't brag about it."

McKinzie blinks as he talks and sometimes shuts both eyes. His Adam's apple, like Alan Berg's, is prominent and jogs when he speaks. Also like Berg, he is prone to epileptic seizures.

"David Lane is not his real name. He has a German name: Vernon Eiden. He changed it to Eden once. He was adopted as a child. He was born in Iowa and went to school in Denver. He has several sisters and one married a black man. Dave's not close to her. His father was a pretty well-to-do preacher. Dave was a real estate agent but told me that he lost his license because he wouldn't close a deal with an interracial couple."

McKinzie pushes his empty plate aside and adjusts his cap. "Dave doesn't believe in forcing the races together. It will lead to a race of mongrels and the white race won't exist anymore. He doesn't believe in slavery or anything like that. Just separation. Slavery is immoral, wrong. It's making other people do the work for you. Dave studied all this, hour after hour. He'd sit and read. He never had a thing against Jews until he began studying history. Nothing. I understand that. I've felt that some of the nicest people in the world are Jews who turned their backs on their religion."

He furtively surveys the restaurant once again. "Dave was always against pornography and making women pose nude in magazines and seeing them treated as sex objects. He'd look at a centerfold of *Playboy* and say, 'She's going to be someone's mother someday.' Dave believed that beautiful things are being destroyed. He feels the white race is beautiful and wants to save it. So many white women get involved with black men because they're sympathetic to them, not because they love them. And it creates such unhappiness with themselves and their families. They turn to a black because they feel that only a black man could be their friend, or maybe a Chinese, but not a white man. Dave felt that white men have become the enemy of women and minorities. Women's liberation hasn't liberated anyone. It's caused a schism between white men and white women. White women don't like white men, because they think they're rotten. I was broken-hearted about a year ago when a white woman I like married a black man. It's like homosexuals. They give up on the other sex. White women give up on white men. Dave hated that. He was an idealist.

"He felt that Vietnam was a tragedy. Young kids sent over there and came back with no legs. You don't do that to people in your own country for no reason. There are guys in [Denver's] Fitzsimon's Army Medical Center right now with no arms because of that war. They want to eat in restaurants and chase pretty girls but they can't. We built up South Vietnam at the cost of our guys and then we just left. Terrible. That really bothered Dave."

McKinzie touches the edge of his plate and takes several moments to consider another issue.

"Dave didn't believe that the Holocaust ever happened and I'm skeptical myself. Why does the press keep harping on the Holocaust? We hear over and over about the six million Jews that died but not about the twenty or thirty million whites that died. Jews call whites *goyim*. That means 'cattle.' That's how they look at us." He throws another searching glance across the table. "I just wish I could go to church every Sunday and be a good Mormon. But I can't."

His posture indicates he might stand and leave the restaurant.

"There was a deep-rooted bitterness in Dave. He said that when he was young and still living with his mother—this was after his dad had split but before he was adopted—things were so bad they had to eat rats. Dave's anger was something you had to sense in him. You couldn't really see it. He blamed his sore hands on rickets, from when he was a kid and his diet was so bad.

"Dave had a first wife but it only lasted about a year. They couldn't have any kids. She divorced him. I think he just really wanted to be married to the right woman. He wasn't a womanizer and he wasn't looking for one-night stands. He needed a home and wife. After his second divorce, he had no roots. He felt he had no life left, so he became more committed to his political ideas. If he'd had a good marriage, he'd probably be free. He was just a home-loving man."

# 13

## "I TURNED HIM INTO A MONSTER"

When Berg was running The Shirt Broker, one of his customers was Ev Wren, a red-faced man with a bright, cheerful way of speaking. Berg once told him that his secret ambition was to be a disc jockey on a jazz radio station. This pleased and amused Wren, who had spent his life in television and radio. In the 1950s he was one of the original Butter-Nut Boys on nationwide TV commercials, dressed in a striped jacket, singing and dancing with a cane, selling Butter-Nut coffee. In the sixties he worked in radio in New York, before returning to Denver to program several local stations. While living on the East Coast he had become fascinated with a radio personality in Manhattan, a late-night talk-show host named Long John Nebel. Nebel delighted in arguing with those who called the show, or poking fun at them, or creating the impression that he didn't give a damn whether they liked his act. Wren listened, at times laughing, at times offended, but always curious about what Nebel might do next. *This*, he believed, was good radio, what the medium had long been and could still be, an unpredictable, untamed wonder compared to the stiff entertainment of TV. After a few years he left New York but never forgot Nebel or the thrill of tuning him in at night.

By the 1970s, Wren, like many radio professionals, felt that talk shows were the coming phenomenon. These programs had been around in the 1960s and had featured several interesting practitioners, like Nebel, but it wasn't until the seventies that AM radio really began looking for something besides the Top 40 format that had been dominant for years. As the number of FM-radio receivers had spread, first in homes and then in cars, the AM band had lost some of its music listeners. AM needed an alternative, and talk radio gradually began to fit the slot. Not only was it different from what was heard on FM, it coincided with, or helped create, the growing need people had to examine, in public, their personal feelings and ideas; their desire to express opinions about current events; and their dissastisfaction with how the news media presented reality. For a matrix of reasons, with the 1970s, people increasingly wanted someone to talk to, even a stranger, and radio was there to fill the void.

One day, while walking through the Cinderella City shopping center in suburban Denver, Ev Wren was surprised to see the tall redhead, now sporting a beard, approach him on the mall. He was even more surprised when Berg said he was hosting a radio talk show on KGMC. "Hell you are," Wren replied, promising to tune in the program and tell Berg what he thought.

Wren listened and was struck by how small-time the station was. It had a weak signal and on occasion it appeared that no one could find it on the dial. One day, in spite of considerable prodding, Berg couldn't get anyone to call him. He joked about it for several minutes but his frustration clearly was taking hold. "Okay," he finally said, "call me up and I'll give you a Christmas tree." He repeated this before going to a commercial.

"I was driving in my car listening to him," says Wren, "and after he thought he'd gone to the advertising spot, I heard him say, 'Well, that's one way to get a call. Give them a fuckin' prize.' I went to the first phone I could find and got on the line and told him to always remember to turn off his mike."

Sometimes, when no one called his show, Berg did monologues chastising the audience for not picking up the phone. When that failed, he played a record.

After listening to the program for a while Wren concluded that it simply wasn't lively enough. Berg himself wasn't dull but management had him interviewing sponsors who had purchased ads during his air time: a woman who ran a beauty salon came on to discuss hairstyles; a man who made dentures talked about his vocation. The interviews, Wren felt, were awful. He told Berg that *he* had potential but the format stunk.

In 1976 Bob McWilliams sold the station to Corky Cartwright and Marvin Davis, one of Denver's two billionaires and the subsequent owner of Twentieth Century-Fox. The call letters were changed to KWBZ and in September, Cartwright, in need of programming assistance, hired Ev Wren as a consultant. Wren had two strong pieces of advice. First, despite the fact that the sponsor interviews were bringing the station badly needed advertising dollars, there should be no more such programming and no more interviews at all, unless someone like presidential candidate Jimmy Carter came through town (he was on Berg's show) or the interviews were spicy and daring. Second, he felt that if Berg was turned loose he could become the best talk-show host Wren had ever heard. "It was his ability to converse and think fast that impressed me," he says. "He was never at a loss for words. He took charge. He *ran* his show."

Wren's dictum for making KWBZ successful was that the station should inform, provoke, and even shock the audience: "I told Alan that Long John Nebel had this thing—he would keep you pissed off all night long. He'd slam the phone down and it was really entertaining. I said, 'Do a little of that but don't fabricate it.' I turned him into a monster. So that when people would go to work the next day, they would say, 'There's an idiot on the radio. Did you hear him?' I told him that he was here for one reason—to entertain them. He picked that stuff right up."

Rudeness in the media may have once been considered offensive but things were different by the middle of the 1970s. People seemed more frustrated or angry than in the past and wanted a focal point for their anger—either someone to yell at or someone to help them express what they were feeling. The condition was culture-wide. It was there in movies like *Network*, in which a TV broadcaster goes into an unstoppable rage while reading the evening news. It surfaced in the films of Clint Eastwood and Charles Bronson, in which the hero takes justice into his hands, stalking and killing those who have harmed innocent people. Revenge was the theme. It was there in the New Wave music that began in England and came to the United States in the mid seventies, music that was driven by anger and barely controlled hysteria. The parallels between the best New Wave musicians—an Elvis Costello, say—and the Alan Berg of that period were many and varied: Both used hostility as a prop; both were gifted in the manipulation of language; both began from a neurotic, ultramodern point of view and commented on the world from that perch; both were essentially comic; both had the ability to make pop art out of fragments of conversation or experience; both were obsessed with love and sex; both grated badly on ears that don't like the rude reality of the modern world.

Pop music may have been a good way to capture and exploit the prevailing mood, but talk radio was even better. It was thoroughly democratic, open to hundreds and thousands of listeners, available to anyone with a phone or a dime. In the 1960s pop artist Andy Warhol said that in the future everyone in America would become famous for fifteen minutes. Talk radio was the fulfillment of that prophecy.

Berg may have already understood or intuited all of this but Ev Wren spelled it out to him. KWBZ was a struggling daytime station with a mere thousand watts of power. Its ratings were so low they weren't listed in the Arbitron book. Contrariwise, as competitive as the Denver radio market was, KWBZ was the only station in the area devoted solely to talk; if it made enough noise, it might find an audience. Alan Berg was Wren's strength for accomplishing that—he was obviously the most unusual thing in town.

Under the new strategy one of his first guests was a masseuse from a local massage parlor. Berg had her describe the action in her place of business. The station got as many calls off the air as on, "hate calls," as Wren puts it. Within days the FCC had been inundated with protests, reportedly the largest such outburst in Denver's radio history. Sex had worked, so naturally the next topic to pursue was religion. Every time Berg honestly stated his convictions—he was agnostic and would believe in God when he met Him—angry callers filled the lines at KWBZ. The station was soon gaining notoriety, Berg was becoming known locally, and the ratings were starting to climb.

"All you had to do was switch the dial, tune in Alan, and you'd say, 'What the hell was that?' " says Wren. "He was always talking about something you'd never heard on the air before."

One day a man called the show and told Berg that he was about to leave his apartment in Cherry Creek, find a woman in the neighborhood, and rape her. He had phoned the program before; everything about the call—the man's screams, his weeping sounds when he lost control on the air, and his tone of angry helplessness—indicated that he was serious. Berg tried to stall him, to change his mind, to soothe him, to penetrate his misery:

CALLER: "Remember when I called and said I was in Cherry Creek?"

BERG: "I certainly do."

C: "I've raped three women since then."

B [off mike]: "Put a trace on this call."

C: "What?"

B: "Nothing. Go ahead."

C: "They don't do nothin' for me. How come, Alan?"

B: "Would you tell me where you are now so we can get some help for you?"

C: "I'm thinkin' of rapin' another woman I saw this mornin'. None of these women I've raped have turned me in. I've heard nothin' about it. How come?"

B: "Where are you?"

C: "I'm in the four-hundred block of Detroit Street. But that's cuttin' it pretty close."

B: "What do you mean 'cutting it close?' Do you want help or not?"

C: "I've got a compulsion to rape women."

B: "Why?"

C: "I was in the pen once, they didn't do nothin' for me. I want some help."

B: "Tell me where you are and I'll get some help and some protection so you won't get roughed up. I'll give you my word on that."

C: "I just wanna rape 'em. I'm so tired of rapin' women." [He begins to scream.]

B: "Tell me your story. Come on. When was the last time you raped?"

C: "In Aurora, a couple of weeks ago. She was struttin' around like she was somethin' else."

B: "She was, in other words, making you feel less than a man and ignoring you. Is that what you're saying?"

C: "I have an irresistible compulsion, just like smokin'."

B: "I understand. I'm sympathizing. When did the rape before that occur?"

C: "It was in the backseat of her car. She pulled into a parking lot and I jumped in and said, 'Okay . . .' It was nighttime."

B: "How old are you?"

C: "Almost forty. I was in the pen twelve years. I didn't get no therapy. Just locked up like an animal. Didn't bother to help me. I was in Canon City [home of the Colorado State Prison]."

B: "When did you go there?"

C: "Nineteen sixty."

B: "Who was the warden?"

C: [garbled name]

B: "Who were your guards?"

C: "Richtofen."

B: "Who was your cellmate?"

C: "Didn't have no cellmate."

B: "Your prison number?"

C: "Nine-eight-oh-five-one-nine."

B: "What can I tell you that might help you?"

C: "Recommend me to someone who can help me and make me quit doin' these naughty things."

B: "Let's keep going and talking and maybe we can get a breakthrough. Okay? Do you still feel that you're going to go out and rape someone?"

C: "Yeah, I'm gonna do it."

B: "Why?"

C: "I've got this irresistible compulsion."

B: "Yeah, you have an irresistible compulsion. Okay. Didn't you say [on a previous call] that jogging helped you?"

C: "Up and down Cherry Creek. Jog up and down. I can name every duck in Cherry Creek."

B: "And every chick, not that there's anything funny about this. Have you decided whom you will rape next?"

C: "I've got her picked out and staked out. I always wanted her."

B: "What is it about her that you like?"

C: "What is it about a piece of strawberry pie or pumpkin pie? I don't know. She could be black, white, Hispano, pretty, fat, or ugly. [He breaks into screams again.] I don't wanna rape no more!"

B: "Now just calm down. I wanna help you. I'm your friend."

C: "You my buddy, Alan?"

B: "I'm your buddy. You there?"

C: "I can't help myself. I gotta go do it."

B: "You can help yourself. You're not gonna go do it."

C: "I gotta go do it."

B: "No, now—"

C: "I'm gonna go do it." [The line goes dead.]

B: "No, but . . ."

Berg was obviously shaken and apologized to the audience for not being able to hold the man longer. At the time he wasn't aware that it took hours to trace a call of this nature. The police were informed but no rape occurred that day and the caller was not found. Berg told Ev Wren he felt particularly bad about not dissuading the caller because as a lawyer in Chicago he had once helped free a defendant who had raped an elderly woman. The man never phoned his show again.

With the growing success of KWBZ, Berg was entering a new phase of his radio career—the most controversial one, the one where his own anger and frustration obliterated everything else. As he had once told Laurence Gross in an early KGMC appearance, conquering alcoholism doesn't necessarily make one a happier person, just more able to survive. In the mid-seventies Berg wasn't happy. His tumultuous affair with Audrey Oliver had waned and his marriage was nearing its legal end. By 1975 Judith had returned to Chicago and taken up residence there. He couldn't live with her, couldn't remove her from his life, and hadn't found anyone even remotely capable of taking her place, although he had tried. Berg was not given to one-night stands. He met new paramours, became intensely involved with them, and almost always talked of going to the altar.

"He wanted to marry all of the women," says Judith, "and all of their dogs."

Several of these women made a point of calling Judith and telling her that while they had been seeing her husband, they wanted her to know one thing: All Berg talked about was her. All he seemed to care about was his wife. "Do you know how strange it is to be told that by another woman?" Judith says. On certain occasions, the women phoned her for other reasons. While spending the night with them, Berg had had a seizure and they had become frightened. What was wrong with him? How did one treat an epileptic? They thought he might die. Naturally, they turned to his wife.

"These women loved that quick, funny, enticing man Alan could be, but when there was trouble—when he got sick—they called on me," says Judith. "Alan detested men who had affairs. But the epilepsy was a nightmare and brought on crazy things."

One night in 1976, on a visit to his wife in Chicago, Berg had a violent seizure, which continued until he passed out. When he regained consciousness, Judith took him to a hospital at Northwestern University, where doctors prescribed Valium and other drugs. Soon after leaving the hospital the seizures came back, again and again, and then he went into one that didn't cease. Judith called an ambulance and Berg was once more driven to Northwestern, given shots to calm him and, while lying on the bed and shaking in a half-conscious state, tested at length. Doctors performed a painful spinal tap, checked his urine, his blood. Within a few days they determined that he had a large brain tumor and that his options were grim: If the growth was malignant it would kill him without fail; if benign, because of the size of the tumor and its precarious location, if he chose to have surgery there was a good chance his ability to speak would be impaired and he would lose much of the strength on the right side of his body. His surgeon, a man from Argentina, wanted Berg to make a decision immediately. The doctor was brusque and told the patient exactly what the possibilities for disaster were. Berg liked the Argentine and felt good about putting himself in the man's care.

For the operation he was strapped into an upright chair and a team of surgeons cut a circle around his skull, much the way one would get inside of a can. Their original plan had not been to open the full circumference of his head, but when they saw the mass of tumor they had no choice but to keep carving in order to get at all the foreign tissue. The operation took eight hours and then Berg was put in intensive care for a testing of his vital signs. He responded poorly and the doctors told Judith there was reason to be concerned. She watched the unmoving figure on the hospital bed, wondering what would happen if he lived but couldn't go back to the radio station—couldn't talk. His existence without words was unimaginable. Staring at him day after day as he attempted to recover, at the wrapped head and the body covered with sheets, she prepared herself for the worst.

"It was like he was dead," she says.

One morning she saw his finger move. A sound came from him, an animal groan, then he tried to speak but only grunts were audible. He wanted to write something on a piece of paper but his hand wouldn't form a word or even a letter. Judith thought he was permanently retarded. A few more days passed and he spoke a full word, then two, then a sentence. As best he could he indicated that if his mind was this damaged, he didn't want to live and be handicapped, a body to be huddled around by nurses. The more his capacity to speak returned, the more he raved about his problems. This process wore him out and annoyed his doctors, but it also got his brain and tongue working together again.

Once the recovery process began it went fast. Berg was soon talking with facility and at his usual blinding raspy speed. The Argentine surgeon was astounded. Not only had the tumor been safely removed but within weeks of the operation the patient was out of the hospital, speaking and acting like his old irascible self, ready to get back on the air. Following the surgery, the grand mal seizures left him forever, although the petit mal remained for the rest of his life.

"All I know," he said in later years, "is that I went into that operation and I knew I was going to make it. Maybe I should be religious over that, but I'm not. I'm not an atheist either. I believe there's a God within everybody. I say that on the air and people get furious with me. I say, 'Until I know better, I'm it. I'm God.' I have control over myself, if I want to use it. I don't have a death wish. At all. I have a living wish and every move in my life has been toward it."

If the success of the brain surgery did not make him religious, it also did not make him a calmer, more benevolent force on the radio. When he went back to KWBZ he was, if anything, more hostile and belligerent than before. During this period he frequently visited Chicago, and his growing anger was obvious to his wife, who watched him, disheartened.

Judith's contention is that his loutish phase—when he hung up on callers for the pure hell of it and filled the air with a boring rage —was not an act but a direct result of his personal despair. He had survived the surgery, but for what? To work for a small salary at a tiny radio station in suburban Denver? His radio career was a failure, just like his legal career, just like his marriage. He didn't seem able to make a real emotional commitment to another human being, with the possible exception of Judith, yet their love and entanglement was so complicated as to almost defy definition. Getting a divorce wouldn't solve problems but create more. In a way they were all each of them had—but having each other was the central dilemma.

"People would ask me, 'Who's helping you with your marital troubles?' " says Judith. "I would say, 'My husband is.' And he would tell people that his wife was getting him through his problems with his marriage. Neither one of us knew what to do about it. Sometimes, the what-ifs keep you alive."

If a new female admirer tried to get close to Berg, he pulled away or disappeared entirely. The ones who didn't want to get close dropped him. He thought of moving back to Chicago and rejoining Judith, but why? He didn't appear to be a husband in any regular sense of the word. That knowledge disturbed him, pricked his conscience and deep reservoir of guilt. He was intensely aware of his behavioral patterns in love affairs and his lack of follow-through, but knowing this only heightened his disappointment in himself. So he talked about his affairs on the radio, turned them into self-lacerating humor, one-liners, show business. It was easier to make fun of himself than to change.

"At the time Alan was angriest at himself," says Judith, "he was given a public platform for his feelings. He was angry because of what had happened to us. He was falling apart inside and it showed. The radio was the only thing he knew where he could go and do anything that would be right. Nothing else was working. So he just went on."

His anger was not entirely personal.

"I first met Alan in 1971, at the KGMC radio-station picnic," says Judy Wegener, from her basement in suburban Denver. She is ebullient, has blond hair, blue eyes, and a good voice for radio, a voice that holds a man's attention. Her basement contains a barber chair, a pot-bellied stove, a copper fire hydrant, a stuffed goose, and several old farm implements. She smokes and bats her eyes, a nervous habit, as she talks. "It was in midsummer and he was the only person there in a three-piece plaid suit. It was hot and he had that shock of red hair. My first impression is like he said about himself: He was Howdy Doody in a business suit. Unbelievable.

"He was on the air right before me and I was on in the early afternoon. My show started out as what was called 'girl talk.' It was sex talk, basically. It was going over in Los Angeles, so we decided to try it here. We got into real emotions and what you should do about your marriage. That was back in the early seventies and it was pretty racy for the Denver area. We were working at Cinderella City [shopping center], behind glass windows, so people could watch us while we were on the air. You got controversial, they knew right where to come and get you.

"Alan wasn't controversial at the start. The sad thing is that he started out answering legal questions and then brought in more facts about his life. People would call in and say, 'You're a drunk, you've been disbarred,' and would make the other obnoxious remarks that people do. Alan left himself open, not realizing how you really make yourself vulnerable in that position. A lot of his nastiness came from trying to protect himself. We were really naïve back then. We didn't know the impact we were having. We didn't know if we were talking to thousands of people or five. I used my own name. I said I had three small boys and am married to an Englewood fireman and said where the boys went to school. I had no idea how vulnerable I was making myself. I had kidnapping threats on the kids. Alan and I had to get the fire department to teach us how to check our car ignitions for bombs. At first we were playing at something on the radio, and having a good time. Then the times got nastier and the people got nastier and it got scarier. We were just finishing up in Vietnam, there was Richard Nixon's demise, abortion was hot, everything was. It got to be a bigger game, just heating up and heating up. You can't imagine the letters I got: 'How dare you comment on abortion, being a wife and a mother!' I was Jezebel and I was going to die as she did in the Bible—being ripped apart by dogs."

She lights another cigarette, caught in the memory of another career. Today she works for the U.S. Census Bureau, in relative anonymity. It's not only safer but, compared to her radio days, a far better-paying job. When she was at KGMC the station's talk-show hosts made a pact, swearing never to mention on the air how much they were earning: $5 an hour for the twenty hours a week they were in the studio, plus a few tradeouts at restaurants and other businesses. The hosts felt that if the listening audience knew how cheaply they were being employed, their mystique and credibility would be diminished. No one would want their advice. As a lawyer Berg claimed to have made as much as $100,000 a year. A decade later his salary was $100 a week.

"The things Alan said on the air about himself, he said out of honesty," Wegener goes on. "But you get tired after a while of what other people throw at you. They were totally ignorant of his past and how far he had come. That's when he started to toughen up. It got to the point where his hang-up thing became his trademark. I don't care how good the caller was, Alan felt he had to hang up and insult him in some way."

She contends that once Berg became insulting on the air, many of those around him encouraged him to be even more obstreperous. Also, the more obnoxious he got the higher were his ratings.

"I left there in 1977. At KHOW [the station Berg went to after leaving KWBZ] he hit the apex of hanging up. I quit listening to him because it was just stupid. I think the people around him were afraid to tell him what they thought. I'd say, 'That's rude, Alan. You don't do that.' He'd say, 'Well, that's show biz. That's what you have to do.' He put up barriers and seemed to not want to get involved with callers. It was like a monster in a way. He'd sit and argue in the staff meetings and say, 'We're not here to preach or to teach, but to entertain.' His idea of entertainment was: Harass them until they say something naughty. That was frustrating because he had so much depth and so much knowledge. He was smarter than anyone else. But when he was at KHOW a lot of people listened just to hear how outrageous, how bad, he could get. At one time he was playing to a lot of kooks. He didn't realize how serious some of them were taking him. If it was enough to make me angry with him, then you can imagine what it was doing to a demented person. We had people who called us—we've had documented cases—who didn't talk to anyone else in the world.

People who had not been out of their house in years. They thought the whole world was out to get them. Alan got a letter from someone who thought he was trying to control his mind."

She inhales deeply, sips iced tea. She does not appear to be a person who is easily intimidated.

"When I heard that Alan had been killed, I pictured a loner standing there screaming as he pumped bullets into him: 'Now, you S.O.B.! Now I'll tell you what I think.' It was incredibly ugly, almost like a story he may have told about his days in Chicago. I thought the loner who thought Alan was trying to control his mind was the most dangerous.

"There was a little group of Nazis in Aurora who called us and talked about having a survival camp near Colorado Springs, where they took ten-year-old kids and taught them target practice. We were liberals, Alan and I, antigun and anti-NRA [National Rifle Association]. I got calls from this group and so did he. They told me to shut my fat mouth. They hit low: 'I'll get you, I'll get your kids, your husband, your dog.' When Fred Wilkins walked into Alan's show that day at BZ and said, 'You will die,' I decided I wouldn't go back on the radio for anything. I felt for the safety of myself and my family."

She snuffs out the cigarette. Her facial expression suggests someone who knows the decision she once made was right. A few minutes later, when her son comes into the basement, a robust young man with quick movements and a broad smile, she glances at him and seems very pleased.

"The last time I saw Alan was about a year before his death," she says. "He spotted me at a Village Inn, where he was eating breakfast. He ran up and grabbed me and gave me a big hug. He had a warmth, almost a joy, that I hadn't seen the last years I was working with him. The people surrounding him now were good for him. I could feel that. He was changing back to what he'd been on the radio in the early years. He was coming of age, doing his own style. I liked what he was doing. He would listen and let the depth come in."

# 14

---

# *REVOLUTION NOW*

---

Robert Jay Mathews was born in Marfa, Texas, in January 1953, but it was in Arizona that he first encountered radical politics. As a high school student he became interested in the tax-protest movement around Phoenix and he claimed to have started an antitax group of his own, the Sons of Liberty, when he was seventeen. Police, he once said, shot at him because of his beliefs. Gunfire was one reason he decided to leave Arizona but there were others: too many laws in Phoenix, too many urban problems, too many people and not enough of them were white. Mathews liked Caucasians; the feeling was more than a preference, beyond a mere prejudice. From the time he was a teenager he had a fanatic racial pride, a conviction that white Gentile men had created the best things in Western civilization and were the only group that could preserve it from decay. Through reading European history, and he contended that he had read a lot of it, Mathews reached a dramatic conclusion: The United States was in decline and only a revolution—a purging of the country's blood—could save it from collapse.

In Arizona he began studying a map of North America, looking for the perfect place to move. His finger traced a path from one end of the nation to the other, back and forth, before settling on Metaline Falls, Washington, an isolated village in the extreme northeast corner of the state. If one were traveling north, it would be the last town in the United States before the Canadian line. In the early 1970s Mathews loaded his belongings into his pickup, drove from Arizona to Washington, and one day after arriving in Metaline Falls, found work at the nearby Pend Oreille lead and zinc mine. Within a few years his family and his bride, Debbie, had joined him in this remote edge of the Northwest. His father, John, was a retired air force officer and his brother, John junior, would become a schoolteacher in Metaline Falls.

Mathews's family did not share his political or racial philosophy—in time his brother would adamantly oppose it—but his relatives moved north at his urging, followed where he had led. Mathews was five feet seven, 160 pounds, with brown hair, prominent sideburns, and hazel eyes. He was a handsome young man, dark-complected, had a strong jaw, and was once described as "looking like a Mexican." Not a large or imposing figure, he did emanate a sense of purpose, an intensity in his eyes that indicated something serious was brewing within. He was bright and he was forceful. Most people who came in contact with him recognized that and liked him, even if they knew of his politics and despised what he stood for.

The change of scenery from the Southwest to Metaline Falls did nothing to alter his views. One day at work a fellow laborer at the mine taped a pinup of a naked black woman to his locker—Mathews exploded, ready to fight. Even photographs of other races were a threat. Minorities were virtually absent from the Metaline Falls area, and a white man living there could imagine that he was existing in a country that wasn't ethnically diverse or full of crowded, complicated cities. A man could dream of starting over here, of rebuilding his life from scratch. Mathews also loved the landscape the town was set in. Canada's Selkirk Mountains rose in the distance. At dawn full-grown deer walked across the main street of Metaline Falls. Heavy snow only made the hills and evergreens more beautiful. God's country. It was the kind of climate one would find in northern Europe, where the Aryan and Scandinavian peoples had flourished before their heirs came to America. In centuries past those ethnic groups had given rise to Norse and Viking sagas, grand tales of the courage and strength of northern warriors in battle. They had no fear of death: If they perished heroically, the Valkyries (the handmaidens of Odin, the Supreme Being of Norse mythology) would whisk their souls away to Valhalla, where they'd be enshrined in the great hall of immortality. A modern-day religion, Odinism, has sprung from these sagas. Bob Mathews was familiar with it; he liked it. He regarded it the same way he regarded the northwestern landscape—both could inspire a man to become a hero.

If Mathews was drawn to the countryside of Washington State, he was equally drawn to a political group at the other end of the nation. Through his convictions he became aware of William Pierce and the National Alliance, operating out of Washington, D.C., and Arlington, Virginia. Mathews found Pierce's neo-Nazi philosophy to be all-encompassing. It wasn't merely antitax or antidemocratic government; it wasn't simply antiminority, calling for racial separation or white supremacy, like the longheld views of the Ku Klux Klan. The National Alliance, like Pierce's fictional hero, Earl Turner, went all the way: demanding the deportation of blacks and other nonwhites and the extermination of Jews. It wanted to purify the gene pool.

Mathews admired William Pierce, and through the National Alliance he became acquainted with other young neo-Nazis. He met Tom Martinez, a high school dropout and custodial worker in Philadelphia whose difficulties in finding a job had carried him toward the extreme right. Martinez was married at nineteen and soon had a wife and child to support. It seemed that every time he went looking for work, the position had just been filled by a minority applicant. In spite of his surname, Martinez claimed to be a mixture of Castilian and Swedish heritage. He certainly didn't consider himself a Chicano. And it angered him that when he finally did land a job with the Philadelphia Housing Authority, he felt it was only because someone thought he was Mexican.

Mathews met William Soderquist through the National Alliance. Soderquist not only had a Scandinavian name and looked Germanic—with his high brow and bushy light-blond hair and a large Beethoven-like head—he had something else that most political movements desire: intelligence. That comes in handy in strategy sessions and gives respectability to organizations and their theories. Soderquist had brains; no one doubted that. Born in 1963 and reared in Salinas, California, he was a child prodigy of the radical right. At eleven he became a volunteer for the local John Birch Society. At sixteen he joined the National Alliance, and three years later he was a featured speaker at the outfit's national convention in Chicago, where he talked of the exploits and glory days of the S.S. (Hitler's Schutzstaffel) in Nazi Germany. In high school he had been in California's MGM program, an educational plan designed to bring out the excellence in those with "mentally gifted minds." Soderquist was articulate, widely read, and convinced that Adolf Hitler had been historically and morally justified in trying to impose "Pan-Europeanism" on the Continent. The young theoretician doubted that the Holocaust had really occurred. When challenged on this notion, he would calmly reply that indeed there were casualties in every war and for that reason some Jews had without question died. Then he would add that a lot of Christians were killed too. At the Chicago convention his speech was considered a resounding success.

Mathews and Soderquist hit it off well, even though they were separated by a decade in age, among other differences. Like many radicals, Mathews had a puritanical strain. He didn't enjoy alcohol, and the idea of hunting for pleasure—of killing an animal for sport—was offensive to him. Driving, he would unthinkingly swerve his car off the highway to avoid hitting a rodent. If he used a gun, it was a means to an end, not something to value in itself. Soderquist, conversely, liked to talk about guns. He was fluent in the language. He enjoyed drinking and when he got a little money in his pocket he would spend it on cocaine. He bore some resemblance to Earl Turner, who was a flawed human being first and a revolutionary second. Soderquist was a remarkable mixture of intellectual prowess and emotional softness. Despite his great admiration for Bob Mathews, when the younger man got into trouble the person he always turned to was his mother.

After several years at the mine Mathews left his job for a laboring position at the Lehigh Cement plant in nearby Ione. There he met Kenneth Loff, a native of Long Island and in his late twenties. Loff had grown up in an ethnically varied neighborhood and the best man at his Catholic wedding had been a Jew, but over time his feelings about race had altered. He felt that the United States had changed for the worse since his childhood, and that his own children were not going to be presented with the same opportunities he had had. When Mathews began talking with him about what was wrong with affirmative-action programs, with quotas demanding that businesses hire a certain percentage of minority workers, with busing children from one racial neighborhood to another, with tariff laws that allowed foreign-produced goods into the United States and put American workers out of jobs—all of this caught Loff's attention. In turn he told Mathews about the Aryan Nations compound across the border at Hayden Lake, Idaho, and how he went there on occasion and how Mathews should make the trip himself.

Mathews took his advice and listened to the preachings of Richard Butler, watched the compound's rituals with interest, but didn't join the group. His ideas weren't quite the same as Butler's or perhaps they were and only his time frame was different. Mathews wanted the revolution to start immediately, not in 1991, as William Pierce had written in *The Turner Diaries*, and not in some vague distant Armageddon, as the Bible had stated and Butler was forever talking about from his pulpit. Pierce and Butler were, after all, older men, and it would be young men who commenced the battle and won the war. Pierce was a writer and Butler a minister, but Mathews was a man of action, as one could see by studying his eyes and the hard set of his mouth. He conveyed it with a word or a glance. He had the inner fire.

By the late 1970s Mathews, with some help from his parents, had saved enough money to buy fifty-three acres outside of Metaline Falls. He and his wife moved into one mobile home on the land and his parents, John and Una, moved into another. Within a few more years Bob and Debbie Mathews had adopted a son, Clint, a blond-haired, blue-eyed little boy, whom Mathews doted on in his writings about the need for revolution. It was necessary for the future of the children, he told those he was trying to convert to his ideas. That's what he said in the letters he had begun sending to *The Newport Miner*, a local newspaper. His words stirred so much response the paper ran his picture on the front page.

Besides radical change Mathews had another goal; had he achieved it, his life might have taken an entirely different turn. He had hoped, somehow, to make money from his land. Initially, he tried raising bees, then cattle, then chickens, then turkeys. But nothing worked. He considered buying a trout farm but eventually abandoned the scheme. To supplement his income and spread his beliefs, he distributed William Pierce's National Alliance literature in the Northwest. Long hours of toil didn't bother Mathews; he labored endlessly on the farm, searching for the magical formula that would put extra money in the bank. The more he failed, the angrier he became. How could this landscape be so alluring, so satisfying to his vision and spirit—and so lacking in business possibilities? It was an old western dilemma: When you get away from it all part of what you leave behind may be financial hope. Times were never outstanding in the Metaline Falls area, but in the past the town had sustained five taverns; now it had one. With the unsteady nature of mine work, the recent troubles in the timber industry, and the ever-rising inflation (which *had* come to eastern Washington), the situation was rife with frustration, especially for an ambitious man. Bob Mathews was ambitious, not perhaps for worldly gain but for something that included financial respectability yet went beyond that. He believed that his country was leaving behind men like himself, hardworking, honest men who had a right to expect more. Everyone else—blacks, Chicanos, women, homosexuals—expected more these days, didn't they? More understanding or the chance to make more money? Guys like Bob Mathews were always a step or two behind the beat of social change, unable to catch up.

When Mathews told people of his hopes and dreams, his message was squarely in an old national tradition: He wanted a better life for his son than he had for himself. In addition to the virulent racism in his words, there was something else disturbing and different in his talk. In his quest for that better life, he no longer felt bound by certain elements that might have affected a man like himself in the past—patriotism, legal constraints, a belief in long-range sacrifice. He wanted his dream to come true right now.

In 1983, after a long fight with cancer, John Mathews, Sr., died. Bob soon quit his job and began spending less time at home. In years past he and his brother had argued about politics, but those days were gone. The two men went their separate ways, John junior to teach school in Metaline Falls, Bob to travel widely in the western United States, recruiting among friends and acquaintances for a new organization, the White American Bastion, which he was ready to start on his farm. He wanted them to join other young men who were going to resettle themselves and their families in the area. The group, said Mathews, would eventually gain control of a small patch of eastern Washington, purge it of blacks and Jews, then widen its influence from there. The White American Bastion would create its own nation-within-a-nation, designed along lines to please Earl Turner and William Pierce.

In mid-1983 Mathews invited William Soderquist to the farm outside Metaline Falls, so the two of them could discuss strategy. Uncertain of his future and thinking of moving to Montana, Soderquist accepted the invitation and brought along Richard Kemp, a friend from Salinas. Six feet, seven inches tall, gawky, with a shambling gait and a thoroughly innocent face, Kemp had not long ago regarded himself a liberal-minded high school student. After considerable persuasion from Soderquist, the tall youngster decided that his sympathies lay more with the far right than the moderate left. By 1983 he was ready to explore his politics a little further under the tutelage of his good friend, so he rode north with Soderquist toward Metaline Falls.

That summer the two Californians helped Mathews build a two-story barnlike structure, the "Barracks," which would serve as headquarters for the White American Bastion and as a residence for foot soldiers like Soderquist and Kemp before they could build homes of their own. To generate money for the Bastion, Mathews's first idea was to get a contract with the U.S. Forest Service and clear land for the government. It quickly became apparent that his vision could not be financed by anything as modest as felling trees. Surely there were faster, easier ways to make some real money than that.

Dan Bauer, whom Mathews had met at Aryan Nations, worked on the Barracks too. Ken Loff, the leader's friend from the cement plant, dropped by on occasion. Mathews had come in contact with other recruits at the church—a magnet for not only those drawn to the Reverend Richard Butler's message but, in some cases, those who were tired of his rhetoric and looking for something more. In 1981 a bomb had been placed at the compound and gone off in the night. Damage was insignificant but it did serve to give the Aryan Nations publicity. Denver Parmenter and Randy Duey, two Washington residents, read about the incident and decided to drive up to Hayden Lake and investigate Butler's Identity Christianity for themselves. Parmenter, the son of an air force officer, had been born in Wiesbaden, West Germany, but grown up in Florida and Texas. After high school he spent three years in the army, mostly in Turkey, before returning to Washington State and enrolling at Eastern Washington University, near Spokane. During college he'd met Duey, a balding young man who had also attended the school and now worked as a postal carrier. Duey's thinning hair, moustache, thick glasses, and furtive eyes gave him the look of a left-wing revolutionary, something out of *Doctor Zhivago*. Parmenter had huge hands, was tall and lumbering and had sort of a friendly back-country grace about him. One wouldn't have taken him for a radical. His appearance didn't reveal much of his native intelligence or the fact that he was an effective public speaker and had once run for student-body president at his university. His looks didn't indicate that he had a drinking problem and, by the early eighties, a marriage that was beginning to topple. His wife, Janice, didn't care for his politics and made her feelings known, which incensed the Aryan Warrior.

At a 1983 Aryan Nations talk on the dangers of communism, given by Colonel Gordon "Jack" Mohr, Parmenter met Bob Mathews. The latter invited him to Metaline Falls, and before long Parmenter and Duey were making the trip to the Barracks. When they arrived, Mathews took Parmenter for a walk and told him how passive the extreme right had become, how it was doing nothing to stop the dilution and expunging of the white race. The men discussed the idea of setting up a small "cell," a term used by Louis Beam, the Grand Dragon of the Texas Ku Klux Klan, in his writing on guerrilla warfare. The cell would have one purpose: to show force.

At Aryan Nations headquarters Mathews met two other men who would find their way to his property in the late summer of 1983. One was Bruce Pierce, a native of Frankfort, Kentucky, a high school dropout, and a former newsboy for *The Atlanta Constitution*. The son of a man who hand-made cherry-wood furniture, Pierce had married soon after leaving school, fathered a child, and then gotten divorced in 1979. Within the next several years, he remarried, had more children, and came to Aryan Nations, looking for a spiritual home. Approaching his late twenties, Pierce was no longer held by Butler and was impatient with an organization whose idea of revolt was going into the woods and shooting at pictures of former Israeli prime minister Menachem Begin, and at six-pointed stars. Pierce was precisely the sort of man Bob Mathews was looking for—ready to bust loose. One felt that just by looking at him. He had a physical stature—large shoulders, big thighs, he stood up straight—that few others at the compound could match (a number of them looked drained and pale). Pierce was unique in another aspect as well. If Soderquist and Parmenter represented the more intellectual end of the far-right spectrum, and if Mathews was a blend of thought and action, Pierce was action personified. He was like a buck in rut.

The final member of the original nine men who came to Mathews's farm to set the cell in motion was David Lane. He'd spent enough time writing articles for Aryan Nations, enough energy being the propaganda minister for Butler, enough effort on a group that was more interested in words than change. The leader that Lane had long been searching for had finally emerged. Bob Mathews may have been fifteen years younger than he was, but what did that matter? The old guard liked to talk; ultimately, its members had too much respect for American institutions and too much fear of the consequences of action. The new generation wasn't like that. It didn't give a damn about the shibboleths that had placated earlier radicals, or at least kept them from picking up a gun. This new generation understood violence, had grown up with it in Vietnam, in the streets of large American cities, in movies or on television, across the front page of every newspaper every day. It was more comfortable with challenging authority, with the notion of bloodshed. And young radicals weren't old enough to remember World War II and the infamy attached to the cause of Adolf Hitler. They weren't interested in contemplating history, but making it. Lane appreciated that. It wasn't long before he was referring to Bob Mathews as his best friend.

In September the original nine held their first meeting at Mathews's, calling themselves simply "the Group" or "the Company." They stood in a circle, prepared to recite an oath of loyalty and commitment to their race and cause, an oath Mathews had written for the occasion. They were also prepared to denounce "mud people," their term for blacks. Before saying the oath a white baby was placed in the circle, as a symbol of the Caucasian future and a reminder of whom they were taking this pledge for. Initially, Denver Parmenter was going to use his daughter for the ceremony, but his wife was also staying at Mathews's and strongly objected to the idea, leaving her husband embarrassed and angry. Ken Loff's child was substituted and the ritual went according to plan.

"From this moment on," the nine men chanted, "I have no fear of death, no fear of foe, and pledge to deliver our people from the Jew."

At the meeting Mathews outlined the objectives of the group, using *The Turner Diaries* as a blueprint for his goals. Step One was forming the cell. Step Two was establishing priorities. Step Three was setting up a war chest: They discussed robbing pornography stores and pimps, as this would not only finance their organization but also harm the people and businesses they felt were bad for society. Step Four was recruiting new members. Mathews intended to lure new blood from the Klan, from Identity churches around the nation, from survivalist groups like the Covenant, Sword and Arm of the Lord, from others who were ready to make a commitment. He wanted troops, and he didn't care if they had criminal records or a last name like Martinez.

Step Five was assassination: either of Jews or Gentile traitors who went along "with supporting the destruction of our race." Mathews assigned each member of the Group an assassination target; the most prominent were former secretary of state Henry Kissinger, Chase Manhattan Bank president David Rockefeller, and the three heads of the television networks, as the news media was felt to be poisoning the minds of the white race. If in the future, Mathews told the men, they became dispersed while fleeing from authorities, or if they were facing death, they must do everything possible to carry out one last mission: Hunt down their assassination targets and kill them, no matter the risk.

Denver Parmenter's victim was to be Fred Silverman, whom the Group thought was the president of NBC television, headquartered in New York. Silverman had departed the job some time before, but they hadn't heard the news.

# 15

---

# *A JOB AT LAST*

---

In the autumn of the year follow-
ing Berg's successful brain surgery, Marvin Davis decided to sell
his stock in KWBZ. Ev Wren helped find a buyer, John Mullins,
Jr., and the purchase was consummated. Before long Mullins was
sitting across from the talk-show host during his program and waving his arms in panic or slipping him notes telling him not to discuss
this subject or that. After it had happened once too often, Berg
said into the microphone, "Okay, let's hear from you ladies out
there. Let's talk recipes. If you have some interesting recipes for
cherry pie, apple pie, or any other exciting cooking tips, give us a
call . . ."

---

Within a few months both Berg and Wren were gone from KWBZ, unable to reach a working arrangement with the new management. Wren steered Berg in the direction of another station in Denver, KHOW, which took a chance on the host and gave him a show. In the past KHOW had featured music aimed at a youthful market, but on February 28, 1978, Berg took over the 6 P.M. to 10 P.M. time slot with his loose, cantankerous style of talk radio. In some ways he was approaching respectability: KHOW promoted him, the station had a full professional sound, as opposed to the tinny quality of a small-time broadcast studio, and it owned a seven-second delay system to keep obscenity off the air. He even began conducting a dating service via his program, where he brought together men and women looking for companionship or marriage; in many hands, the program would have been the essence of commercial radio, designed to garner listeners and aimed at particular sponsors. In Berg's it was an opportunity for a lot of titillating chatter, some of which approached the tasteless. The station didn't seem to mind, at least at the start. Nighttime radio was even more competitive than daytime—it was on during the same hours as prime-time television. In the late 1970s in the Denver market, radio was struggling and often losing that competition.

Before Berg's arrival at KHOW, most of the station's 6 to 10 P.M. listeners were teenagers, who tuned in expecting to hear rock 'n' roll. When they heard a man with an abrasive nasal voice talking fast and making provocative or insulting remarks, they called the show and said things on the air like, "I hate you" or "You suck." Berg returned the compliments, which generated even more, and before long he owned the highest evening ratings KHOW had ever had. At night the station's reach and audience were far wider than Berg had ever known at KWBZ, and he was soon being heralded in the newspapers and other media as the West's Last Angry Man, baying the moon and spewing venom into the night. He regularly hung up on people, characterized almost all callers as "boring," and when women phoned and said he was damaging the values of their children, he asked if he could come to their homes and hold their bodies. It was while at KHOW, in 1979, that a poll named him both the most popular and most disliked radio personality in Denver.

"It was just a hateful show," he recalled a few years later. "I got caught up in that role for a while."

Despite his ratings, trouble was hard by. Doubleday, the book publishing conglomerate in New York City, owned KHOW, and Alan Berg made them nervous. Their broadcast corporate headquarters, in Minneapolis, was interested in buying other media properties, and while they were making plans to do this the FCC was being bombarded with complaints about their radio station in Denver and one of its uncontrollable employees. Orders came down from Minnesota to Colorado—tame Berg or else. He was impervious to such talk. On Saturday night, August 11, 1979, the head of KHOW's programming, John Lund, waited until Berg had finished his show at ten o'clock before informing him that he was fired.

"Alan told me later that he walked over to the Petroleum Club building, walked around it, and went back to the station," says Ev Wren. "He went up to Lund and said, 'Tell me you're kidding. I don't believe this.' Lund said, 'We're going back to music.' Alan called me and he was crying and saying, 'I'm through. No one will ever hire me again.' I called Gary Stevens, who worked at Doubleday and had met with Alan before they ever put him on the air. I asked him why they'd fired him. He said, 'He was a pain in the ass. He wouldn't conform. He wouldn't knock off the anti-Christ stuff or the sex talk. The guy's good and I'll recommend him for another job but I don't want that headache in Denver.' "

While hosting his dating show at KHOW, Berg had met Linda Gotlin, an attractive, gray-haired woman who was divorced and had two children. On the topics of love and marriage she was quite independent-minded, and that disturbed Berg. As usual, he broached the subject of matrimony not long after learning the name of her cat. On one occasion, when they were making plans for a weekend trip to San Francisco, he bought a dress and insisted she marry him in it before they returned to Denver. She carried it onto the airplane but never took it out of the box.

"Twice a week was enough for me to go out with someone," she says, ensconced in her shadowy Denver living room, stroking a beautiful gray feline. "Alan would say, 'I want to spend at least an hour a day with you.' I'd say, 'That's impossible.' I needed my time away from him to enjoy my time with him. He'd be upset because I wouldn't go down to the station with him to watch him do his show. Watch a radio show! Why would I want to watch him do his show when I could hear it on the radio? In 1979, I wrote him a letter saying I needed space. He called me during a break in his program. He'd gotten the letter and said, 'How could you do this to me?' I said, 'I don't care if you are the number-one radio personality in Denver. I need my space.' Three weeks later he was fired from KHOW. I felt sorry for him. He lived by the ratings."

The affair was far from over. It lasted, off and on, and between and around several other women, until the summer of 1982. One day after Berg complained that she wouldn't move in with him, she loaded her cat into her car, drove the two of them to his apartment, sat down in his rocking chair, and began rocking and staring at him hard, eventually saying that she had come there to live. Within an hour he became so upset with her decision he left the apartment. She took her pet and went home.

As other women besides Linda Gotlin had discovered, Berg was footloose himself but furiously possessive of the opposite sex. The only subject he would never discuss with Judith was the men she met and dated in Chicago. He was fanatically jealous.

"On my birthday one year," says Gotlin, "I had dinner with my ex-husband. The next night . . . well, Alan could be insane about it. But I knew he was never going to hurt me in any way. He just wanted more from me and I couldn't give him more. I was never hurt when he went away and I think that bothered him."

In August 1979 Berg was forty-five years old, unemployed, and apparently unemployable, at least in talk radio in the Denver market. He was never far from despair, and the firing from KHOW gave him the chance to give in to it completely. Ev Wren tried to reassure him, told Berg that larger markets all over the United

States would be interested in his talents, told him that working together they would find him a better job than he had ever had, told him that under no circumstances should he let this temporary misfortune lead him to take a drink.

"I'll kill myself before I'll do that," Berg replied. "And I've been considering that too."

On the Monday after being booted from KHOW a strange thing happened to the talk-show host. John Mullins, who had caused him to leave KWBZ in 1978, asked him to return to the station. In spite of his recent firing, Berg was known in Denver and potentially a valuable asset. The host fumed; he may have just been let go, he may have been without financial support, but he would be damned if he would consider an offer from the man who had waved his arms at Berg in the studio and driven him to solicit calls from women about cherry pie.

When he had finished denouncing and threatening Mullins, he took the job. While he was working out the details of a contract with KWBZ, KOA, the largest and classiest radio station in the city and region, called and said they would be willing to try Berg out on an all-night program if he would be less abrasive and more manageable. He was flattered. He sought Ev Wren's advice and it was simple: If KOA really wanted him, the station would accept him on his own terms or not at all. Berg took the job at KWBZ.

"The first day back at BZ was fine," Wren says. "The second day no one called him. He phoned me during a commercial and said, 'Ev, I'm embarrassed. I can't do it anymore. To be back in this shithole. . . . What the hell am I doing here? This is depressing, degrading.' "

Wren not only played something of a maternal role with Berg— reminding him to pick up his paycheck (he lost one on occasion), to pay his bills, to become more organized in general—he also thought up ways to promote the talk-show host around town and to keep his mind off his return to KWBZ. Wren was convinced that Berg would make an excellent speaker at social functions, so he tried to find engagements. He conceived of an album, *The Best of Berg*, featuring verbal exchanges and comedy snippets from the radio show, which could be sold both locally and nationally. This last idea was unprecedented, a new form of entertainment in the record-and-tape marketplace. The two men also discussed writing a book together, an account of Berg's radio experiences. Nothing developed; by his own admission and that of everyone around him, Berg's staying power on these projects was dismal. He acted and reacted and felt and thought in the moment, for that moment, creating instantaneous dialogues or monologues or verbal dramas. That was his gift. His potential for real success on talk radio, instantly obvious to Red Buttons and Slappy White and other well-known comics who appeared on his show or met him when he emceed functions around Denver, was a direct result of his spontaneity, which was total. Hearing him on the radio could produce an actual physical sensation, a rush of energy, a stimulation of the senses, like music. He had immediacy, not follow-through. He talked like a demon but couldn't sit still long enough to write a letter to Judith. His voice was perpetual motion, working, churning, and when he talked on the radio he was absolutely *live*, live in a way that the media does not often encourage and sometimes will not tolerate. He was the First Amendment in action. The album and book ideas were bound to be stillborn.

He stayed on at KWBZ, gradually building an audience but wondering if he shouldn't, finally, leave the job or Denver or the radio business for good. In addition to financial problems (his own and KWBZ's) and professional doubts, other troubles were still with him. The death threats and bomb scares had never stopped. In early November 1979, after media reports indicated that the Ku Klux Klan had been engaged in racist activities in the South, Berg delivered a tirade against the organization on the air, so angry he nearly lost control. He seemed personally hurt by *all* instances of racist behavior, hurt in that place that cannot be contained or mollified.

"Alan was fearless when confronting truly dangerous people," Ev Wren says. "If they called and told him that if he said one more nasty thing about them, they would kill him, he would blister them for two solid hours."

If he was fearless on the air, he wasn't after leaving work. On November 6, 1979, Fred Wilkins walked into the studio and told Berg that he was going to die. It left the talk-show host terrified. He demanded that Wren drive him to the Englewood police station so he could get a gun permit. The police chief, along with Wren, tried to talk Berg out of this, and when that failed the chief refused to issue the permit. He told Berg he could carry a gun in his car if he laid it on the seat or strapped it to the steering wheel, but not if he kept it concealed. Berg had no interest in complying with those rules, and over a period of time his desire for a weapon began to subside, but not the death threats.

"There was one scare in particular," Wren says. "The same voice would call the producer [who screened Berg's on-the-air callers] several times a month and say, 'I know what Alan Berg looks like, I know what kind of car he drives, I know where he lives, and I'm going to kill him.' We tried to trace this caller but just never had enough time. We would get many screwball calls, making threats, but when this voice called, Alan got concerned.

"Two or three days after the Fred Wilkins incident, we were having coffee in a shop and a guy walked in and came over to us and said, 'Well, Alan, I'm glad to see you made it through another day.' Alan said, 'I don't think that's very funny.' It really bothered him. It was serious by then."

In early 1981 Slappy White, who was performing at a comedy spot in Denver, was the master of ceremonies at a "roast" for Berg. White and the talk-show host's radio colleagues, current and erstwhile, took turns insulting Berg from the dais of a local nightclub, where an audience had assembled. When his friends had finished insulting him, Berg was invited to the podium to offer a rebuttal. As he came forward, all the speakers rose and exited the dais, leaving him standing there alone, the victim of their final joke. The crowd was amused, Berg was pleased with all the attention, and for an evening his position as a local media personality was rewarding. He would have enjoyed himself even more had not three or four of his ex-lovers come to the event on their own, just to observe.

Each time Berg spotted one he became more upset and worried, and tried to avoid being seen; at evening's end he slipped out the back door with his new woman on his arm.

The feeling of being appreciated locally couldn't last. Within weeks, KWBZ dropped its talk-radio format and resumed playing music. Berg spent his final show trying to find a way—through donations or locating a buyer—to keep the changeover from occurring. He left the air saying, "Freedom of speech is disappearing in this country. This [talk radio] is one of the last vestiges of it because we're not controlled."

Once more he was out of work. The time had definitely come, Wren and Berg believed, for him to seek a job outside Denver. Under Wren's guidance, the two men sorted through hours of Berg's tapes, spliced the best segments together, sent them to stations around the country, and ran an ad in *Broadcasting* magazine. KTOK, in Oklahoma City, was soon interested in Berg, and flew him there for an audition. The station offered him a starting salary of forty thousand dollars, a car, and an apartment, plus talent fees for reading on-air commercials, significantly more money than he had ever made in the radio business. He said he would inform them of his decision within a couple of days. Back in Denver Wren told him the salary was impressive but his act would play in Bible Belt Oklahoma for about two weeks before they ran him out of town. (Wren's distinction between a Colorado radio audience and the one in bordering Oklahoma is subtle and probably accurate. The attitudinal change from the Central Time Zone to the Mountain can be traced back to the historical differences between farmers and miners or prospectors. The first group was settled on the land, the second was more transient and in a riskier business. Both are deeply conservative but the Rocky Mountain West still prefers to think of itself as a little wild and woolly. The Midwest knows better.)

While debating with himself about the Oklahoma City offer, Berg was asked to fill in one afternoon on KOA. Roughly half the off-mike callers that day urged KOA to hire him, the other half urging the station to do the opposite. KOA made no move in either direction. Ev Wren had also sent an audition tape to WXYZ in

Detroit, the fifth largest market in the United States. Berg was soon being flown to Michigan for a meeting with WXYZ's management. By that time Oklahoma City was calling Wren and demanding an answer from his friend. The day after the meeting in Detroit, WXYZ offered Berg a first-year base salary of $50,000, with talent fees on top of that. His second-year salary would be $70,000, and the third year it would reach $110,000, plus the fees. The Detroit station presented Berg with a contract and he signed it. The following morning he called Wren from Chicago, told him the news, and added that since he was in his hometown, where a radio station had expressed interest in him in the past, he thought he might as well drop by for an audition.

"You just said you signed a contract with WXYZ," Wren told him. "What in the hell are you talking about?"

"Oh, they [Chicago's WIND] have a weekend deal . . . pays big money too."

"Alan, did you really go through law school?"

Both men began laughing. Then Wren announced that a Cincinnati station also wanted to talk to Berg.

When he was home again, the talk-show host called Oklahoma City and told KTOK he was going to turn them down. After the station matched the Detroit offer, Berg said he would think it over and let them know. Think about what? Wren asked him. Hadn't he made a commitment to WXYZ? Wren had long known that his friend was worried about finding and holding a job in the radio business, but he was beginning to understand how pervasive this feeling was. Berg wasn't just profoundly insecure, he also loved being wanted, whether by a woman or two or by more than one radio station. While keeping Oklahoma City on hold and making plans to move to Detroit, he confessed to Wren and to Beth Ames, another close acquaintance whom he had met through radio, that he really didn't want to leave Denver. He had rebuilt his life once in a new location and the hardship of the experience was still with him. If he went to Detroit he would go with only his Airedale for companionship; as much as Fred meant to him, the dog was hardly an adequate buffer for the loneliness he felt would be waiting in a large, unknown city. It had taken nearly a decade to establish a professional reputation and new friends in Denver. He felt at home in the town; he felt accepted.

As Berg continued to fret over the decision, he had a great deal to think about. His evolution on Denver radio had been natural; he hadn't started out with the idea of becoming a madman of the nighttime airwaves. Somehow, it had just happened, fulfilling a need within him and within the local population. By the early 1980s radio stations across the country were hiring talk-show hosts like Berg because they were insulting, rude, offensive. Their provocativeness was becoming a commodity that could be packaged and sold, like pizza or shoes. There was money in being outrageous. Everyone in America, it seemed, was angry and frustrated and wanted to cut loose on the air, angry at their government or the Russians or the Iranians or the Arabs or their job or their kids or husband or wife. Talk radio was spreading apace, with programs about sports, gardening, raising children, politics, religion, sex, about letting off general steam; it was the perfect venting medium. More than a hundred years earlier Walt Whitman had listened to his countrymen speak and written that he could hear America singing. In the late seventies and early eighties, talk radio became the sound of America singing, arguing, whining, bitching, confessing, and letting raw feelings, private problems, and political or social opinions hang in the air for everyone with a radio to absorb. The need to emote and connect was everywhere and deep. The global village once predicted by futurist Marshall McLuhan had in some ways arrived; we were all next-door neighbors. It was possible to drive in one's car at night, tune in a show several states away, and learn more about the intimate life of a stranger in three minutes than one knew about a best friend's. People just had to talk.

The notion of being packaged and promoted as a wild man and then sold to Detroit did not appeal to Berg. The seventies were over and he had begun to move away from the bombastic act he had aired at KHOW and KWBZ. He was ready, as he once put it, "to incorporate more of me into my program—sometimes serious, sometimes funny. I want to do all of me, the purest me of any me around. I don't miss telling people off all the time now. I'm not mellower, just broader-based." Could he be that way in a bigger and more lucrative market, or would management make other demands?

He not only had a history in Denver, and friends, he also had a particular chemistry with the audience. Many callers seemed to like Berg in spite of himself; they listened to his flights of fancy and tirades with patience and indulgence, like parents observing a bright and gifted child whom they don't quite understand. They accepted his oddities as such things are often accepted in a small town: He's strange but he's ours. The chemistry went further than that. In predominantly white, Christian-oriented, middle-class Denver he had an edge. He was an outsider in the city and region in a way he would not have been in a larger metropolitan area with a greater ethnic and cultural mix. In Colorado he would forever be genuinely different and that gave him a sense of purpose and delight, almost an identity. The enemies were close by here: convention and complacency, and in some instances, narrowness and bigotry. He needed the enemies to rub against, to stoke his moral indignation and fire. He liked to talk about evil—to try to ferret it out and pin it down—and in some ways that was easier in a place like Denver than in Detroit or New York. Denver would always make him mad.

"I stick it to the [Denver] audience and they love it," he once said. "I first learned what I was doing here after I lost my job at KWBZ. I got an overwhelming number of letters from people who hated my guts but wanted me back on the air so bad they could taste it. They didn't understand exactly why they needed me but they missed the hell out of me when I was gone. I'm an addictive personality. Addictive personalities create addictions in other people. We addict them to us. I meet closet listeners of mine all the time. They can't stand me but they sneak back and listen 'cause they don't know what I'm gonna do next and they wanna be there. That uncertainty drives them up the wall; it excites them. They don't have much excitement in their lives. I give them something to feel—some emotion. Compared to what goes on in Denver, I'm damned exciting. I'm not waving a big flag for myself but Denver is not a very exciting community. Everybody here is dying to bust out, to feel. But I've got to really dig in there to get people worked up enough so there's some action. Denver's not like New York, where the nerve endings are hanging off people's noses. I'm angrier than anyone who calls my show. Anger is one of the greatest motivators in the world. Rage destroys, but out of anger has come a lot of my creativity."

Several days after he had signed the contract in Detroit, two KOA executives called Berg, invited him to breakfast, and made him an offer. A few hours later he said he would start work at their station within the week. Two more days passed before he could find the courage to call Detroit's WXYZ, which by now was planning promotional spots for their new *Alan Berg Show*. He stopped answering his phone, certain that he would have to listen to a corporate attorney in Michigan explain how he was being sued for breach of contract. WXYZ didn't want to see him again—not even in a courtroom.

On Monday, February 23, 1981, he began at KOA. His debut resulted in a barrage of protest letters and calls to the station. KOA had long been regarded as a respectable institution; where, many people wondered, had their standards of good taste gone? One local newspaper columnist wrote that "Mr. Hate," Alan Berg, had been hired to replace "Mr. Nice," Pete Wehner. These negative responses upset Berg, who had never been indifferent to criticism. More than once he had deserted a restaurant before finishing a meal because the people in the booth behind him were talking about what a fool Alan Berg had made of himself on the air.

What people were telling KOA now hurt his feelings, but that wasn't the issue, was it? The station had decided to hire him and showed no signs of reneging on its word; they hadn't placed any strictures on him either. He could say what he felt. KOA was behind him and that made him feel good. His salary was twenty-seven thousand dollars, about half what it would have been in Detroit or Oklahoma City. That was fine. He was on the best and most powerful radio station in his part of the United States, where he had always secretly wanted to work. He was right where he wanted to be, where he would stay.

In the winter of 1981, not long after Berg began at KOA, the Denver Broncos hired a new football coach named Dan Reeves. Arrangements were made for the talk-show host to introduce the coach at McNichols Arena during the halftime of a Denver Nuggets basketball game. Reeves, a former professional football player with the Dallas Cowboys, had spent a number of years with that organization as an assistant coach, and in early 1981 he knew virtually nothing about Denver. He had certainly never heard of Alan Berg. For the ceremony at McNichols, the arena lights were dimmed, and Reeves and Berg walked to center court and stood facing the fifteen thousand people who had come out to watch the game and meet the coach. The public-address announcer said that here to introduce the new man in charge of the Denver Broncos was KOA radio personality Alan Berg.

A good portion of the fifteen thousand spectators rose from their seats and booed, hurling insults and curses at the tall, bearded man in the spotlight at midcourt. Berg smiled and waved up at the crowd. Reeves, a quiet, polite, religious man from rural Georgia, was appalled by the fans' behavior but even more dumbstruck by the actions of the man standing next to him. Alarmed, he turned to Berg and said, "Who *are* you?"

It was the operative question of his life. Who was he? By the early 1980s, with his decision made to stay in Denver, with his job at KOA and his age approaching fifty, Berg was closer to answering that query than ever before. He wasn't one person, capable of living within a single coherent identity, but multiple people, a juggler of lives, a chameleon, a man who not only had several distinct personalities—or extremes of one personality—but one who created even more pasts and experiences to make himself more dimensional. He might propose marriage to one woman on Sunday night and another on Monday. Weren't two different men saying those words?

The radio only reinforced his tendencies. People who called his show made up things about themselves—why couldn't he? On the air he was merely a response to whatever stimuli came in over the phone, whatever the moment demanded.

Interestingly, in 1982, when he tried to make the transition from radio to television, he failed. For a few months, Berg hosted a noontime telephone call-in program on Denver's Channel 4, the sister TV station of KOA. It competed with soap operas and *Leave It to Beaver* reruns and lost to them in convincing fashion. The show was amusing and lively, but Berg on Channel 4 was not the same as Berg on KOA. Something vital was lost in translation. On radio, he was a disembodied voice, stirring up the mind, conscious and unconscious, engaging the fancy of a listener, as radio has always done. Half of the fun of tuning him in was trying to imagine what he looked like or was doing while talking to callers. Television took away that dimension. It was too real. He was an image on a screen and no longer inside one's own mind, jarring one into a sensation of freedom. No wonder he failed on TV.

Beth Ames is a seamstress who lives in Boulder, Colorado. In 1977 she heard a radio talk-show host upbraiding an elderly man on the air, telling him not to call again until he had dentures and could speak clearly. She laughed, she thought it was the height of bad manners, and she kept listening to the show—not because she liked it but because she wanted to know what Berg would do next. In time she sent him program ideas and met him. At KHOW Berg oversaw a radio contest in which the winners got to visit the studio and join him during his show. Several people won but were afraid to come to the station and sit with him. Beth filled in for them and went on to host a number of programs herself, when Berg was indisposed by his car or his dog or a woman. She was one of the very few people ever allowed inside his home.

"It was a zoo," she says. "If you walked into his apartment you got a real clear sense of him. There were shoes in the kitchen cabinets. He had one hundred and fifty pairs. He had no dishes, no silverware. He only liked to eat out. At a restaurant, if you don't like what's served, you argue with the waiter and send it back. In someone's home, you're stuck with what they give you. He loved sweets and was comfortable eating them at my apartment. And coffee. That we could do. But you wouldn't get him to sit for a meal too often. He liked to walk, just walk around shopping centers by himself, just walking and looking.

"At his apartment Freddie's food was in the refrigerator and he had lots of coffee, but not much else. I don't think he ever used the dishwasher. It still had the instruction guide inside. Once when I was there, he brought me a paper plate with Oreo cookies on it and we watched TV. That's as close as he would get to being a host. For five minutes he would pretend that he was a regular person. There were books and papers and magazines and shoes and records and notebooks and ties and dog food and all this stuff everywhere. He'd get sick of it after a while and stay home all weekend and clean. I'd take a vacuum over and he would make it spotless. He'd always ask my advice—do you use Windex or Ajax? He never let me help. He'd clean it all up and then everything would get messy again. When you were there, you didn't have a sense that this was a place for someone who was even marginally at peace with himself or the world."

Part of Berg's identity was that he refused to choose one self; he would live between the choices and on the margins. If this was frightening and meant existing inside of chaos, he could handle that. And when he couldn't, he would phone Ev Wren or Beth Ames or his ex-wife or his current girlfriend and burst into tears. An observer might have called Berg existential, but he went the existentialists one better. If they believed that a modern individual has to invent his identity, Berg was becoming adept at reinventing himself from one moment, or one phone call, to the next. In public, a shifting identity keeps an audience off balance, amused, entertained, aware of your mystery. But alone . . . it can be terrifying. There's no one to play to or off of, no resonance inside. Berg's terror—his shaking in his sleep, his frenetic behavior, his insecurity—all these were real, not parts of an act. He had no idea what he might do next, or who he might be. There was an easy way out of the dilemma, but the world was too intriguing to him, his curiosity about other people was too deep, and he was too fascinating to himself to violate the "living wish" he had discovered after surgery.

While working at KOA he had begun to change, to solidify, if only slightly. The station did not attempt to guide or restrain him in direct ways, but it did wield an influence. His rudeness was waning, though at times he lapsed into it. On March 5, 1982, he had a long-distance radio interview with Ellen Kaplan, a current phenomenon in the news. She had recently seen former secretary of state Henry Kissinger and his wife, Nancy, at the Newark airport and confronted him with a startling question: "Is it true that you sleep with young boys at the Carlyle hotel?" At that point, according to Kaplan, Nancy Kissinger stepped forward and tried to choke her.

The flap was too juicy for Berg to ignore. After calling Kaplan in order to interview her, he characterized her as "a vile human being" and indicated that Nancy Kissinger should be commended for grabbing her throat. Kaplan soon hung up on Berg, but for the remainder of the program he kept returning to the subject, unable to let it go. "They say women should never be struck," he said on the air. "There's one that deserves it. . . . I'd commit suicide today if I thought I'd have to spend the rest of my life with that woman. . . . I've decided I want a blind date with Ellen Kaplan. . . . You want to know something? She'll show up and I'll fall in love with her. She's just the kind of woman I get involved with."

Many people did not find this funny. Kaplan's boyfriend called KOA and demanded an apology. The attorneys for General Electric, which owned the station at the time, thought a brief suspension of Berg might avoid a lawsuit. To the talk-show host's dismay, KOA management went along with this plan and gave him a few days' vacation. The whole matter left Berg defiant and depressed, but there was another long-term effect: He would never again be so blatantly abusive to a guest on his show.

He was changing in other ways. In a 1982 interview, when asked about his anger, he thought for some time before responding: "We like to say a lot of heroic things about why we're angry, right?

Because we don't like indecency or wrong. But I think it's mostly all premised on not liking yourself. When all is said and done, there are just too many things you know about yourself that aren't as pure as you would like them to be. It was unbearable to me that I was prone to corruption [in his Chicago law practice]. All of the sudden I was doing all of the things I'd always been ridiculously critical of. I learned that lying was the single most destructive thing in my life. And practicing law like that is a form of lying. Maybe it reminds you a little bit of your father, whom you never saw any guts in in your whole life. You suddenly say, 'I'm not the opposite of him. I'm weak, too.' You have to sort that out for yourself."

He appeared to be happier than at any other period of his radio career. Talking into the KOA microphone, rolling his chair across the studio floor, chain-smoking filterless Pall Malls, pointing one hand at the ceiling, talking faster now, he often became so excited that he clutched at the edge of his desk for ballast. He was having the time of his life.

"It's strange," he said at the end of 1982, "but in the past year I've felt more love for my show than ever before. Maybe I'm making more of a breakthrough. Sometimes, I question myself. I say, 'Am I doing this program because I think it's so important that I'm on for the folks out there?' No. It's important for me. It's a great catharsis for me. I can do tremendous emotional things for myself on the show. I can get myself up when I'm down. If I'm depressed, I write down on a piece of paper what my show will be tomorrow. That gives me something to look forward to that I love.

"First and foremost, I'm trying to entertain. Mostly myself. I've spent my whole life trying to entertain people. I'm trying to entertain you right now. If anyone in this business ever says they are trying to make a serious significant contribution to society, they're fulla shit. There ain't a guy in this business who doesn't have an ego on the line, who isn't insecure and frightened to death. Me included."

Then you don't, he was asked, have any moral purpose in doing your show?

"My moral purpose is to kill myself," he said, laughing. "To figure a way out of here. If I had any moral feelings for this city, I'd leave tomorrow."

He went into a soliloquy about how several beautiful women had fallen in love with him but drifted away because they grew tired of hearing him whip himself. Then he discussed love and sex: "Sex doesn't maintain. Love should maintain. They blend with one another and they don't have anything to do with one another. I love my ex-wife, love her the same way I loved her when I met her. But I'm not 'in love' with her, and I feel very guilty about what I did. I'm the classic romantic. I've got to be in love with someone. My being in love has been one of the most destructive things in my life."

Why, he was asked, did he keep whipping himself?

"I must be punished."

But *why?*

He exhaled cigarette smoke and began to laugh, a deep, mature laugh colored with a certain nervousness. He took another long drag.

"I secretly want to be a Christian and don't recognize it," he said, laughing again.

# 16

___

## *BAD CHEMISTRY*

___

                        Soon after the initial gathering of
the nine men at Bob Mathews's farm in September 1983, several
recruits made surveillance trips to Spokane, about one hundred
miles south of Metaline Falls and the largest city in the area. They
went there to look for black pimps to mug and pornography stores
to rob. By late October Mathews had selected his target: Spokane's
Worldwide Video Adult Bookstore. Mathews, Randy Duey, Bruce
Pierce, and Denver Parmenter had all planned to commit the robbery on the evening of the twenty-eighth, but Parmenter arrived
late at the rendezvous point, so the other three left without him.
Shortly before eight, the trio entered the store, tied up the two

employees with tape (they ran out before the job was done), and searched the business for cash. When the male sales clerk, Kenneth Taylor, offered resistance, Duey hit him on the left cheek. The thieves were armed, but beyond the punch no show of force was needed. They stole $369 and got away without difficulty. After the police arrived at Worldwide Video, Taylor described one of the gunmen, apparently the leader, as resembling a Mexican.

Two weeks later, Parmenter, Duey, Soderquist, Dan Bauer, Pierce, and Mathews drove to Seattle in two cars. Money was scarce. Under a false name Mathews checked all six of them into one room of the Golden West motel at the north end of town. For the next several days five of the men surveilled the movement of armored cars approaching and leaving a K mart store and a Fred Meyer department store, while Soderquist studied another business target in a different section of town. At night they met back at the motel to compare their findings. Surveilling, they were armed with a variety of rifles, pistols, and shotguns.

The group noticed a newspaper report stating that France's Baron Elie de Rothschild, of the internationally renowned Jewish banking family, planned to visit Seattle in the immediate future. He was coming to attend a fund-raising event of the Jewish Federation of Greater Seattle, held downtown at the Four Seasons Olympic hotel. Bob Mathews could hardly believe it; the opportunity was too good to let pass. Anyone closely affiliated with the radical right, or with Identity Christianity, had heard the sermons of Reverend Jim Wickstrom, of Tigerton, Wisconsin. Wickstrom traveled the Midwest preaching the Identity faith and shipped taped messages to his followers around the nation. No phrase rolled off his tongue with the same bitter relish as when he was condemning the "House of Rothschild." The very name seemed to make him shudder with hatred and pleasure. In 1983 he was sentenced to eighteen months in prison for impersonating a public official.

Mathews sent Dan Bauer and Denver Parmenter to the University of Washington library in Seattle to look through Jewish publications and learn more about the baron's visit. When they reported back, Mathews decided his men should set off a bomb in a ballroom of the Four Seasons, killing Rothschild. But how to do it? They discussed placing an explosive on the floor above the ballroom and blowing it downward at their target. They considered a suicide mission, in which one member of the gang would walk up to the baron and detonate a charge, destroying at least both of them. But who would volunteer for the job? Would Mathews have to choose which Aryan Warrior to sacrifice? They talked of other options, but finally concluded that they had neither the time nor the materials to make a fail-safe bomb and complete a successful mission.

Mathews went back to his robbery plans, selecting the Fred Meyer store as the best site. Then another problem arose. Dan Bauer had originally been drawn to the Aryan Nations compound and later to Metaline Falls because of his religious convictions. Even though he had come to Seattle to conduct surveillance for a robbery, when faced with the prospect of committing the crime, he wanted no part of it. It was wrong, he believed, for the men to engage in illegal activities, no matter what the ultimate purpose or goals. Mathews strongly disagreed, but Bauer's doubts caused others to raise questions, and eventually the robbery was called off. Several members of the surveillance team drifted away from Metaline Falls and it appeared that Mathews's grandiose schemes were at a dead end.

Bill Soderquist, in spite of his pledge to be an Aryan Warrior, returned home to see his mother, visit his girlfriend, and snort cocaine with his friends. Richard Kemp stayed in the Metaline Falls area and found work at a sawmill in Ione. Parmenter went back to Cheney, Washington, to rejoin his wife, Janice, and daughter, Kristin. His feelings about the Group were at best mixed. Some time later he met Randy Duey in a Cheney bar, and after a couple of drinks Duey poured beer on his companion and they got into a fistfight. Parmenter had a violent temper; Scotch set it loose. He and Duey were estranged, but not for long. The two men were bound together in this adventure into radical politics, their fates entwined at least until they had gone further than the stickup of a dirty bookstore. This special linkage between them was not an uncommon thing in the thirty or so people Bob Mathews would choose for his revolution. As a whole they had a volatile chemistry: Before 1984 only two or three had criminal records, or even criminal tendencies. By December of that year they had committed more than 240 acts of crime and conspiracy. Within the group itself there were several pairs—two men usually—who had a particular interaction, a potential violence. Soderquist and Kemp were one such pair. Parmenter and Duey were another. In both cases, one man (Soderquist and Parmenter) was primarily a thinker and the other (Kemp and Duey) was more of an actor, prone to kill. David Lane and Bruce Pierce made a similar duo. The blending of these personalities would in time play itself out fully and end in disaster.

Mathews wasn't discouraged by their failure to rob the Fred Meyer store in Seattle. He soon went to the Aryan Nations compound to meet with two young men, David Tate and Gary Yarbrough, who ran the printing press for Richard Butler. Only twenty, Tate had become involved with Butler's Church of Jesus Christ Christian because his parents were members there. Yarbrough, nearly thirty, had been recruited by Aryan Brotherhood inmates while serving time for burglary in an Arizona prison. "The initiation rite for joining the Brotherhood is simple," according to one ex-con in Denver. "You just walk up to the biggest, meanest nigger in the joint and take him on."

While incarcerated, Yarbrough had come into contact with Butler's literature, which was mailed to the prison. Upon his release this short, thin, hard-looking redhead went north to Idaho with the express purpose of finding Butler and telling him that his ideas were false. Before long, Butler had convinced him of the opposite and Yarbrough was employed as his bodyguard, carrying a rifle or other firearm and wearing a Nazi-like uniform and cap. His disdainful eyes perfectly matched his outfit.

One evening in November 1983, Mathews, Yarbrough, and Tate met in the printing room on Reverend Butler's compound to look into the possibility of turning out counterfeit currency. Aryan Nations had purchased a four-thousand-dollar offset press, Mathews and his colleagues had a fifty-dollar bill, and before the evening was over the machine was printing fake money. Howard Witherwax, who was a member of the church, the head of its security force, and Butler's son-in-law, oversaw the duties of the compound guards. When he got wind of the counterfeiting operation, he went to Yarbrough and posed some questions; the redhead told him that what took place in the printing room was none of his business. The son-in-law queried Bruce Pierce, who was also on the premises, but learned nothing from him. Finally he went to David Tate and was told that the young man had done the layout for the counterfeiting job. When Witherwax informed Butler, the minister suspended Pierce and Mathews from the compound. He wanted no truck with illegalities, not on his own property, anyway. On December 3, he went to Southern California to hook up with Randall Evans and Frank Silva, two Klan leaders in that state. In the San Fernando Valley outside of Los Angeles, fifteen men, including Butler, were arrested for attending a KKK cross-burning. Criminal charges were filed against them and then dismissed, but not before a local judge took the opportunity to characterize the defendants as "slimy, no-good, yellow-bellied scum."

By the time Pierce and Mathews had been told to leave the compound, they were ready to break all ties with Butler's church. Gary Yarbrough would soon follow their lead, bolting Aryan Nations and moving his wife and three young children into an attractive mountain home at nearby Sandpoint, Idaho. Yarbrough's actions would grab the attention of several people in the area; they thought of the redhead as a poorly paid dishwasher at a nearby restaurant who devoted his spare time to an eccentric group of religious converts at Hayden Lake. Where did he get the money to live in this new home? No one was startled enough to take such thoughts to the police.

A portion of the counterfeit money produced at the compound on that November evening found its way into the hands of David Lane, who transported it to Ken Loff near Metaline Falls. Mathews had designated Loff as the group's banker and a "legal," someone who would aid the men in their crimes but not be directly involved in illegal activities, another concept borrowed from *The Turner Diaries*. With Loff, Lane dyed the money green and rubbed coffee grounds into it to make it look real, used, and ready to be spent again. On the evening of December 3, while Butler was at the cross-burning rally near Los Angeles, Bruce Pierce went into a Radio Shack store at the Valley Mall in Union Gap, Washington, near Yakima. After selecting a clock and batteries, he walked to the cash register and gave the sales clerk, Dennis McRae, a fifty-dollar bill. "It looked a little funny," McRae later recalled, so he didn't immediately accept it but turned it over in his hand, feeling the paper, staring at its face. Pierce grabbed the bill back and pulled a twenty from his wallet. McRae completed the transaction, but watched Pierce as he left the store and went into another business on the mall. From the front of the Radio Shack McRae observed him trying to pass another phony bill. He called the police, who quickly arrived, found Pierce hiding in a restroom stall, arrested him, and notified the Secret Service (counterfeiting is the agency's bailiwick).

The Secret Service recovered fifty-two fake bills in the Yakima area. They were easy to identify—all were fifties and all had the same serial numbers on their face, since Mathews had undertaken the counterfeiting operation with only one bill. Bruce Pierce pleaded guilty to passing phony currency and was released, with the obligation to show up for a prison sentence beginning at a future date. Pierce said he would be sure to do that—while he, Mathews, and others were already laying plans for other, more daring escapades.

By December the hard-core group around Mathews was starting to refer to itself as the Order, the name of the inner-circle members of the revolutionary command in *The Turner Diaries*. (Later, some of the men would refer to themselves as the Silent Brotherhood or—in German—Bruders Schweigen.) On the morning of December 20, a few weeks after Pierce's arrest, Bob Mathews went into Seattle's Innis Arden branch of CityBank, displayed a pistol to a young woman teller, and demanded that she give him the money at her window. When she had done this, Mathews herded her and several other female employees into the bank's vault, not locking its door. As he was carrying out the robbery, the bandit told the women no one would be hurt if they followed his instructions, and then apologized for the inconvenience, adding that he had a sick child at home and desperately needed money for medical care. Before fleeing he wished all of them a Merry Christmas.

One of the stolen bundles of cash contained a packet of red dye that detonated as soon as it was taken outside the bank. The force of the explosion knocked Mathews to the ground and covered him, the money, and the surrounding snowfall with the dripping red liquid. He jumped up, got his bearings, and left the scene. Part of the $25,956 was ruined, and he gave David Lane the tedious chore of cleaning the salvageable bills with turpentine.

In one way the robbery had been an unqualified success. It was possible, Mathews had learned, to commit a real crime, something more than rifling the cash register of a magazine store—and to get away with it. Knocking over a bank this easily emboldened him. In the weeks ahead he would drive his cohorts around Seattle, take them past the bank where the heist had occurred, and talk proudly of the deed. He liked to discuss his exploits, unconcerned about who might be hearing the words or what they might think. It wasn't so much that he trusted his listeners; rather, what was the point of being a revolutionary, an outlaw, if you couldn't share a few good war stories with your kinsmen during the struggle, if you couldn't wink at them and whisper "eighty-eight" (the eighth letter of the alphabet was *H* and when you put two of them together it meant "Heil Hitler!"). Even the story about the dye blowing him off his feet was amusing, because he had survived. He would never fall prey to that trick again.

Mathews had learned a tremendous amount recently and was looking forward to the New Year. Nineteen eighty-four—ever since George Orwell had published his novel by that name, the date had had an historical ring to it. Mathews wanted it to be a special twelve months. He planned to enlarge the Order and its influence, bring in more money for the war chest, move beyond the first timid steps of revolt and into the more challenging and significant areas of action, of change—things like political assassination.

Born in Chicago in 1934,
Berg's first nickname in
life was "Peachy Puss."

Because of his temper
tantrums and his hair,
which was turning red,
his childhood nickname
became "Fumy Plumey."

Berg, second row from the bottom, third from right, with
his 1947 graduation class at Chicago's O'Keeffe grammar school

The groom's wedding party, from left to right: Ruth, Alan, Norma,
and Dr. Joseph Berg.

Berg and Judith Halpern were married in Denver in 1958.

Berg and Judith honeymooned in San Francisco before settling on the South Side of Chicago.

Berg began his career as a struggling young attorney in Chicago.

Always meticulous about his appearance, Berg would one day own a clothing store.

In the late 1960s, Berg opened The Shirt Broker in Denver.

After a decade of losing jobs, Berg was hired by Denver's most prestigious radio station, KOA, in 1981.

Berg's hair was grown long to cover scars from brain surgery.

In 1983 Berg and Linda McVey began spending a lot of time together. His beloved Airedale, Fred, often tagged along.

Berg attending a theatrical performance in Denver with a friend, Doatsy Peifer

Berg was driving his black Volkswagen the night he was killed.

Robert Jay Mathews, the
founder and leader of the
Order

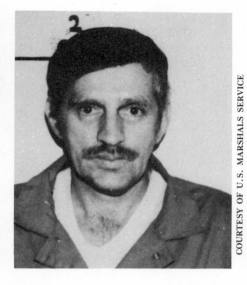

Before joining the Order in
1983, David Lane had
debated with Alan Berg
on Denver radio.

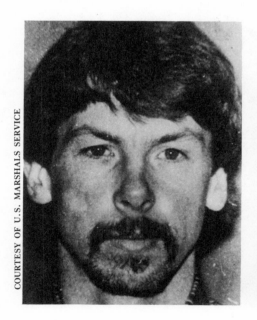

After his arrest in 1985,
Bruce Pierce asked to be
deported from the United
States.

Richard Scutari was the
Order's head of security.

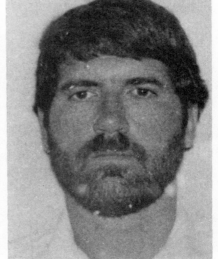

In the spring of 1984 Jean Craig traveled from Laramie to Denver to conduct surveillance on Alan Berg.

Denver Parmenter was one of the first Order members to confess to the FBI.

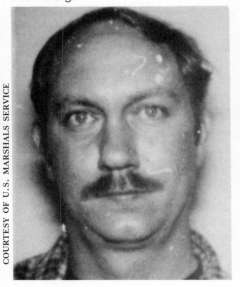

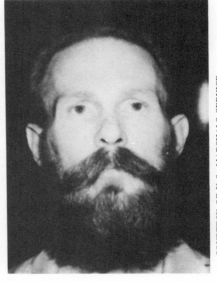

The federal government accused Randy Duey of murdering Walter West in the Idaho woods.

The gun that murdered Alan Berg was found in the home of Gary Yarbrough.

Berg in the late 1970s, while working at Denver's KHOW, the most controversial period of his radio career

# PART THREE

—

# LOSING IT

—

# 17

——

## *SELF-KNOWLEDGE*

——

Throughout his radio career Berg had frequently talked about his Jewishness and poked fun at it. The anecdotes often centered on ethnic stereotypes—like his tight Uncle Harry, back in Chicago—subjects that can at best be tricky and at worst be vulgar or bigoted. In Berg's hands, they were comic. He brought Uncle Harry alive, made him seem funny and human; somehow, this old man's habit of stealing cream cheese from grocery stores helped illuminate a whole culture and made one appreciate it. While reading commercials for a fur store in Denver, Berg would deliver monologues about Jewish women in Miami who insisted on wearing their mink coats on summer days at the beach. The ad would be lost but he was so irrepressible no one seemed to mind.

"There were so many important aspects to his Jewishness," says Judith. "The ability to learn about different things and experience them is much of what Jewish ethnicity is about. Jews want you to have all these experiences and come out with more Jewishness. Alan did that—he had the brilliant mind and was the achiever—but he came out with more Alan. He was caught between the different cultures. He saw the problems with all of them. His humor was in those gaps. A lot of Jews give money to a cause and get their name in a Blue Book and that's the extent of their Jewishness. That's what he wanted to prevent forever. He wanted to have his *own* mind. He was criticized for that, and he resented it. Did he assimilate or leave the fold? No, he just had a lot of brains, a lot of guts, and a lot more feeling than a lot of other people."

By the time he went to work for KOA his interest in Judaism and his own Jewishness had expanded and deepened. In September 1981, on Yom Kippur, the holiest of Jewish holidays, the day set aside for fasting and the atonement of sins, he opened his show by asking Gentiles in the audience to call and explain to him why they didn't like Jews. Why, he asked, has anti-Semitism been prevalent during so much of Western history? What is at the root of it? Perhaps if some callers would answer these questions, he and those listening could learn something that might alleviate the problem. As provocative as his questions were that day—and as uncomfortable as they made a number of Jews in Denver—they seemed to go well beyond Berg's penchant for grandstanding and show business. He really wanted to know.

A few months into 1983 Berg's father died. The talk-show host went to Chicago for the funeral and was faced with a difficult choice. KOA, in concert with several Jewish organizations in Denver, had recently decided to send him to Israel, where he would conduct his program and broadcast reports on the country back to Colorado. Dr. Berg succumbed to a longstanding illness shortly before his son's departure. The death was wrenching. Two months earlier, Berg had made some bitingly critical remarks about his father, which appeared in a newspaper interview. When he saw them in print, he became upset and angry, feeling he had betrayed the older man. The death only added to his sense of wrongdoing.

Where did his obligation lie now? To spend time in Chicago with his mother and sister or to go on the excursion abroad? After some mulling, he made arrangements to leave four thousand dollars in a drawer in his Denver apartment—half for Judith and half for Beth Ames, in case he died—and flew to Israel on schedule. The trip was a success from a journalistic viewpoint but also made an impact on him that was not immediately obvious. His feelings about Israel, like those about his Jewishness, had long been mixed, and after returning to the United States he did not seem greatly changed by the visit. Yet overseas he absorbed a lot, felt a lot, and learned a good deal about the Israeli state. Months later the residue of the voyage would find its way onto the radio.

In mid-June of 1983, a fellow talk-show host at KOA, Peter Boyles, invited Roderick "Rick" Elliott to be a guest on his program. From Fort Lupton, Colorado, Elliott was the publisher of the *Primrose and Cattlemen's Gazette*, a sporadically produced journal, and the founder of the National Agricultural Press Association. In these capacities, he often traveled the West and Midwest, talking to gatherings of financially troubled farmers. All bank loans made since the early 1970s, he told them, were illegal under federal truth-in-lending legislation; if the farmers would file lawsuits using his guidelines, they could banish their debts and keep their land. The message was attractive. The farm-debt situation had been worsening through the early 1980s and Elliott's words simplified a complex and disastrous economic reality for many rural people. Their anger over these troubles was often bitter, and he gave it a focus. He sprinkled his oratory with the same kind of references that could be found in the *Primrose and Cattlemen's Gazette:* Farmers' problems were the result of U.S. government policies, 'which were controlled by a conspiracy of banker and Jews, or Jewish bankers. (In September 1984 Elliott would be charged with twenty counts of felony theft and conspiracy to commit felony theft, all as a result of his failure to repay more than $230,000 in loans to ten people. He was convicted and sentenced to eight years.)

At the time Elliott appeared on Boyles's show, he had a friend who was a columnist for the *Primrose and Cattlemen's Gazette*, Colonel Francis "Bud" Farrell, retired from the air force. Farrell was an associate of David Lane, who had also done some writing for the *P&CG*, most notably a piece called "Death of the White Race." In June 1983, Lane was working nights at the periodical as a security guard. Boyles was prompted to have Elliott on his program after Farrell published a series of articles for the paper, entitled "Open Letter to the Gentiles."

As the discussion between the talk-show host and Elliott was being broadcast, Alan Berg was driving to KOA to work the next shift. He heard Elliott and was intrigued by him. When Berg arrived at the studio, he asked Boyles if they could get the guest back on the radio the following day. Berg opened his program of June 15 hooked up, via the telephone, with both Elliott and Farrell. In addition to the subjects of farm debt and anti-Semitism, Berg had another concern in mind. A friend of his, U.S. Representative Patricia Schroeder (D-Col.), a member of the House Armed Services Committee, had been informed of Farrell's articles and the fact that the U.S. Marine Corps advertised in the *Primrose and Cattlemen's Gazette*. She was disturbed by this, contending that the federal government had no business supporting such a publication. There were rumors of Schroeder using her influence to stop the Marine Corps ads from appearing in the paper. Berg, in turn, was upset by *this*. More than once in his radio career he had been the target of boycott threats—both by advertisers at radio stations and by listeners who patronized their businesses. Some of the threats had been carried out. Berg thought Representative Schroeder was out of line and the *P&CG* had the right to sell ads wherever it could.

The program of June 15 was heated; like much talk radio, it jumped from one topic to the next—from the Holocaust to Christianity to Israel—without transition. After Farrell and Elliott had left the air, one of those who called Berg was David Lane, but whether he is a speaker in the following excerpted transcript, filed in a Denver court, is unknown. What is known is that the show cast a shadow from the time it was aired to the evening Berg lay murdered in his driveway.

Berg: "If I were to read these [Farrell's articles] as a Jew—I mean I am trying to remain objective here—my own emotions are very opposed to what you're doing. But my emotions should not interfere with your freedom of speech. . . . I'm not sitting here telling you that Jews are perfect, okay?"

Elliott: "I'm not saying that Christians are."

Berg: "See, when you make these indictments against Jews, one of the really nice things when you question the Holocaust would be to have some facts available and the facts are available if you care to look at them."

Farrell: "We'd like to sit down with you and debate them with you."

Berg: "Well, it's so simple. In fact, it would be far more valuable to you to write—let's say—the Holocaust Museum, be it in Washington or Baltimore. Write, let's see, the United Jewish Federation. They'll send you all the information you want, with all the documentation, with the names [of Jews who died in World War II]. Did you see the recent Holocaust convention that took place in Washington?"

Elliott: "Yes."

Berg: "Okay, what do they do there?"

Elliott: "I have no idea."

Berg: "You see . . . if you were interested in how they did all the tracing and searching and the checking out of each person, who was in fact in the camps. They documented this. This is not a game. This is not made up. This is reality. . . . I would be the first to tell you that if we say six million [died] . . . you know, somebody could have made a mistake. It could be five, it could be four, in fact it could be seven."

Elliott: "It could be two, also."

Berg: "Well, is that really the issue, though?"

Elliott: "That is not the issue, except that you people are making up the issue, to try to say why Pat Shroeder did what she did."

Berg: "I disagree with—I think Pat Schroeder was wrong. . . ."

Elliott: "She is saying we're anti-Semitic, when that is not a fact."

Berg: "Sir, that speaks for itself in the very comments you're making. You're not anti-Semitic. You're anti-Jewish."

Elliott: "I am not and I—"

Berg: "You are accusing the Jews of a world conspiracy to take away your Christianity. That is not exactly a love affair with Jews, is it? . . . I am not too thrilled with Christianity but you have a right to be a Christian the same as I have a right to be a Jew. . . ."

Farrell: "Alan, let me ask you a question. . . . You're not married?"

Berg: "Fortunately, for the women out there, I'm not."

Farrell: "Say you're married. . . . Now could you be loyal to a wife and a girlfriend? How can you explain dual citizenship then? How can you explain dual loyalty?"

Berg: "I don't think it's difficult to explain at all."

Farrell: "Well, you see this is the difference and so much of this is coming out. You've got a country that's in trouble. The economy is in trouble. . . ."

Berg: "Are you familiar with Israel's economy?"

Farrell: "Well, there's hyperinflation."

Berg: "How much inflation?"

Farrell: "I know that it's much greater than ours."

Berg: "Would you perceive the Jew of Israel as a rich person?"

Farrell: "The figures I had [say] that every family in Israel got over ten thousand four hundred dollars, the equivalent of that of [U.S.] taxpayers' money."

Berg: "That's the most fallacious—sir, you will never see more collective poverty and merely getting along than you will in Israel. . . ."

Elliott: "All you have to do is go to West Virginia."

Berg: "What does West Virginia have to do with it?"

Elliott: "It's just as plain poverty as you'll see in Israel, and probably worse."

Berg: "I don't doubt that it's true. . . . I would urge you to take a trip to Israel or to look at how the average Israeli lives. They're living hand-to mouth. Are you familiar with that?"

Elliott: "I'm familiar [with] hand-to-mouth, but again we're getting to the point of what we're talking about."

Berg: "But see, you accused the Jewish banker of this conspiracy and . . . here is the state of Israel, barely getting along. It's unbelievable. You have to be there to see it . . . a country trying to hold on to a little piece of land. . . . Let me urge you again, all right? If you want some facts instead of whistling 'Dixie' here—"

Elliott: "I am *not* whistling 'Dixie.' "

Berg: "You're whistling because everything you have said is a lie, okay? But I think you have a right to advance your lies. . . . I'm still protecting your right to lie, okay? . . . As long as you lie, I like it open like this because, you see, you have no facts. You have made up and you have inferred a thought, like all fanatics, like John Birchers, like Klansmen, like all of these folks."

Elliott: "You're crazy."

Berg: "I'm crazy, sir. You're a healthy person. Thanks so much for calling, and I stood up for you, believe it or not. [He hangs up the phone.] All lines are open: eight-six-one-TALK, eight-six-one, eight-two-five-five. What do you think about this thing here? It's kind of sickening. It really is. I mean here is a man who has laid out—what, about ten to twelve things?—wrong on every one—all documented—all available to anyone who cares to look. We are going to take a pause on KOA and we will be right back. . . ."

New caller: "I would like to address the Pat Schroeder issue but before I do I have got a few things that I would like to say about Jewish people. And I hope you will let me say it because I think it is important. I am talking about Jewish people as a nationality, like Italians or Mexicans or whatever and not as a religion. . . . I myself am a Christian, okay . . . but Alan, some of the best people I have ever known in my life are Jewish people. They have been close friends, they're warm—"

Berg: "I don't think that means anything connected with this argument."

Caller: "Yeah, well, it's important that that be said."

Berg: "I don't think it is important. I think it is nonsensical, stroking, almost anti-Semitic. . . ."

Caller: "What I am trying to get at is I just felt so much hatred, you know, through the radio there about Jewish people and the reason people don't like them is that they're proud hardworking people. . . . And as businessmen they will clean your plow in the free-enterprise system. Because they are going to get out there and hustle."

Berg: "Maybe we should learn from them, instead of hating them, right?"

Caller: "Right."

Berg: "Okay, I must go to the news. . . . Thank you for your call. . . . I feel they have a right to say that. I also think it is incumbent upon me to challenge his faulty thinking."

New caller: "Just calm down a little bit."

Berg: "No, I will never calm down so long as people think this stupidly and resolve issues based on no factuality. I'm always going to get—I hope I never quit getting angry."

Caller: "Oh—I mean—definitely get angry but try to be a little more subtle and—"

Berg: "Give me an example. Isn't that how the Jews got theirs in Nazi Germany? By being—you know—by saying that they really don't mean it?"

Caller: "No, you have to stand up and say what you want to say."

Berg: "The era of the Jew taking a backseat to anybody is over, dear, and the next Jew that does will get annihilated by mentalities like the people that talked on this show."

Caller: "Oh, I agree with you."

Berg: "Thank you very much. Lines open. That's the German Jew philosophy: 'Let's not make too much noise about the whole thing'. . . . Okay, let's go back to the phone here. Westminister [a suburb] you are on KOA."

New caller: "Hello, Alan. How are you?"

Berg: "All right."

Caller: "First of all, I just want to say you make me so mad sometimes I would like to strangle you. But sometimes you make me love you. It's fifty-fifty, I guess."

Berg: "Well, that's part of love. . . ."

Caller: "I had one other thing to say. Thank God for Alan Berg and the fact that you do speak up like you do. . . . You talked about in the past and Nazi Germany, where the Jewish people were too passive."

Berg: "That's exactly right. The Israelite Jew took on a posture . . . one they will not step back from: 'We will never be victimized again like this. Or if we are, you're going with us.' "

Caller: "Definitely."

Berg: "That is their goal, their quest, and I respect them with all my heart for that. . . ."

New caller: "Hi, Alan. You had a rough day today."

Berg: "I didn't have a rough day."

Caller: "Yeah, well, you had a lively day."

Berg: "My dear, dealing with people like this is dealing with duck soup."

Caller: "You had a lively day then."

Berg: "Yes."

Caller: "You're going to have the John Birch Society after you."

Berg: "Oh, God! . . ."

New caller: "Yes, sir. While I agreed with you fundamentally that the guests you had appeared to be bigots, I have an objection to the way you handled them."

Berg: "Well, you go right ahead. . . ."

Caller: "Basically, I think an earlier woman was correct. You tend to dominate these conversations and act more like a prosecuting attorney than a moderator."

Berg: "I am challenging the prosecutor. . . . I am giving them the sources and they are still screaming, 'You're wrong, Alan, you're wrong.' What kind of thinking ability is that? How dare you challenge what in fact has been proven over the decades."

Caller: "I realize that but I think you would have a better indictment of people like that if you allowed them to talk. They will indict themselves."

Berg: "They certainly did. . . . All of these Holocaust memorials were set up for the very reason that we are contending with today.

For all those who will continue throughout the years to try to negate what happened in the Holocaust. That's exactly why these . . . were established, so that we have the facts available instead of the paranoid thinking that you heard advanced today. . . ."

New caller: "Alan, I tuned in a little late. I was just driving down the street and, uh, did you have Farrell on earlier?"

Berg: "Yeah."

Caller: "Damn. I wish I would have heard that. It's been a month but I read some of those editorials and, uh, is he still printing them?"

Berg: "I'm not sure. As I understand, it was a six-part series."

Caller: "I'm a rancher and a cattleman and I'm also a writer and my response to Mr. Donovan [an advertising salesman for the *Primrose and Cattlemen's Gazette* who had called Berg earlier]—when I read that kind of garbage in a magazine and a newspaper or whatever you want to call it [and it] claims to be an agricultural-oriented thing—when they lend themselves to publication of that sort of trash and that madman rambling—they make their whole publication suspect. As far as I'm concerned, I wouldn't spend a nickel to buy the damn thing or I sure wouldn't spend any money to advertise."

Berg: "I have been to the stock show the last two years. [Berg did radio programs from Denver's National Western Livestock Show, held each January and drawing farmers and ranchers from all over the United States. It resembles an enormous county fair.] I never met more caring people in my behalf."

Caller: "Sure."

Berg: "I met more farming people—it changed my whole view of farmers. It really did."

Caller: "Well, most of them, you know—you're going to find a cross section."

Berg: "Well, naturally, you're going to find everything, but collectively those people had fun with my show. They enjoyed it, I think. They liked me as a Jew. I think they liked me."

Caller: "Well, the important thing is they like you as a person. The hell with where you—"

Berg: "Exactly. My point is I saw a real lovingness at that show and this [today's program] is the kind of stuff that is—is just hate stuff."

Caller: "Well, it is. It's hate stuff and it's trash and I haven't even bothered to discuss it with any of my neighbors. I don't even think it's worth discussion. . . ."

New caller: "I'm a truck driver. I listen to your show all the time. . . . I'd like to say that the Jews—they follow a certain code and a pattern of life. God blesses them and that's why they're successful and people don't understand that."

Berg: "Yeah, well, I don't know how the Jews follow, per se, any code of life any more than anyone else. . . . It isn't very confusing. Jews want no more than anyone else wants. . . . They want success, they want security, they want peace of mind. Doesn't everybody?"

Caller: "Uh, yes. Everybody's like that. But it's hard times."

Berg: "We sure have a crazy way of affecting it, don't we?"

Caller: "Yeah, that's for sure. . . ."

Berg: "We just had a notification from Pat Schroeder's press secretary, who's advised us that she does not want to talk about it [the possible advertising boycott] because she considers it a non-issue. I dramatically disagree with her. I think Pat Schroeder owes us a phone call on this one. I think she should be on the air discussing this and she's a lady I've long admired. But on this particular one . . . this is not her stance in doing most things. . . . She could say, 'That Berg's so rude, I won't talk to him.' Hey, I took a pretty good pie in the face from Pat Schroeder once, at a fund-raiser. So for the pie in the face, I could get a call on this one. . . . I think it's very much an issue, as to what your role in influencing or not influencing [what] government spending would be. . . ."

Berg: "Could you remember the Holocaust Awareness Week? I had a Christian minister on my show."

New caller: "Yes, I do, I certainly do."

Berg: "And he has worked endlessly on the Holocaust story, teaching it, and I brought him on specifically because I had done my show from Israel and I said, 'I want to get a voice other than a Jew talking about this.' "

Caller: "Uh, huh. Well, I want to advance this point. I'm, well, a Christian. I've talked to you a number of times before. We've had wonderful conversations. But you know these people claim to be Christians and that does something so outrageous to me. I—I can hardly stand it, because I say, 'You turkeys, you're making the rest of us look bad. I don't support or advance any such nonsense.' "

Berg: "I know that. . . . Rick Elliott, who is editor of the *Primrose and Cattlemen's Gazette*, has advised us that in fact he's had a threat on his life based on what we have discussed here on the air today. This, I think, is a valid point to bring up here. This is not the way to handle it. [This] is usually done on me. I'm always getting the threats on my life. This is not going to solve anything whatsoever. . . . I don't like what Rick had to say. I don't like what Colonel Farrell had to say, but we're discussing something and hopefully we'll make some sense out of this thing. I [am in] no way arguing or advocating—or have I at any time in the show—violence against these people or anyone else who doesn't agree with me. . . . To the callers out there who threatened them, you're all wet too. That's no way to handle this at all. They're not advocating violence. If they were I might have a different thing to say. So cool that kind of stuff, if you will please. So Rick, I hope that solves the problems for you. . . . Threats of violence [are] certainly no way to solve a problem. Let's keep that in mind. . . . Unfortunately, history didn't keep that in mind. . . ."

New caller: "I'm a farmer and rancher from, ah, out in this part of the country and I consider myself conservative, even though I don't agree with you or Pat Schroeder on many issues. But I am highly insulted by the approach that the *Cattlemen's Gazette* takes not only on this issue but almost every conservative issue."

Berg: "There's a big difference between being conservative and being a fanatic right-winger."

Caller: "And they are actually doing a—a great disservice to the causes they profess. . . . And I resent that they use the word *cattlemen* in their title. I don't think they represent the, uh, average, cattleman at all in their point of view, although most cattlemen are conservative. . . ."

Berg: "This is opening a whole new door for me. . . . Isn't it interesting in that all the stockmen I met there [at the National Western Livestock Show]—their wives and their kids . . . were such nice loving people? They really were. . . . I mean, if that's conservative, then [it's] certainly healthy. . . . The reason I dig these people so much—I saw they enjoyed my humor more than most of the so-called hip city people."

Caller: "I think that's right. . . . I drove in from the field. I got stirred up. I wanted to tell the urban people I don't think this paper reflects the average point of view. . . ."

New caller: "Is there an alternative to boycotts?"

Berg: "The alternatives are simple. Let it flow. Let people choose to believe what they want. Challenge it in open forums. I think short of inciting a riot, which is criminal activity, I believe let people say things that they want to say, as ugly as they may be. That, to me, is true freedom of speech. . . ."

Caller: "Why is it that Jews have been hated throughout history?"

Berg: "I think because, obviously, it stems from religion way, way back [and] from the fact that the Jew was something different, as most people perceived it, and they saw that they wanted to blame somebody for the problems of the times."

Caller: "I have not called you before but I have been so riled up and so disappointed in the kind of people that there are in the world. It really makes me sick."

Berg: "Now, see, when you hear voices on here don't think these are rare voices. These are representative of tens of thousands of people. . . ."

New caller: "It just shakes me up so bad that people turn their backs on the Holocaust and say, 'It didn't happen.' . . . What hurts me more about the Jewish people is the way they let it happen. . . ."

Berg: "It will never happen again."

Caller: "It will never happen. . . ."

Berg: "The only place I could ever see that same thing happening again is here in the United States. . . . The only reason that I am fighting for them [the publishers of the *Primrose and Cattlemen's Gazette*], if you want to call it fighting for them, is that it always scares me if we do anything to interfere with freedom of expression, being [that] it always ends up hurting the minority. . . ."

New caller: "Hi, Alan. I'm nervous."

Berg: "Take your time."

Caller: "Okay. I wanted to agree with you. I was really appalled [by] the attitude toward Jewish people. I grew up in the South and it's terrible but you get accustomed to prejudice, like against different minority groups."

Berg: "It's very easy to fall into that trend."

Caller: "Yeah, well, I wasn't aware of how many people had prejudice against Jews."

Berg: "Don't forget, the Jews have their own fashion of being very clannish and very prejudiced in their way, too. . . . It's a part of living. We kind of cling to our own and we don't understand what's different. We're afraid of difference, when difference is the way we learn more. . . ."

One result of the show was that the *Primrose and Cattlemen's Gazette* lost advertising revenues; eventually, several employees, including David Lane, had to find work elsewhere. During the program, Berg had referred to Bud Farrell and Rick Elliott as "jerks." Three months after this aired, Elliott filed an $8 million defamation suit against Berg, Peter Boyles, and KOA. By the time it was legally dismissed, in January 1985, KOA was under new management, Boyles worked at another radio station in Denver, and Alan Berg was in a cemetery in Forest Park, Illinois, buried next to his father.

# 18

—

# *"AWFULLY CLOSE"*

—

On January 30, 1984, Bruce Pierce and Gary Yarbrough entered the Spokane Valley branch of the Washington Mutual Savings Bank, slipped a note to a teller, and stole nearly $3,600. Before the robbery, they had placed a call to the police, warning them of a bomb about to explode on another side of town. The robbery went smoothly and the men got almost ten times the amount Pierce had helped steal from the pornography store the previous October. The year had started well.

Earlier in January, just before Alan Berg was to do another live remote broadcast from the National Western Livestock Show, he received an anonymous call from a man saying he would kill him there. Police were informed of the phone message, Berg was asked by KOA management if he wanted to avoid the stock-show broadcast, and he said no. Death threats had lost some of their sting, although he usually sat in restaurants facing the front door and looked over his shoulder in parking lots. A recent occurrence had left him more resigned to public abuse. Berg's name and address had mistakenly been printed in the 1984 telephone directory. Some strangers called and left messages saying how much they liked his show; others said he was a "nigger-loving hook-nosed Jew pervert." Berg talked of suing Mountain Bell, but decided against it. The media attention surrounding such a case would only publicize his address more widely. He would probably have to move, a distasteful thought. He liked living at 1445 Adams, had spent months finding a safe top-floor apartment on a well-lit busy street. He considered changing his phone number, but finally did not even do that, anxious to forget the whole episode.

His broadcasts from the National Western took place without incident. Police did accompany him there and manhandled one person who was suspiciously lingering in Berg's vicinity, but he turned out to be a shy fan. No connection was made between the anonymous call and anyone who appeared at the stock show. A few weeks later Detective Dan Molloy, of the Intelligence Bureau of the Denver Police Department, got a report on David Lane from a paid informant. Lane had recently followed Berg, the informant said, on two occasions, tailed him around town but done nothing more. The report characterized Lane as "harmless" and Detective Molloy accepted this description as accurate. No one told Berg of Lane's activities; they weren't significant enough. Lane had no history of criminal activity, had never been arrested, no history of violence, no serious involvement with guns or other weapons. He just had odd views on people who weren't Gentile or white.

In late January, CBS-TV aired its *60 Minutes* program on several of the country's most controversial and obstreperous talk-show hosts. It featured Steve Kane of WNWS in Miami, Gary D. Gilbert of WPKX in Washington, D.C., Howard Stern of WNBC in New York, and Alan Berg. If Berg did not really distinguish himself on the show, he came across as more interesting and multidimensional than the others and gave a good definition of talk radio: "It's the last neighborhood in town. People don't talk to each other anymore. Talk radio is the last place for them to hear human voices. So many people are isolated today. They don't have a chance to communicate." Months after the piece was broadcast, CBS producer Alan Weisman said, "Of all the talk-show hosts we interviewed for that program, Berg was the most intelligent. He'd been a trial lawyer and had a first-class mind."

That was hard to tell watching the TV set. The *60 Minutes* interviewer, Morley Safer, took a rather dim view of the hosts and never really depicted Berg or any of them having a lengthy or interesting conversation with anyone. Berg and his colleagues, the message seemed to be, were irresponsible, perhaps even abusing the right of free speech. During the interview, Berg told Safer, "You're even ruder [than I am]. You go around sticking microphones in people's faces and intimidating them and violating their rights, and when they try to explain to you, that part ends up on the cutting-room floor." This quote wasn't broadcast, ending up in a can or somewhere on the cutting-room floor.

The *60 Minutes* program didn't really damn talk radio; it simply made no effort to understand how it is an alternative to the large, established media, how it allows nonjournalists to voice a public opinion, how it releases a lot of anger and frustration generated by the endless parade of tragedy depicted in the conventional media, how it sometimes broadcasts unchained chaos, as opposed to news shaped to fit a tight "objective" format, or how someone like Alan Berg went beneath the surface of the body politic and aired out the confusion and conflict lurking there. That's not easy to do in fifteen minutes.

A few moments in the show were memorable:

Safer: "But what are the people who listen to call-in shows actually hearing? Those who listen to Alan Berg get a mixed bag of mayhem and malarkey, political science and pop psychology, common law and uncommon sense, all of it laced with aggression, abuse, and sarcasm. . . ."

Berg: "A woman filed a lawsuit against me early in my career.

I think it was the second year I was in the business. Her husband had a coronary while he was listening to my show, so she filed suit against me because he became so angry listening to my show that she felt I was the causal connection for the death. . . ."

Safer: "Isn't there something a little dangerous about this kind of broadcasting?"

Berg: "There is a danger. I agree with you. I think that's the danger that we exhibit in all free—all rights of free expression, be it columnists who write in newspapers—"

Safer: "Yeah, indeed. But—but you say yourself, you often go on there, you don't know quite what you're going to say."

Berg: "Hopefully, my legal training will prevent me from saying the one thing that will kill me. And I've come awfully close."

# 19

## "YOU CANNOT HAVE A JUDEO-CHRISTIAN ETHIC"

The Reverend Pete Peters nervously taps his coffee cup, glancing across the dining room of a Holiday Inn near Fort Collins, Colorado. He has neatly trimmed hair and a moustache, he wears a large western belt buckle, and has a great sense of purpose in his eyes. He looks like a Fundamentalist preacher, which some people might call him, although he himself has a number of profound disagreements with many Fundamentalists. Peters is thirty-eight, grew up on a ranch in Nebraska, and now heads the Laporte Church of Christ, just north of Fort Collins. His ministry has a reach far beyond the one hundred or so members of his congregation. The church sends tapes of his sermons to nearly every state in America as well as to South Africa, Canada, and France. He's regularly on the radio in California, Missouri, and Indiana. "Last week," he says, "we mailed out eight hundred tapes for the tape ministry." The church has a newsletter and plans for a cable-TV program. It has a print shop and is publishing a book.

Peters believes in the Identity doctrine, which holds that Northern Europeans, and not Jews, are the Covenant—or Chosen—People of God. (Circumcision, according to biblical interpretation, symbolizes spiritual purity and God's covenant with Abraham.) It was his faith that led Peters to appear on *The Alan Berg Show* in February 1984.

"In January 1984, I chose to have a great patriot, a man who loves his country as well as Jesus Christ, come and preach at our church," Peters says. "Named Colonel [Gordon 'Jack'] Mohr. Retired colonel from the United States Army. I didn't know him at the time. I'd read about him and heard some of his messages on cassette tapes. He'd spoken on talk shows all over the U.S. and on television shows. But I'd never met him personally. When he came, we advertised to the local populace that he was coming, and we were packed every night. Friday, Saturday, and Sunday. I put him on the plane Monday morning and came back to my office. Someone called and said, 'Have you seen the paper out of Fort Collins?' Across the headline on the front page, in about the size of print for the bombing of Pearl Harbor, was EVANGELIST OUTRAGES AREA JEWS. I suppose my life has never been quite the same ever since."

He sips coffee, and frowns. "Basically, the article said that Mohr was anti-Semitic and had incensed local Jews. As a result, there were editorials and letters to the editor about Nazism, racism, anti-Semitism, and whether this thing should be allowed. I wrote a letter to the editor, saying we would make available any message he preached and we'd like to know where he was in error, and how he fits anywhere into being a Nazi. We described how he was a war hero, was given a field commission under General Patton in World War II, fighting the Nazis, and was highly decorated in the Korean conflict. He was tortured, the whole works, for his country.

It disturbed me what they were trying to do. A smear campaign.

"*The Denver Post* came up to do an article. It hit the national papers. In the process, I guess Alan saw that and said, 'Hey, this would be a good one.' You know how controversial he was. He really liked to talk on anything that had to do with Jews, and communism. He called Jack Mohr to be on his show, which I thought was fine. Then as an afterthought he thought to have me on the show also. That night, he had me hooked up in Fort Collins and Jack was down in Mississippi, at his home."

Colonel Mohr, a sixty-nine-year-old member of the Christian Patriots Defense League, was trained in survivalist tactics and sabotage. In the summer of 1984 he would give a workshop in his specialties at the Aryan Nations World Congress. On the night of February 13, 1984, he was plugged in to *The Alan Berg Show* via long-distance telephone, and his mission on the program was to discuss and explain the connection between the worldwide communist conspiracy and Jews. The conversation did not last long. Berg was less aggressive than he could be, but too much so for Colonel Mohr. After a few brief exchanges and interruptions, things slipped out of control, with Berg asking the men if they wanted "to end it right here."

"I'll hang up on you," Mohr answered.

"Go ahead," Berg countered. "Both of you. Cowards. Bail out right now."

Mohr hung up, while Peters had been lost in the clash between the two other voices.

"I didn't hang up, but when Jack hung up it cut me off," Peters recalls. "My wife was listening in the other room. She came in and said, 'Why did you hang up on him? He called you a coward.' I said, 'I didn't hang up.' So I called back."

Reconnected, Berg and Peters talked on the air for quite some time, an unenlightening, disappointing experience for a listener. Berg was intent on addressing the issue of Jews as part of a communist conspiracy, and repeatedly mentioned the frustrated efforts of many Jews to get *out* of the Soviet Union. Peters was concerned with another question: Were Jews or other ethnic groups the Chosen

People of Scripture? Berg showed little interest in pursuing this query, while Peters did not have much to say about the role of Jews in international politics. Before long it was apparent that the two men had no common ground, but they kept talking, missing one another at every turn. They didn't quarrel, as Berg and Mohr had done, and they didn't even argue. They bypassed each other in the night, two mutually contradictory forces on the radio airwaves.

"Basically," says Peters, "I received exactly what I was expecting. He had complete control. He sat there with his finger on the button and he had that tape-delay loop, so he could cut off anything you want to say. He was a professional intimidator. He used that for his own end. I spent the night before reading Proverbs, read the entire Book and underlined every passage dealing with a scoffer. You don't answer a scoffer to his own folly. If you listen to the tape, you know that I was very courteous and wasn't about to answer back on his level. That's like throwing fuel on the fire.

"Overall, I thought Alan was very kind to me. Kinder to me than anyone I'd ever heard on his show. I didn't listen that often. We never had any words. His main tactic was to keep you from talking. So I just had to make do with the short end of the stick."

Peters takes another sip before attempting to reconstruct what happened on the program. "Jack had done all the research all these years on the communist movement, to make the connection between the Jewish Zionists and communism. He'd done an excellent job of that. And has all these figures in his cranium. They're in my library but not up here, because I'm a preacher. I said to Jack, 'You talk in the area of the connection of the Zionist Talmudic Jewish movement being connected to communism and I'll talk in the area that I'm capable of talking in.' Which is mainly that there's been a terrible case of mistaken identity. Whereas most of the Christian world today are saying that the Jews are the Covenant People of the Scriptures—the descendants of Abraham, Isaac, and Jacob—I'm saying that they are not, and that can be proven by their own writings and by Scripture. And I'm saying that the Anglo-Saxon, Germanic, Scandinavian, and kindred people are. As I told Jack and tried to tell Alan, that's what I'm capable to talk on. But Alan didn't want to talk on that. Alan was a master chess player. He played psychological games. He immediately found the weakest spot of his opponent and then kept needling in that spot. Had I known Jack was not going to be on the air, I would have done my homework and been able to answer in the areas I was expecting Jack to answer in. Alan did not want to talk about the Jews not being the Covenant People of the Scriptures. He knew my strong point and he did not want the Bible, in terms of chapter and verse, being talked about on his radio talk show. In fact, he said, 'You're not going to read the Bible on my show.' I've found out that you can be controversial on any subject you want but as soon as you begin to touch this Jewish issue and indicate the possibility that the Jews are not the Covenant People of the Scriptures, the wrath of hell will come down on you. The big guns of the media will be turned on you and your life will never be the same.

"Probably every big-name evangelist has a common denominator, and that is that they all say the Jews are the Chosen People of Scripture. Jerry Falwell. Billy Graham. Oral Roberts. You can name others. As a result they are able to be on the airwaves that are basically controlled by Jewish people. The political significance of that is obvious. As long as the Christian world believes that the Jews are God's Chosen People, they're going to be supporting their government, as they send more money to Israel to buy more Uzis [machine guns] to kill more Arabs. If you have a man like myself come around and question that position, actually your life becomes in jeopardy.

"I don't hate anybody. When you start to preach this, all the sudden you're being told that you're preaching hatred. I love people. I love my race, my country. I love the world that Jesus Christ died for. I recognize all these wars and battles that are going on and I believe that much of it would stop if we recognized who we were and our obligation to keep the law of God. I reached my conclusions from reading the Bible. Let me give you an example. When I say, 'the Covenant People of the Scriptures,' I'm talking about a covenant that was made by a man named Abram. His name was later changed to Abraham. It was in Genesis, the seventeenth chapter, the first several verses. God said to Abraham that he was going to have a child and he would be the father of a multitude of nations. God would be the God of him and his descendants forever. Just take one example. The Jews have never formed a multitude of nations. They're a minority in the world, a small minority. They don't match the Scriptures."

He pauses for a moment and a question is raised: How do you define anti-Semitism?

"Have you ever seen any Jews killed in the United States?" Peters says. "It's really interesting to me that myself and my church have been accused of being anti-Semitic, when all I've ever done is say, 'Hey, there's been a case of mistaken identity.' All the sudden that's anti-Semitism. I have never seen anti-Semitism in my life. I'm a midwestern boy. Maybe it goes on somewhere, but I've never seen it. I have a hard time seeing how Jack was anti-Semitic when he points out that Karl Marx was the son of a Jewish rabbi. When he says that the Talmud teaches that Jesus Christ was a bastard conceived by a prostitute during her menstrual period. That's in the Talmud. Anti-Semitic? In my opinion, it becomes a propaganda term that certain forces in our land are throwing out to keep people from facing the facts. I don't believe that anti-Semitism is a problem in the United States but a trumped-up thing. I'm not saying that there weren't Jews killed in Germany but there were just as many Christians killed. You see, every race has suffered. It just seems like, perhaps, some keep better track than others. Keep reminding."

David Lane attended the Laporte Church of Christ, but how often is unknown. Peters claims that he never saw Bob Mathews in his sanctuary, but others say Mathews was there on at least one occasion in late 1983 or early 1984. During those months the leader of the Order was having an affair with a young woman in Laramie, Wyoming, named Zillah Craig. Laramie is something more than an hour's drive north and west of Fort Collins. Zillah's mother, Jean Craig, had discovered Peters's church and made her way there from time to time, taking along her friends, but this eventually stopped. Peters's religion appealed to them but his politics fell short.

198

By the late winter of 1984, Jean Craig and her associates had cut their ties with the Laporte Church of Christ and on Sundays began meeting at the home of Dennis Schlueter, of Fort Collins. Schlueter was like-minded, and in his home they were free to discuss their real feelings and plans.

Peters drinks coffee, before going on to reiterate how little he knew Lane, Mathews, and Jean Craig. Then he returns to the topic of Jews and Israel. "I think it's a bastard state. It's certainly not the nation in the Bible that was going to be born in a day. One of the ways that Fundamentalists get support for Israel is that they point out that in 1948, under the U.N. Charter that allowed it to exist, this was the fulfillment of prophecy. That's totally contrary to Scripture. The nation born in a day was in 1776 and is called the United States of America. The word *America* means 'Heavenly Kingdom' in the Gothic language. It's the new Jerusalem of Scripture, the Zion of Scripture. . . . I've watched farmer after farmer bite the dust, losing their farms, can't get decent loans. If we had the loans and grants that are sent to Israel, we wouldn't be losing our farm community, which in my estimation is our backbone. So a lot of things can come from this truth that would help out the country."

Peters says he is in the process of forming a group called the Moral Minority. "In the future I'd like to challenge [Moral Majority leader] Jerry Falwell to a debate, the theme being the farce of the Judeo-Christian ethic. You cannot have a Judeo-Christian ethic. They're diametrically opposed to one another. One teaches that Jesus Christ was the son of God, the other that he was a bastard. How can you synthesize the two of them? . . . If something happens to me, I already have someone who will take my place so the work will go on. To get the message out across the land. There's a strong possibility that something could happen to me, because of telephone calls and things like that. Let's drop it at that.

"If you want something juicy for your book, in terms of who killed Alan Berg, it could very well have been a Talmudic Jew, because of what he said that night on the talk show. After I was off the air, someone called in and asked him about the Talmud.

He said something to the effect that if you want to see a Talmud, I'll take you down to the synagogue and show you one. The Talmud says that any Jew who shows the *goyim* the Talmud is worthy of death. So a Talmudic individual could have said that this man was going to let a *goyim* see the Talmud and the Talmud says that if he does that he is worthy of death. I see nothing in the Bible that says someone should go out and kill a man like Alan Berg. But I do see it in another book, called the Talmud. I know you don't have the nerve to put that in your book, because you'd never get it published."

# 20

## THE DRAGONS OF GOD BUY AN OLDSMOBILE, A HONDA, AND GUNS

Two people who heard parts of the February 13, 1984, *Alan Berg Show* were Warren McKinzie and David Lane. At the time they were living together in the Denver suburb of Lakewood, although Lane would soon move out. He was increasingly nervous, convinced that cars were driving slowly past his residence, surveilling him. He thought they were from the Anti-Defamation League or the FBI. People were calling his number and hanging up without identifying themselves. He believed his phone was tapped and worried that someone might try to assassinate him. Lane kept a gun in his vehicle and made plans to leave Colorado for good. He had more pressing business in Idaho and Washington.

While Berg had been interviewing Pete Peters and talking with other callers, Lane and McKinzie had spent the evening driving around town, looking for nightlife.

"We were in the truck and I turned on Berg," says McKinzie. "Dave said, 'Turn it off. I don't want to listen to that filthy little Jew.' Berg was attacking Mohr and Peters and everyone like that. Me and Dave had talked about Berg and we agreed that he was the best thing that the right wing had, because he was rude. Dave thought Berg was an advertisement for what Dave was saying.

"We went home and I turned the program on again. Berg was shooting down people right and left. He kept asking for 'one shred of evidence' about a Jewish conspiracy and communism. I told Dave he could give him evidence. I said, 'Why don't you call him?' He said no. I picked up the phone and dialed. I figured I'd be put on hold and have to wait a long time, but the call went right through and the girl said, 'Do you want to talk with Alan Berg?' I gave the phone to Dave and he took it. He told me to get an article out of his briefcase and I did."

On the air Lane quoted a passage from *Parade* magazine, stating that Soviet leader Yuri Andropov had Jewish blood in his background. Berg seemed a little taken aback by this piece of information, as if he didn't quite know how to respond. "I can't really argue with that," he told Lane. The discussion was neither long nor heated. Lane made his points, quoted several other passages, and hung up, satisfied that he had answered Berg's challenge. After the call, Berg said the voice on the other end of the line had sounded familiar.

"I taped the conversation," McKinzie says. "I was fascinated. I didn't know Dave could be so cool and calm on the radio. We used to play that tape if a friend was over. Dave would chuckle about it. He felt he'd really beaten Alan Berg and shut him down.

"When Dave hung up the phone that night, he said, 'Yech!' but he didn't say that he was going to kill him or anything. He didn't listen to Alan Berg that much. I listened to him. I thought Alan Berg was funny. When he was insulting people he was, but I stopped listening when he tamed down. But I used to listen when

I was working and sometimes I called because it was late at night and I was alone and wanted to put my two cents in. He made me laugh. He was the most creative asshole I ever heard. One night he was talking about being an alcoholic, and I called and said, 'Would you recommend the radio business for washed-up alcoholics and rejected lawyers?' The radio went silent. Before this call, he'd hung up on me so I decided to make him mad. Another time he was supporting affirmative-action programs on the air and I had a friend call him. I'd already called that night. My friend asked him why he didn't give his job to a black. He couldn't answer that."

In the weeks following Lane's call to the show, he played the tape both at his Lakewood apartment and for other friends, including Bob Mathews, in Fort Collins. He was proud of the dialogue and took pleasure in his performance on the air. After listening to the exchange between Berg and himself, he occasionally used a throwaway line, just to amuse his companions. "Somebody," he would say, "ought to shoot that guy."

By winter's end, Mathews had assembled a team for his next mission. Using information gathered the previous November, when he and five Aryan Warriors had visited Seattle and conducted surveillance, Mathews returned to the Fred Meyer store on March 18. With him were Bruce Pierce and Randy Duey. They waited until the Continental Armored Transport Service truck arrived and its courier, George King, went into the store, before entering themselves. As King was wheeling a cart full of money through one of the aisles, Pierce confronted him, Mathews took his gun and told him to lie on the floor, and Duey stood guard, blocking the way in case anyone came near. The theft took less than a minute. Their getaway car had no reverse gear, but in spite of this limitation the men escaped with forty-three thousand dollars.

For the past several months the Order had been sputtering, unfocused and inactive, some of its original members falling away. The Fred Meyer robbery galvanized the band of revolutionaries. In late March Denver Parmenter visited Duey at his home and was shown the newspaper clippings on the holdup and seven thousand dollars cash—Duey's share of the proceeds. Until then, Parmenter hadn't really believed that the Order could accomplish much of anything. He soon left his job as a machine operator, went back to Metaline Falls, and devoted himself to the cause. By spring David Lane had also arrived in northeast Washington to stay. Richard Kemp was preparing to quit at the Ione sawmill and plunge deeper into the business of the Order. Mathews had recently picked up a new recruit, Andrew Barnhill, once associated with the Covenant, Sword and Arm of the Lord near the Missouri-Arkansas border. Barnhill was short, with soft seductive eyes and full lips. Under pressure, he tended to smile. Like other members of the Order, he often disguised his appearance with facial hair and other ploys. Clean-shaven, he bore a resemblance to the actor Robert Blake playing Perry Smith, the killer of the Clutter family in the movie *In Cold Blood*.

Mathews had also come across Robert Merki, a middle-aged ex–aircraft engineer who once worked at Boeing. Since leaving that career Merki had attempted to make a living growing hydroponic vegetables (raising them in a nutrient solution) and then tried silver refining. That didn't pay off either. Merki's wife, Sharon, had five children from another marriage and he himself had two. Like virtually everyone else in the Order, his financial situation was grim. In 1982 he and Sharon were arrested in Oregon for passing counterfeit one-hundred-dollar bills. They were released on bond but instead of attending their trial they took an extended vacation in Central America, eventually stopping off in Costa Rica. Under false names they returned to the United States in November 1982, and Merki renewed an association with white activists, begun several years before. He met David Lane, and by 1984 he was rendezvousing in a motel in the Denver suburb of Arvada with Bob Mathews and Gary Yarbrough. At the time Merki was living in Boise, Idaho, and struggling to support his family by selling advertising for bowling-alley scoring sheets. Mathews had brought along some of the fake fifty-dollar bills printed at the Aryan Nations compound the previous November. Merki examined them, found them poorly made, and burned them over the motel toilet. He could do better than that. At Mathews's suggestion he decided to help Lane find a press suitable for good counterfeiting and show him how to run it. Besides printing phony money, he knew something about falsifying identification documents and could reveal a number of tricks to the Order.

In late March Randy Duey and Denver Parmenter traveled from Washington to Missoula, Montana, to perform a ritual that other members would repeat in other locations of the Northwest. At the Missoula courthouse they met Bruce Pierce, who had been spending time in local graveyards gathering a list of names of people who had died in infancy. Had they lived, they would now be in their late twenties or early thirties, about the age of Pierce, Duey, and Parmenter. Using these names, Pierce forged IDs, took them to the courthouse, and obtained copies of the infants' birth certificates (in some states such birth certificates are stamped DECEASED in red letters, but not in Idaho). He gave Duey and Parmenter each a certificate and, in effect, a new name. The two men used the certificates to register as voters in Missoula and to apply for Social Security cards. The next step was getting a fake driver's license, or two or three. Duey was now Swift Dana Nelson and Parmenter was Bruce William Fry.

For a few brief moments in March 1984 it looked as though the Order might have an Aryan air force to complement its foot soldiers. Mathews enlisted two planes and supposedly skilled pilots, but one of the crafts, a Luscombe 8-A, crash-landed in a hay field and damaged some Idaho power lines. The other, a Cessna 172, nearly hit a commercial airliner in bad weather above the Pullman-Moscow airport, and was permanently grounded.

On Wednesday, April 18, Mathews, Parmenter, Pierce, Duey, and Yarbrough left Metaline Falls, traveling west. From Missoula Richard Kemp and Andrew Barnhill joined in the cavalcade. Under aliases, all seven men checked into a Motel 6 at Issaquah, east of Seattle, and looked through ads in the local papers for cars. With money that a bank teller had placed in an envelope, Pierce went to the house of a seller and purchased a white van, handing the envelope full of money to the man. Pierce suddenly remembered he'd written an important message on the envelope—could he have it back? The seller complied. It was a fingerprintless way to buy an automobile. Barnhill purchased a blue Chrysler the same way. After closing this deal, the seller wanted to take a picture of him with his new car. Barnhill was terribly sorry but in a hurry and had to decline.

On April 22, Easter Sunday, Gary Yarbrough bought a ticket and went into the Embassy, an adult movie theater, in downtown Seattle. He was carrying a small bag. Fiddling with the contraption inside the bag for several minutes, he then left it not far from where several patrons were watching the film. When he had slipped away from the Embassy, the theater cashier, Emma Cochran, received a phone call from someone who said, "You'd better get those people out of there because the place is going sky high."

A hissing sound filled the Embassy and the bomb exploded, destroying two theater seats, damaging six others, blowing uphol- stery to the chandeliers hanging from the thirty-foot-high ceiling, and striking one person with debris. Twenty people were viewing the movie and none were injured, although police at the scene later said the force of the explosion was great enough to kill. Yarbrough and the Order regarded the bombing as a success; it had not only brought physical destruction upon a corrupting influence in society—the dirty-film industry—it also laid the groundwork for tomorrow, a much more important piece of strategy.

On Monday, the twenty-third, a member of the Silent Brother- hood called the Embassy again, reporting that another bomb had been planted at the theater and was about to go off. Mathews hoped this would cause the Seattle Police Department to dispatch a large number of officers to the scene, create a traffic jam in the heart of the city, and divert attention from the north end of town. Not long after the call was placed, George King, who had been robbed by the group in March at Fred Meyer's, pulled a Continental Armored Transport Service car into Seattle's Northgate Mall. Immediately he was approached by a white van and a blue Chrysler, the men inside wearing ski masks and surgical gloves. Posing as window washers near the armored car were Yarbrough and Randy Duey, who had donned a wig. The men had expected King to back the vehicle up to the entrance of a mall department store, but he pulled in nose first. As he did, the Chrysler drove behind him, pinning the car in. Mathews jumped from his automobile, went around to the front of the armored vehicle, and held up a sign: GET OUT OR DIE. Kemp waved a shotgun. Duey and Pierce, flashing handguns, took control of King as he climbed down from the car. Yarbrough and Barnhill stood guard. Parmenter, who had driven the Chrysler, stepped from the automobile holding a mini-14 rifle. As he was watching the robbery unfold, an elderly woman came across the parking lot toward him, apparently baffled by what she was seeing, utterly lost. Parmenter screamed at her to stop coming at him— stop walking! She didn't seem to hear. Clutching the gun he yelled again, louder this time, and she snapped to, focusing her eyes in alarm and stopping cold. She turned and disappeared.

George King had been stuffed into the rear of the armored vehicle and held at gunpoint while the men unloaded his cargo. Within minutes they had transferred the cash to the van, leaped back into the Chrysler, and driven away, Kemp tossing nails out the window to discourage anyone trying to follow their route. The cars they had originally brought to Seattle were parked at a nearby Royal Fork restaurant. Abandoning the van and Chrysler, they got into the other automobiles and drove to Newport, Washington, north of Spokane, where Duey and Parmenter lived. Along the way Kemp was stopped by police and issued a speeding ticket, but he aroused no other suspicions. At Newport the men counted the take: nearly $500,000. Each of the seven got $24,000. Yarbrough gave $40,000 to Thomas Bentley, an assistant pastor at the Aryan Nations church, the Order regarding this as a tithe, a standard percentage of their income going to their faith of choice.

Bob Mathews wanted to spread the bounty well beyond Aryan Nations and the Far West. He hoped to give money to Louis Beam, the Vietnam veteran and Ku Klux Klan leader in Texas; to Glenn Miller, another Vietnam vet and Klan leader in North Carolina (several of his followers took part in the 1979 shootout in Greensboro that left five members of the Communist Workers Party dead).

Mathews wanted to provide funds for Robert Miles, who ran the Mountain Church of Jesus Christ the Savior in Cohoctah, Michigan. He once spent six years in a federal prison for his plan to blow up school buses shortly before court-ordered busing was to start in Pontiac, Michigan. Miles admired Mathews and stood in awe of this new generation of Aryan Warriors. In a computerized message sent across the nation—available to anyone with a home computer and phone linkup—Miles predicted the future: "Soon, our own version of the 'troubles' will be widespread. The pattern of operations of the IRA [Irish Republican Army] will be seen across this land. We, the older and less active spokesmen for the folk and faith, are being replaced by the young lions. These dragons of God have no time for pamphlets, for speeches, for gatherings. They know their role. They know their duty. They are the armed party which is being born out of the inability of white male youths to be heard. They are the products of the failure of this Satanic, anti-white federal monstrosity to listen to more peaceful voices, such as our own. We called for the dog federals to let our people go! We called for the government in Le Cesspool Grande to let us be apart from their social experiments in their mongrelism. But to no avail. And now, as we had warned, now come the Icemen! Out of the North, out of the frozen lands, once again the giants gather. Soon America becomes Ireland re-created."

With their newfound cash, Order members did what any group of upwardly aspiring young men might have done after robbing a bank or winning a lottery. Parmenter bought a 1981 blue Olds Cutlass. He paid $4,500. Duey bought a Honda Civic, apparently indifferent to the effect this could have on American auto workers. Yarbrough got himself a blue van to go with his mountain home in Sandpoint, Idaho. Barnhill got a 9mm gun in Missoula, Montana. Bruce Pierce didn't have quite the same latitude to enjoy the spoils of his labor. Or he shouldn't have: On May 9, he was supposed to begin serving his prison sentence for the counterfeiting plea he had made the previous December. He was in hiding at Bob Mathews's home. The tall, handsome young Kentuckian, whom you might have taken at first glance for an attorney or physician, had become harder since his arrest. When you looked into his eyes, they reflected nothing back. They didn't appear to see you.

In late April he and Mathews had an argument that nearly erupted into violence. Pierce and Richard Kemp had gone to Boise and put a bomb under the Israel Aravath synagogue. When it detonated, the building was empty and so the damage was slight. Pierce had felt it was important to send this message to area Jews, but Mathews disagreed. Why take such a risk when virtually nothing was at stake? It wasn't the first time they would collide over strategy—or the last. Mathews liked Pierce's bent for action but resented that he was difficult to control; he was also afraid of him.

While the Northgate robbery was taking place in Seattle, David Lane went to Colorado Springs, purchased a printing press, and hauled it back to Randy Duey's home in Newport, Washington. There Bob Merki showed Lane how to prepare special plates for counterfeiting and churn the money out. They used ten-dollar bills this time, instead of fifties, and employed more than one so the serial numbers would vary. The business went smoothly, until Duey's landlord noticed drawn curtains at the residence in the daytime and became curious. It wasn't long before a sheriff's deputy was knocking on the front door of the Newport house and asking questions. The next day the printing press was loaded into a U-Haul, which was driven to Merki's home in Boise. From that address fake ten-dollar bills continued to flow.

Another new Order member, James Dye of Philadelphia, came to Metaline Falls, was sworn in, and prepared to take on his role in the organization. Dye was thirty-six, an ex-marine who had fought in Vietnam and received a serious shrapnel head wound from a mortar shell. After eight months of convalescing in an army hospital, he was honorably discharged from the service in 1968. Eventually he found work at a manufacturing company in Philadelphia, which lasted until 1981, when the corporation lost its lease and had to move to another part of the country. He was suddenly unemployed. Growing up in a small farming town outside of Pittsburgh, Dye had had little contact with minority people, and in the marines he had got along fine with blacks. Only later, in inner-city

Philadelphia, did he begin to experience racial hatred and fear. These feelings deepened when he lost his job. He joined the Ku Klux Klan, but found it passive, unable to help him or satisfy his emotional longings, so he tried the National Alliance in Washington, D.C. Not until he met Bob Mathews in Philadelphia did he believe there was a group that could hold his interest. The notion of killing or watching death occur was something he could adjust to with more ease than many people; he had seen plenty of violence in Vietnam.

May 9 came and went without Bruce Pierce showing up for his prison sentence. Two days later Jim Dye, Andrew Barnhill, and Denver Parmenter set out across the United States, first traveling to West Plains, Missouri, where they met Randall Rader, an acquaintance of Barnhill's. Rader was in his early thirties, a former rock 'n' roll guitar player with an affinity for marijuana and LSD. In 1974 he had a religious conversion and gave up rock music, cigarettes, and drugs. He met Jim Ellison, who ran the Covenant, Sword and Arm of the Lord in southern Missouri, and by 1979 Rader was living at the CSA, which was being transformed from a religious sanctuary to a compound of far-right Christians, arming themselves with rifles and other assault weapons in preparation for a war Ellison said was imminent. Rader began converting semiautomatic weapons to fully automatic, and constructing explosive devices. He became adept at survivalist training and paramilitary tactics: hiking, map reading, pistol and rifle usage, squad drills. At night he often dreamed of rescuing a ravaged United States under attack by the Soviet Union.

When the trio arrived at Rader's in May 1984, they had two things in mind: buying guns and persuading him to come to Metaline Falls, set up a paramilitary camp, and train Order members in the survivalist arts. Rader accepted and received a thousand dollars for his decision. He also sold Barnhill an Ingram .45-caliber MAC-10 machine pistol for five hundred dollars. Much later the ex-musician would say that when he sold the gun, which he had illegally converted to fully automatic, he did not know what it was intended for. But he did tell Barnhill it would be wise to scratch the serial number off the MAC-10, and that was done.

Leaving West Plains, Parmenter, Dye, and Barnhill went to Mountain Home, Arkansas, and purchased booby traps, detonating devices, C-4 explosives, and hand grenades. Barnhill got a German machine gun known as a P-40. Parmenter got an Uzi, the small Israeli-made machine gun considered superior by gun aficionados, and the gear to make it fully automatic. From Arkansas they drove to Philadelphia to meet Tom Martinez, the longtime acquaintance of Mathews from the National Alliance. Although Martinez had been involved with right-wing organizations for many years, and had once distributed the radical paper *The Thunderbolt*, by 1984 he was thinking of dropping out of the movement. He had a wife and children; what had his association with neo-Nazis ever done for him? He was still a maintenance man for the Philadelphia Housing Authority but ready to move on. At the same time he was drawn to Bob Mathews, and if the short powerful man asked him for a favor, he would be hard to refuse.

Before the three men had departed Metaline Falls, Mathews had told them to inform Martinez about the Seattle Northgate robbery and their half-million-dollar haul. Parmenter thought this was a bad idea. He himself may have had a drinking problem and his share of emotional instability, but he also had a respect for security and a certain healthy skepticism. Bob Mathews didn't; he talked too much and to far too many people. Those around him had observed this with some alarm, not sure what to do about it. In Philadelphia the three Aryan Warriors argued among themselves about telling Martinez and then called Mathews to get a clarification of orders. When they had told Martinez everything, the men looked up two other possible recruits in the City of Brotherly Love: George Zaengle and William Nash. Zaengle had longstanding white-radical leanings and Nash was an ex-con. The duo were suitably impressed with the direction Mathews was taking the Silent Brotherhood, and would soon cross the nation for a visit to Metaline Falls.

Jim Dye made his way back to Washington State, but Parmenter and Barnhill drove south to see Glenn Miller, the Klan leader in Angier, North Carolina, whose recorded phone message featured a frightening simulation of a black man being lynched. On the way to Miller's, Parmenter got a speeding ticket. In Angier the travelers were so taken by Miller's Klan answering service, his newsletter, and his entire operation, they gave him a thousand dollars. If Mathews's success continued, the men indicated, more money would find its way east.

Parmenter then drove to his brother's in Orlando, Florida, while Barnhill spent time in Fort Lauderdale. As the former was getting another traffic ticket, Barnhill looked up Richard Scutari, an underwater-diving and martial-arts expert with political convictions that ran parallel to those of the Order. After talking with Barnhill, Scutari decided to move north to Washington and become head of security for the Aryan Warriors. The fact that he was dark-complected, had a prominent nose, and had an Italian surname would on occasion become a matter of discussion around Metaline Falls, but no one really made an issue of his heritage. They needed all the bodies they could find.

Earlier that spring, Tom Bentley of the Reverend Richard Butler's Church of Jesus Christ Christian had come to the Order with a problem. Word of the recent holdups and counterfeiting operations had filtered back to Aryan Nations, and one church member, Walter West, had reportedly been talking about such matters with outsiders. West had a way with trouble: He drank excessively and beat his wife, Sue, so frightfully that she had gone to a battered women's clinic to escape him. When Bentley conveyed all this the Order agreed it was a serious, potentially disastrous set of circumstances. Mathews promised to find a solution.

On May 27 Randy Duey and Richard Kemp went to see West, who lived near the Aryan Nations compound. They told him they were part of a secret organization and wanted him to join. Their intention, Duey explained, was to take him to an isolated site in the woods and initiate him into their ranks in a private ceremony. West was flattered, slipped into their car, and rode into the forest, where Jim Dye and David Tate were waiting, resting on shovels from Bob Mathews's farm. As the car arrived Dye and Tate hid in the bushes, listening to the three men get out. Peering from the bush, Dye noticed the top part of Richard Kemp, six feet seven and the possessor of a distinctive lumbering walk. When they drew near, Dye heard a hammer blow delivered to West's head, heard the man fall to the ground, heard the gun he was carrying hit the earth, heard him cry out, "What's going on, Randy?" Duey picked up the mini-14 and Dye heard him shoot off the back of West's skull.

David Tate emerged from the cover of bushes, sickened and unable to do his job. Kemp and Duey dragged the dead man to his grave, and Dye, the Vietnam veteran, came forward and cleaned up the brain matter scattered on the forest floor. He filled the grave with dirt, and the four men got into the car and drove away from the obscure spot in the woods, back to Bob Mathews to report the success of the mission. Mathews wasn't the only one pleased with the disposal of Walter West. Kemp was, too. He had earned a reputation as a man who completed hard tasks. He bragged of his exploits, going so far as to tell his friend and cohort Bill Soderquist that his blow alone had killed West, although he later mentioned to Parmenter how surprised he was that the hammer smash had been insufficient and Duey had finished the job. The death of West became something of a joke within the Silent Brotherhood, a joke attached to a ritual. As Kemp swung his arm through the air, other Order members would sing the 1969 Beatles tune "Maxwell's Silver Hammer," a ditty about a young man who kills people with his fancy implement. Kemp became known in the group as "Hammer" or, sometimes, "Jolly." Tom Bentley was perhaps the one most satisfied with the way Mathews had handled the security problem. The dead man was not long in his unmarked grave before Bentley and Sue West began living together.

In early June, Mathews, Duey, Pierce, Yarbrough, Parmenter, and Scutari met in Boise to discuss assassinations. Four names were brought up as targets: Norman Lear, Morris Dees, William Wayne Justice, and Alan Berg. Lear was the innovative producer of a number of well-received TV shows—*All in the Family, Good Times, The Jeffersons.* The last two programs featured black actors, and the

Order, or at least Bob Mathews, felt that Lear's work was antiwhite and detrimental to social morality. Morris Dees was the national finance director for Jimmy Carter's 1976 presidential campaign, a civil rights attorney, and operated the Southern Poverty Law Center in Montgomery, Alabama. Silent Brotherhood members understood that Dees had not only monitored certain white activist groups but had also had confrontations with Texas Klan leader Louis Beam. Both Lear and Dees are Jewish. U.S. District Judge William Wayne Justice, the chief magistrate in eastern Texas, had ordered fifty white and black families in Clarksville, Texas, to exchange apartments in a housing project as part of a desegregation ruling. Mathews kept a manila folder labeled INTELLIGENCE, which contained newspaper clippings on potential assassination victims, like Lear, Dees, and Judge Justice. He called them "white traitors" and said they would be dealt with when his people were in a position to carry out that segment of the revolution. With the exception of David Lane, who was not at the June 5 assassination meeting, no one in the Order knew much of anything about Alan Berg. In the past Lane had told his friends that Berg was a Jew in Denver who had criticized right-wing organizations on his radio talk show. He was outspoken, had castigated Bud Farrell and Rick Elliott on the air in 1983, and came under the general category of being antiwhite.

At the Boise meeting Mathews declared that the time had come for a Step Five operation. Pierce, Yarbrough, and Scutari agreed. Duey and Parmenter held a different opinion. They argued that an assassination would bring too much attention to the group now, just as it was beginning to fulfill its goals. Killing would arouse the local authorities, the state police, perhaps the FBI, and so far the Order had avoided these troubles and gotten away with their robberies. When they were more established and stronger, assassination might make sense. The dialogue developed along those lines, but it was really concerned with something else—the difference between theft and murder. Duey had just lived through an execution and knew how discomfiting it could be for a witness or participant. Parmenter had many doubts, unresolved questions. He was an intricate, intelligent young man, who had originally come to Aryan Nations, at least in part, for religious reasons. He still had Christian convictions and wondered where assassination fit in among them. Stealing may have been reasonably easy—taking money from wealthy businesses and parceling it out among his poor or unemployed friends—but killing . . . that was a more complicated thing.

Parmenter sensed that the group was at a crossroads. If they went ahead with Step Five, he believed, the Order would be subtly changed and divided, if not immediately, then at some time in the future. He wanted to prevent that and tried to do so at the meeting, but when it broke up nothing had been resolved. No target had been selected and no one had been asked to volunteer for such a mission. Mathews did not like the resistance he had encountered but didn't try to change anyone's mind. He concluded the gathering by saying he would talk further with those interested in pursuing the matter and the others could stand aside.

Within a week he and Scutari left Metaline Falls without fanfare, saying only that they were going to meet Bruce Pierce in Boise. David Lane, who had lately been in eastern Washington, departed the area the next day. Pierce had recently rented a house near Troy, Montana, and had been taking target practice in his yard with a .45-caliber MAC-10 fully automatic machine pistol, the same gun Randall Rader had sold to Andrew Barnhill for five hundred dollars. Pierce practiced so often with the firearm that a neighbor, Sherry Flaten, complained to his landlord. Sometimes, the gunfire frightened her to such an extent she lay on the ground and waited for it to end. Her protests did nothing to deter Pierce from emptying the clip of the MAC-10. One target he shot at was attached to a tree —a cutout figure of a human being.

# 21

---

# *"SOMEONE WHO DOESN'T KNOW YOU"*

---

        The woman came to KOA for an appointment with Patrick Connor, a promotions assistant at the radio station, and told him she was a student in need of research materials. Middle-aged and heavy-set, with brown curly hair, she looked like the kind of person who shows up at left-leaning folk-music festivals. She said she was taking a class in Wyoming and her current assignment was on radio. Connor gave her photographs of KOA employees, biographical sketches, and a schedule of their programs. He later noticed the woman in a parking lot near the station, taking pictures of a rear studio door.

One spring day Charlie Bishop, an account executive at KOA,

saw Alan Berg and the woman arguing outside the station. As Bishop walked onto the sidewalk, he heard Berg tell her, "Leave me alone. Stop following me."

"What's the matter, Alan?" Bishop asked. "She looks like a loyal listener."

"She is, Charlie," Berg said, turning away. "And she doesn't like Jews."

In the spring of 1984 there were two kinds of people who knew the talk-show host: those who believed Berg was truly beginning to calm down and find a measure of self-acceptance for the first time in his life and those who denied that; those who thought he had finally met a paramour he would settle down with and those who said that was balderdash; those who felt he was—since the Ellen Kaplan incident in March 1982—more in control of himself, or more controlled by management, and those who said that was false. Both sides could have been right.

In mid-November 1982, General Electric had sold KOA to the BELO Broadcasting Corporation of Texas. The transfer of ownership was completed on August 31, 1983, and Lee Larsen, KOA's new general manager, began working in Denver the following day. Like the sixty-year-old radio station itself, BELO projected a conservative, all-business image. The forty-year-old Larsen, a solidly built blond man with a trace of fierceness in his eyes, also fit that image. He was slightly brusque—the kind of man used to dealing with and solving a lot of problems in a hurry.

"That first day Alan insisted on having breakfast with me at the Marriott Hotel," Larsen recalls. "He also insisted that he belonged on the air in the daytime, as a few months earlier he had been moved from day to nighttime. My first impression was that he was a pretty gutsy character. The stereotype of a real talent. That means he was outspoken, insecure, very focused on himself."

Larsen felt that Berg was made for nighttime radio—his bizarreness and unpredictability were what people expected after dark, and he had the evening ratings to prove this. Larsen kept him on at night until March 1984, when Berg's fellow talk-show host at

KOA, Peter Boyles, took a morning job at rival station KNUS. Larsen then switched Berg to the morning shift, so the two best-known radio personalities in the market could compete head-to-head for the morning AM audience.

In public Berg and Boyles professed a great fondness for one another, but in private Berg relished the opportunity to defeat the other in the ratings. The two men were more or less at the poles of talk radio: Boyles was hardworking, a good interviewer, given to hours of preparation, a devotee of the notion that talk radio is an educational medium. Berg liked to be called an entertainer and claimed to be nothing more than that. He railed often and loudly against how seriously many talk-show hosts took themselves and their programs. Humor, he said on many occasions, was the best way to connect with listeners and those who call your show. The tension between the two men was natural; competing with Boyles was something he had looked forward to for a long time. In the only ratings period that accurately compares them, which came out three days after the murder, Berg lost the first hour by one tenth of a share point but won the second hour conclusively—by almost two full points.

"I was pleased with Alan's work from February to June," says Larsen. "He was always accused of not being prepared and we were working on that issue. He was brilliant and entertaining but not all the time. We were trying to increase the odds, instead of just winging it. With the discipline he was trying to acquire here, he would have been close to awesome."

One of Larsen's favorite Berg programs was ad-libbed, after the talk-show host learned that a parrot had witnessed the murder of a woman in an apartment in Chicago. The bird began talking to investigators, implicated the woman's husband, and a judge had to decide whether to allow this testimony in court. Berg did an entire freewheeling show on the subject.

KOA talk-show host Ken Hamblin maintains Berg wasn't changing at all and was as irascible as ever. In the winter of 1984 the two men went to Vail, Colorado, for several days of live remote broadcasting from the American Ski Classic. They spent the week together in the mountains and rode back to Denver Friday night in a snowstorm. "I could only drive about twenty miles per hour and there is no smoking in my car," says Hamblin. "None. It's snowing and Alan's nervous. He's reaching for a cigarette. I said, 'No smoking.' He said, 'You have a lot of problems. You're an asshole.' I said, 'That may be true but no smoking.' He rolls down the window to stick his head out to smoke. He takes a couple of puffs and when he pulls back in he has this soft slushy spring snow all over his face."

After cleaning himself, Berg turned to Hamblin and said, "Wouldn't it be funny if we came around one of these corners and saw a giant God standing there? And He said, 'I've been listening to you and Hamblin and you've got two weeks to convince your audience that I exist. If you do that, you go to heaven. If you don't, you go straight to hell.' Do you think we could do that?"

"We better get us some asbestos underwear," the driver said, "because we don't have a chance."

Hamblin laughs at the memory and then his always-serious eyes become more serious.

"Alan and I used to sit in Besant's [a restaurant near the previous home of KOA] and trade our hate mail. Someone got my picture and defaced it. It's something to open a letter and see a modification of yourself. Alan would say, 'These guys will never kill you. It will be someone who doesn't know you.' "

Early in 1983 Linda McVey noticed a story on Alan Berg in a Denver newspaper. A longtime admirer of his show, she listened to him by earphone at her job as a dental technician. She read the article, saved it, and occasionally glanced at the picture of Berg that accompanied the piece. That April she tuned in one morning and heard the talk-show host interviewing Stan Getz, the tenor saxophonist, who was in Denver for a concert that evening at the Fairmont hotel. Berg announced he was emceeing the music program. McVey decided to go, but not with the intention of meeting him.

"He scared me," she says, which was why she had never found the courage to call his show. McVey is blond and shy, as reticent as Berg was vocal. She's thirty-eight, from Iowa, and could appear in an advertisement for reasons to live in the Midwest. "I was waiting for the concert to begin and in walked Alan, all by himself. I thought he'd have an entourage. I had had three glasses of wine and I walked over to tell him that I really enjoyed his program and it got me through the day. I said, 'I promise I'm not a groupie, just a fan.' He sort of double-looked me and a little giggle came out of him. As he was shaking my hand, he said, 'Let's go have coffee.' "

After coffee, McVey and Berg spent every night together for a week and many nights together in the following year. There were tempests—he would suddenly disappear or concoct a drama to drive her away, but never succeeded. Unlike some of his previous companions, McVey didn't mind coming to the radio station, sitting near the studio during his program, waiting for him to break for coffee or a kiss in the hall. At his request, she also listened to Peter Boyles's show and gave him reports. More than one observer compared her to a very traditional Japanese woman: still, patient, not averse to walking two steps behind her man. Others, including McVey, disagree and describe her as the rare individual who could tolerate, understand, and positively affect Berg's volatile swings of emotion.

"I think Alan was slowing down, mellowing, and thinking a little more about his life and work," she says from a chair in her Denver living room. Fred, Berg's beloved Airedale, snoozes near her feet (any number of people were upset that she got the dog). "It was more important that his listeners liked him than before. We spent a lot of time together, just the two of us. Alan didn't feel that he fit in, anywhere. He trusted me. We spilled our guts to each other. We loved each other and felt we didn't need anyone else. He didn't feel threatened that I would walk away."

She brushes at her cheek. "He thought of himself as odd and unusual-looking. I thought he was gorgeous."

Fred awakes and for a moment appears interested in the activity in the room.

"He tried to be all things to certain people," she says. "I believe in my heart, and I think Alan did too, that we would get married, but not burn the road to the chapel. We wanted to take our time and make things right."

She glances at the Airedale. "I probably let a lot of things go that I wouldn't have with someone else. I felt Alan needed an oasis, someplace he could relax and not feel that someone would attack him verbally or assail him. Just a breather. Someplace where if he wanted to be quiet and sullen and pouty that was all right. Or angry, or where he could flare up, but not at me. I gave him all the space he needed. Weekends were a real salvation for us, but by Sunday night he would feel the pressures of the battles beginning again. When he felt good, I was so happy it almost made me scream inside."

Berg once announced to her that during the upcoming summer of 1984 they were going to "do something big," implying marriage.

"Norma [Berg's sister] told me that Alan was afraid to do anything like that," McVey says, "because of his fear of what would happen with Judy."

"People always asked Alan and me why we got a divorce," Judith Berg says. "The answer was very simple. We got a divorce so we could get married again."

"I think he would have married Linda," says Tom Wilscam, a Denver restaurateur whose place of business Berg used to frequent. The radio-show host found much to talk about with Wilscam, who was also a recovered alcoholic. "She loved him to death. He'd talk and she'd just sit there and listen to him. You could just see the love in her. He was settling in. They were constant companions. He fought the feeling. They broke up a couple of times, and he'd come in and say, 'She's too possessive.' The macho thing. But he didn't mean it. He was gradually accepting it. He wasn't nearly as torn up and at war with himself as earlier in his life. Maybe he was ready to stop chasing the rainbow."

"One day," says Beth Ames, referring to a time long before Berg had met Linda McVey, "Alan called me and asked to come over to talk about his relationship with a woman he was going to marry. He sat on the sofa talking about this girl and quite literally he could not remember her name. Now what does that tell you? That was not unusual for him. At all. One day he picked a fight with her and out the door. Of the three options at the end, I think they would have gone like this: He would have been single the rest of his life; the next believable thing is that he would have remarried Judy; and the third is that he would have married someone else."

"No question, he was happy with the last woman," says Al Zinn, an attorney in Denver who had known Berg since 1951, and Judith longer than that. "Bergie was more content, more at ease with himself, than he'd ever been. He didn't have to devote time to his social and sexual life, but could spend more time at his work. He wouldn't have married Linda. As a lifelong bachelor, I just know that. His marriage [to Judith] was the best thing that happened to him. But Judy was too permissive with him. He was a maniac in Chicago. No other woman would have stuck with him. He was such a goddamn wreck."

"At times he would drop out, quit answering the phone, and refuse to see anyone," says Anath White, Berg's next-to-last talk-show producer at KOA. "Linda would screw up all her nerve and go to his place and knock on the door. From inside he'd say, 'I don't want to see anyone or talk about it.' She'd keep trying. Eventually, he'd come pretty close to thanking her for it. She knew how to get to him when he wanted to shut out the whole world. That last weekend he told Linda that this was it: He was going to tell Judy that she couldn't keep turning to him. He had to be done with it."

"That last period, when he'd settled in with Linda and it was working on the radio, must have caused an enormous conflict for him," says Dr. Andrea Van Steenhouse, a therapist who conducted an afternoon talk show on KOA. "How could such a dog be doing so well? It must have been confusing. I saw Alan doing less destructive things to himself during the last stretch of his life, and I would like to think that he was going to work things out."

"He wasn't mellowing," says Ken Hamblin. "He wasn't."

"He needed to be wanted to the point of marriage," says Ev Wren, "but he would never have married someone else. It wasn't going to happen. On the radio he had mellowed out a lot but he was not removed from the tirades and harangues. He wasn't going to change."

On Sunday, the seventeenth of June, Berg went to the Denver Zoo with Linda McVey to participate in a KOA promotion being held there. On the eighteenth he arose early and ate breakfast at a Greek restaurant, Gyros Place, just west of his townhouse on Colfax Avenue. The proprietor, Dinos Tsounakos, is thirty-seven years old, with a moustache, sad but friendly eyes, and busy, nervous hands. His place has a red-tile roof and a blue awning, caters to young and old, black and white, lost and found.

"Alan liked Greek food very much," Dinos says, wiping at his counter. "He think we gotta good food here. He was tough on the radio but when he come in here everyone's attitude changed. He made everybody happy. He always come here alone. Never with anybody. It's hard to find people like Alan. He was funny. He was smart. Every morning he would eat the breakfast, read the paper, and carry on a conversation with me at the same time. And he'd finish the three things all at once. I never got so much from anybody as I got from him."

# 22

---

# *REPULSION*

---

After snapping pictures outside KOA's offices and acquiring information on the radio's personalities, Jean Craig didn't write a paper for a class in Wyoming. She passed on what she'd learned to Bob Mathews, who had got Craig's daughter, Zillah, pregnant several months before. Mathews was pleased with the thoroughness of the older woman's research. When he and Richard Scutari, the recent Order recruit from Florida, left eastern Washington in mid-June, they knew what Alan Berg looked like, the kind of car he drove, when he went to work and departed the station, where he lived and ate his meals. As the men made their way toward Colorado, they had all the intelligence they needed.

So did Bruce Pierce and David Lane, moving down separately from the Northwest. On Friday, June 15, under the name of Joe Shelby, Pierce registered at a Motel 6 in Laramie. On Saturday, using the same alias, he checked into a Motel 6 in east Denver. That afternoon Mathews and Zillah Craig were also in Denver visiting the city zoo, a handful of blocks from Berg's apartment. On Sunday Scutari called Annette Hatton, an acquaintance in Stuart, Florida, from the Motel 6 where Pierce was registered. He wanted to say happy birthday. Pierce spoke with his wife in Troy, Montana. Mathews would use the phone to call Zillah in Laramie. These Aryan Warriors liked to talk to their women. David Lane's code name in the Order was "Lone Wolf" and he had no one to dial on the phone.

On Monday, the eighteenth, Andrew Barnhill placed an urgent call to Bob Mathews's home in Metaline Falls. He wanted to inform the head of the Order that he had been arrested in Madras, Oregon, for illegal possession of a concealed automatic weapon. He needed Mathew's advice. Bill Soderquist took the call and Denver Parmenter investigated the matter further with the Madras police to determine the extent of the trouble. Order members who were in eastern Washington at the time—Yarbrough, Duey, Parmenter, Soderquist, and others—decided to hide their weapons and explosives and scatter for a few days. Some went into the woods near Mathews's, waiting and watching his house from a distance. They saw nothing unusual. The Barnhill arrest amounted to little, although when taken into custody he was carrying two false birth certificates. After police looked up the records attached to one of the certificates they discovered that "Keith Alan Merwin" was dead. This was curious but not curious enough to arouse suspicions about Barnhill, who was soon set free.

On the morning of June 18, Mathews wasn't available for Barnhill's call because he and David Lane were in Fort Collins, Colorado, an hour's drive north of Denver. They stopped by the Foothills Fashion Mall to look up a friend. Earlier that spring, Lane had on occasion visited the Fort Collins home of Dennis Schlueter, to discuss his philosophy and meet people like himself. At 11:30 A.M. on Monday, Schlueter, who was a security guard at the mall, took a break from work to chat with the two men. "Mathews indicated they had come from the north," Schlueter has said. "He indicated they had a meeting in Denver later that evening and they had to get going. Lane agreed."

As the men neared Denver in Mathews's dark-blue Chevrolet Cavalier, Alan Berg was interviewing Representative Patricia Schroeder of Colorado. Although the talk-show host had strongly criticized her a year before for not coming on his program to address the issue of marine ads in the *Primrose and Cattlemen's Gazette*, all was forgiven this afternoon. Their conversation was friendly, almost affectionate. KOA was sending Berg to the upcoming Democratic National Convention in San Francisco, and he told Schroeder he was looking forward to seeing her there. He sounded proud of himself for receiving this assignment. Berg said good-bye to her, signed off the air, and left the station. That afternoon he taped a commercial for the American Cancer Society and worked on promotional projects at the Cherry Creek shopping center. At 6 P.M. Judith, in town for her parents' fiftieth wedding anniversary, drove to the shopping center, then she and Berg ran some errands and went to dinner in a western suburb of Denver. He asked Judith if she had enjoyed that morning's program on Pope John Paul II's recent comments regarding sexual pleasure, and what was her reaction to his interviews with Pat Schroeder and Colorado governor Richard Lamm?

Riding back into town, he brought up tomorrow's show on gun control. Morton Grove, a Chicago suburb, had just passed a law making it mandatory for gun owners to register their weapons with the police. Judith had followed the situation closely and kept her ex-husband apprised. Neil Cashman, a spokesman from Morton Grove, was to appear on Berg's program in the morning, along with a police officer from Kennesaw, Georgia, a town that had lately instituted a law requiring each household in the community to have a gun. Berg was excited about the show but he was also worried. What if the debaters were dull? What if no one interesting phoned in? If that happened, Judith promised him, she would call and liven up the debate.

He and Judith intended to visit some mutual friends in southeast Denver, but as he pulled up in front of his address Berg said he was tired. With his Volkswagen idling in the middle of the street, they discussed their options for several minutes. Should they both go into his apartment and feed the dog, then go visiting, or should she go by herself? "I'll be fine by myself," she said.

He glanced at her, put the VW in gear, and took her to her car in Cherry Creek. On the way home he lit a Pall Mall, which he was still smoking when he reached his driveway and stepped from the Volkswagen.

At 9:41 P.M., when police found the cigarette, it was smoldering near Berg's blood. An autopsy report would one day describe how the course of the bullets through his torso had been hard to estimate because his body was twisting at the time he was shot. Two slugs struck near the left eye and exited on the right side of his neck. Others hit the left side of his head and exited from his neck and the back of his skull.

Sixty-seven minutes after Berg was officially pronounced dead, at 9:45 P.M., Bob Mathews called from the Denver Motel 6 to his home in Metaline Falls to announce the success of the mission. The next morning the Order left town, Pierce going west, Lane east, Mathews and Scutari north. On June 21, Mathews obtained a Wyoming driver's license, under the name of Rocky Roy Lund, in Laramie. His picture was taken and affixed to the license, and in the photograph he is smiling and looks happy and tanned—a clean-shaven man who appears satisfied, as if he had just eaten a good meal. His eyesight is 20-20 and he doesn't have any problems with depth perception. With this document in his wallet, he and Scutari began the long drive back to Metaline Falls. By the evening of the twenty-second, they had reached Mathews's farm, and although they were weary and hungry travelers, Mathews found the energy to call a few Order members together so he could show them his souvenirs.

"Did you hear about the guy in Denver?" he asked, spreading on the kitchen table newspaper clippings from the Denver dailies, with their huge headlines and extensive stories about the murder of Alan Berg. The front-page photograph in *The Denver Post* was the most graphic, perfectly reflecting the slackness of the body, the angle of his leg sticking up into the black Volkswagen, the lake of blood.

Mathews displayed the images proudly, smiling and musing over the accompanying articles. He told Bill Soderquist he was surprised by the amount of coverage the killing had generated and couldn't believe it had made the nationwide *Good Morning America* TV show the following day. Mathews was impressed with this Alan Berg, confessing to Soderquist that he hadn't realized the talk-show host was such a *kehilah*, a Hebrew word Mathews used to indicate an important Jew in the American power structure, someone engaged in the conspiracy to undermine the white race and destroy Christianity. He really was worth shooting.

Randall Rader was also present when Mathews took out the pictures. While Rader had been recruited by the Order to teach paramilitary tactics, the former rock 'n' roll musician wasn't prepared for what took place after Mathews and Scutari returned from Denver to Metaline Falls.

"They were laughing about it and joking and seemed to be rejoicing about it," he said, recollecting the experience. "I was repulsed by the scene."

Later he confronted Mathews and reminded the leader that he had been told the group would not conduct or condone assassinations. Mathews listened quietly for a moment, then shrugged and walked away.

# 23

---

# *FIFTY CENTS FOR*
# *A LOTTERY*
# *TICKET*

---

On June 24, David Lane arrived in Philadelphia with thirty thousand dollars in uncut counterfeit ten-dollar bills. He went to the home of Tom Martinez, Mathews's friend from the National Alliance, and the two of them proceeded to slice the money into piles. Lane felt confident handling the currency; since Pierce's arrest for passing bad money last December, the Order had learned a great deal about producing its own tender. These bills were of much better quality than the earlier batch. The serial numbers were varied, the denomination smaller and less suspect. Lane had been given strict instructions by Mathews when they had parted in the Rockies. He was to transfer a portion of the

---

money to Martinez, who was not to spend one bill of it in his Philadelphia neighborhood of Kensington, but move it in another part of town. Lane may have had doubts about giving the currency to Martinez—hadn't the maintenance man recently talked of dropping out of the white movement?—but this was Mathews's wish and he didn't want to let the boss down. Besides, Lane didn't dwell much on money. It was hardly the primary interest in his life. Unlike many of his kinsmen in the Silent Brotherhood, he didn't need to buy a new home or expensive weapons or a better car. His yellow Volkswagen ran well enough to get him from the Far West to Philadelphia. Recruiting new members, laying the plans for the revolution, financing it through any available means, avoiding the police or FBI so he could continue the work that had to be done —these things stirred David Lane. He wanted to win the war and live to see that, not become "a glorious martyr," as he had once written in an Aryan Nations publication. He didn't care anything for being rich.

Martinez was probably a good racist anyway. Years ago, he told people, a young black man had killed one of his friends. Ever since then, his hatred of minorities had been genuine, unassailable, in spite of that surname. Hadn't Bob Mathews, in late May, flown Martinez from Philadelphia to Washington State, just so the leader could spend several days persuading Martinez to join the Order? Hadn't Mathews trusted him implicitly—telling the visitor about the armored-car robberies that had occurred, the counterfeiting operation, the future plans? On May 27, on a drive to the Spokane airport, where Martinez had a return flight, Mathews had gone so far as to say that "a guy in Colorado" was going to be killed for the revolution. When Martinez asked who, Mathews told him to keep his eyes and ears open. The custodian read about the Berg murder in the *Philadelphia Daily News*. As he and Lane were cutting up the counterfeit money, Martinez asked him what he knew about the killing.

Lane laughed. "Hell," he said, "I drove the getaway car and I was in shock. We watched that Jew-kike while he was eating dinner. We waited for him for six or seven hours. We had real good intelligence on him."

Lane didn't tell Martinez about something else that happened on the evening of the eighteenth of June in Denver, something that would surface later, when other Order members or those at the periphery of the group recounted the story as they had heard it. It took place while the men were waiting in the car for Berg to come home. It was something not uncommon in moments of great stress or expectation, especially when a crime is involved. Lane lost control of his bowels.

Like Randall Rader and Denver Parmenter, Tom Martinez looked upon assassination somewhat differently than he did armed robbery or counterfeiting. "After he told me about being in the Berg killing," Martinez has said, "I just wanted to get the bills cut and Lane out of my house."

Lane soon left Philadelphia for Easton, Pennsylvania, sixty miles to the north, where he paid a visit to his sister and brother-in-law. On June 28, Martinez went to the Beerland package store in his Kensington neighborhood and purchased a fifty-cent Pennsylvania lottery ticket, using a bogus ten-dollar bill. He didn't win, so the next day he went back to the store and bought another ticket. During his first appearance at Beerland, the sales clerk had regarded his ten-dollar bill with suspicion, and when he returned, the clerk jotted down the number on his license plate. A few hours later the Secret Service arrested Martinez. He called Lane in Easton and the news quickly filtered back to a message center the Order had established in Boise, and then to Mathews in Metaline Falls. Martinez was faced with a choice: plead guilty and go to prison for a reduced sentence or join the Order and go underground. If he left Philadelphia immediately, took his wife and family and headed west, the Order would shelter and protect him from the authorities. Mathews called Martinez and wanted a commitment from him— now. He told him to pack and flee. Martinez mulled over his choice for some time, and eventually realized there was a third alternative, very different from the other two, one that had never crossed Bob Mathews's mind.

In late June, after Mathews and Scutari had rested from their trip to Denver, a large meeting was held behind the leader's home.

Even Bill Soderquist, who had been in Salinas, California, with his girlfriend, broke away from her to rejoin the revolution. Among the core of the Order, only David Lane was missing. He was, in the language of the Bruders Schweigen, in deep hiding. Lane's name had already come up in Denver in connection with the Berg matter and police detectives were putting out feelers, talking to his old friends and acquaintances, but he'd left them all behind.

At the gathering Randall Rader talked of his plans for teaching paramilitary training, while Scutari discussed his security rules. According to his guidelines, when Order members were in the presence of blacks they were to act as though these "mud people" were just like normal human beings. Doing otherwise would call attention to themselves and damage the cause. Scutari told them how much they were allowed to drink and that they were not permitted to take drugs. He said they could use only pay phones and when calling were to identify themselves by code names or not at all. The traffic tickets were dangerous and had to stop. No one was to drive over sixty-five miles an hour, even if he was being tailed.

After the meeting, Mathews and Parmenter drove to California for a surveillance mission in the northern part of the state. As the men were riding west Mathews announced that he had a confession to make, but it was more like a boast.

"He advised me of the Alan Berg murder," Parmenter has recalled. "He said he was present. He told me about the surveillance done by an old lady, the mother of Zillah Craig. Jean Craig—she ran a message center in Wyoming. This person had gone and surveilled Berg's home, place of employment, his routines. Mathews told me that they went to Denver, the four of them. He said they were waiting outside his home. He and Scutari flanked the house and Lane drove and Mr. Pierce did the actual killing. Later, Mr. Lane told me that he drove the getaway car from the murder and Mr. Pierce told me that when Berg was shot he went down as if the carpet had been pulled out from under him."

Mathews and Parmenter drove to Lookout, California, to meet Charles Ostrout, who supervised the money-processing room for the Brinks armored-car company in San Francisco. (Mathews knew that in 1981, black left-wing revolutionaries had robbed a Brinks truck in New York State, leaving three law-enforcement people dead; he thought the far right should give Brinks a try.) A married man in his fifties, Ostrout had never shown much interest in hooking up with the radical right until 1980, when he came across Bob Mathews's advertisement in *The Spotlight*, a newspaper of the white-power movement. The ad asserted that white people were being displaced from jobs by minorities and outsiders, particularly the Southeast Asians who had come to the United States after the American military pullout from Vietnam in the early 1970s. According to the ad, Oriental refugees labored for smaller wages than the native working class and were taking money from the pockets of American men.

"His ad hit home," Ostrout has said.

He and Mathews began writing letters to one another and talking on the phone. The Brinks supervisor and his family eventually paid a visit to Metaline Falls. Ostrout disagreed with some of Mathews's views and felt a certain wariness about the direction in which the young man's life was moving, but he found Mathews fiery, captivating, difficult to ignore. By 1984 the leader of the Silent Brotherhood wanted Ostrout to take an active role. He resisted at first, until Mathews brought out some of the money already pilfered by the Order and counted it in his face.

In the past Ostrout had driven the Brinks route in northern California, a run that generally carried about $2 million in cash. He never liked making the trip, he told Mathews, because the other guards were a black man and a white woman. Security on the route was bad, "absolutely ridiculous." He gave Mathews a map of the journey, and said the armored car had to ascend one gradual ten-mile incline, during which it nearly came to a halt, an excellent spot for a heist.

Mathews and Parmenter returned to Idaho and spent several days in Boise laying plans, then went back to San Francisco on the second of July for another discussion with Chuck Ostrout. Options were floated: Should they rob a few dope dealers in the Bay Area—Ostrout knew where to find them—or should they go for a business near San Jose or should they try a bank in Milpitas? They had found another recruit for the Order, Ron King, an operations manager at Brinks, and eventually five men met in Salinas to make a final decision. The fifth was Bill Soderquist, home to see his family and girlfriend for the Fourth of July. By the seventh Mathews and Parmenter were conducting surveillance 110 miles north of San Francisco, around Ukiah, California, near where Ostrout had suggested as the best place for a robbery. For a week the men stayed at a Ukiah motel, Pierce and Randy Duey arriving to join in the preparations.

While these activities were occupying the Silent Brotherhood on the western front, the Aryan Nations compound in northern Idaho was enjoying its greatest moment of triumph. For the past few summers Richard Butler had hosted his World Congress in the Hayden Lake area, and with each passing July it had become more crowded and perfervid. The one in 1984 was the climax: The rhetoric in the summer air went beyond the fever pitch and evolved into strategy for terrorism. For two days in the Idaho woods, classes were held instructing Aryan Warriors how to conduct urban guerrilla combat. The assigned text for the students was *The Road Back*, a book published by the California-based Noontide Press, under the control of Willis Carto. *The Road Back* describes in detail how to create a revolutionary organization, gather intelligence, build communication networks and underground railways. It has one section on sabotaging urban environments, another on biological and chemical warfare. Those attending the class were told how to bomb bridges and railroad tracks, how to bring a city to a dead stop by putting gas in a sewer system and igniting it. At the congress, Colonel Gordon "Jack" Mohr advanced the theory and practice of survivalist techniques. Several keynote speakers said they were in a state of war with the American government, and former Texas Klan leader Louis Beam, now serving as ambassador-at-large for Butler, announced the forthcoming "Aryan Nation Liberty Net": a computer system linking right-wing extremists in every part of the country. It would be on-line soon, Beam said, providing a list of racial enemies and the names and addresses of all national and regional offices of the Anti-Defamation League of B'nai B'rith. For those with special access, the computer contained the names of "race traitors," who had been marked for death. One man on the list was Morris Dees, the Alabama civil rights lawyer whom Bob Mathews had mentioned as an assassination target in June. Another target was Denver lawyer Don Jacobson, a former head of the Colorado Zionist Association who had also taught self-defense to Jews. In 1981 his ten-year-old daughter was harassed by robed Klansmen demonstrating in front of the East Denver Orthodox synagogue. He taught her self-defense too.

On July 21, 1984, during the Aryan Nations World Congress, seven fires were set in downtown Spokane. Speculation in the area flourished: Were those theories about urban warfare in Idaho being tested across the border in Washington? No criminal charges were filed, but damage was assessed at $4.8 million.

Mathews and his men chose a hill not far from Ukiah in the redwood country of northern California. Using the money-in-the-envelope ploy again, Randy Duey and Bruce Pierce wore disguises and bought a van, two pickups, and a Buick Riviera. On Sunday, July 15, the gang checked into a Motel 6 and a Super 8 Motel in Santa Rosa, fifty miles north of San Francisco. Scutari, Kemp, Dye, Yarbrough, Randall Evans (a new recruit from the Ku Klux Klan in Southern California), Mathews, Parmenter, Duey, Pierce, Soderquist, Barnhill, and Bob Merki—all twelve assembled for further surveillance from San Francisco to Eureka. They purchased latex gloves, white T-shirts, masks, bandannas, hats, and Krazy Glue to get rid of fingerprints. On Wednesday, the eighteenth, they observed the Brinks truck on its route through the territory, and that night they met at the Motel 6 for a final strategy session. In the morning they arose early, gathered at the Super 8, said an oath of loyalty and purpose, and went over final instructions. Randy Duey read a prayer and Richard Scutari read the Ninety-first Psalm.

The men put Krazy Glue on their fingers, ate breakfast, and drove to Ukiah in four cars and two pickups. At Ukiah they all boarded the trucks except Merki, who was in another vehicle equipped with a CB radio. He was dressed like a woman—wearing a short gray wig, a beige half-slip, jumbo panty hose, a bra, and falsies. Going south, Merki tailed the Brinks truck for several miles, then passed it and radioed ahead to the rest of the group: The target was on its way. Moving onto Highway 20, the Brinks truck drove past the waiting pickups, and as it did they pulled in behind it, one of them gradually overtaking it on a hill, the others pulling up alongside, pinning it in. The front pickup slowed down, the side cars did likewise, and the armored vehicle had no choice but to downshift and come to a stop. Bill Soderquist held up a sign for the trapped driver: GET OUT OR DIE. Bob Mathews jumped up on the hood of the Brinks truck and repeated the message on the sign. The two guards in the cab were instantly surrounded by armed men: Pierce had a .308-caliber rifle, Dye an assault rifle, Parmenter a makeshift bazooka and an Uzi.

Despite Mathews's orders, the guards hadn't moved. Pierce fired three rounds through the windshield, spraying glass into the cab. The men, one black and one white, climbed out and were held at gunpoint, prone, on the side of the road. Randall Evans blew out the tires. Scutari, a driver of one pickup, was timing the operation and watching a police scanner for any sign of patrolmen in the area. Duey stood by the highway, wielding an Uzi and guiding the traffic past. A white woman guard was in the rear of the armored truck, with the money. When she refused to come out, one member of the Silent Brotherhood shot out her side window. As she was exiting from the truck, its back door swung shut and none of those conducting the robbery could open it. For a moment or two they panicked, fearful that the mission had been botched. They persuaded the woman to use whatever means she had to open the portal. She found a key and the men were quickly inside the rear of the vehicle, forming a human chain and transferring bags of money from the back of the armored truck to the pickups. Randy Duey kept waving the traffic by. Scutari advised them that four minutes had elapsed and the holdup had already been reported to the police.

The Order jumped into their pickups and, tossing nails from the tailgates, drove toward nearby Lake Mendocino. Pierce, looking back, noticed the black guard trying to stand and fired a round at him. The man got down. On the ride Pierce found an extra weapon in his pickup and tossed it to the side of the road. It was the second firearm they had left behind. In the confusion of making the guards cooperate, Mathews had dropped a gun in the cab of the Brinks vehicle. He forgot to retrieve it.

At Lake Mendocino they changed clothes and abandoned the pickups, stashing money, gloves, masks, and guns in the rear of the van. Some of the twelve left in the Riviera, others went into a patch of forest, unloaded the money, and covered it with foliage. Yarbrough drove the van back to Ukiah for reasons of surveillance, leaving four men in the woods to wait for his return. As those in the Riviera were riding toward Ukiah, they were passed by police cars, sirens wailing, moving at breakneck speed toward the crime. Police were visible throughout the area. Yarbrough, the ex-con, took note of this and let a dozen hours pass before driving back to the woods at 2 A.M. to pick up the men and money. In the dark someone lost ten thousand dollars on the floor of the forest but nobody knew the difference.

The blueprint was for the Silent Brotherhood to rendezvous in Santa Rosa, where they would switch to the vehicles they had driven to California. Their next stop would be Reno, Nevada. Amidst the chaos of coordinating the movements of twelve people, Soderquist and Evans were left behind. When they didn't connect with one another in Santa Rosa as planned, Soderquist became paranoid and headed for home in Salinas. Evans, who forgot to recover a shirt and a gun he had stuffed under a bed in a local motel, decided to hitchhike to San Francisco, and from there caught a bus to Reno. After spending a day in Nevada scrubbing down the van in an effort to remove all fingerprints, the men ditched the vehicle in Sparks, then drove north to Boise and Bob Merki's house. The task there was to count the money and burn the bags. They counted and burned, counted and burned some more. By the time they were finished, the money had been arranged in well-formed piles and all the piles had been added together. The Order had come a long way since nabbing $369 one night in Spokane. In the rear of the Merkis' home was a printing press that had turned out almost $500,000 in false currency. That was loose change compared to the $3.6 million in the front room.

The Ukiah job, like the Berg mission, was another turning point for the Bruders Schweigen. A number of questions followed the heist: What would become of all the money? Who would divide it up? What would happen now that they had carried out two identical robberies and the police and FBI would certainly be looking for a specific gang of West Coast bandits? For weeks two related fields of tension had been building within the group and the sudden arrival of $3.6 million brought them to the surface. Parmenter, Pierce, Yarbrough, and several others felt that Mathews had assumed too much authority. The men had more or less been willing to acquiesce to his demands when they were a struggling organization searching for its next dime, but the situation had changed. They had killed two people, bombed a theater and a synagogue, counterfeited broadly, and stolen more than $4 million. They had succeeded so quickly and so well that it wasn't until after the Ukiah robbery that they became aware of the need to switch into the second gear of the revolution. Leadership roles needed to be divided now, so the group could spread out and avoid arrest. The troops had begun pressing Mathews to relinquish some control, and were also annoyed at him for leaving the gun behind at Ukiah, the first real mistake the Order had made. When this was brought up at a gathering at the Merkis', several men shouted at Mathews, and Yarbrough went for him with his fists. The two were separated, but their anger was out in the open. The rift had come.

Mathews had another problem. Not only was he being challenged in general by the Order, he was also confronted by the one individual present who upset him the most. Bruce Pierce was still wanted by the law on his counterfeiting charge and he desired his freedom—from Mathews and the rest of the gang. He wanted to take a good chunk of the $3.6 million and start his own branch of the Silent Brotherhood, away from Metaline Falls. He would be a satellite of the revolution. He could recruit, rob, murder, and promote; alone among the members of the group, Pierce could say that he had done it all for the cause. Now he wanted the rewards. In the past Mathews had complained about Pierce—the young man was too headstrong, too impulsive for anyone's good. He was useful, but he was also scary. What Mathews had seen one night in Denver had stayed in his mind.

A compromise of sorts was reached at the meeting. Each of the twelve participants at Ukiah got $40,000 in cash, which Mathews described as $30,000 in bonus money and $10,000 in salary for the next six months. In the future he hoped to have them all on a yearly income of $20,000, and this was the first installment on wages. In addition to his salary and bonus, Pierce took $800,000 for the purpose of setting up his new cell within the Order. Ken Loff, Mathews's old friend from the Lehigh Cement plant, had been designated as the group's banker. He lived near Metaline Falls and Mathews gave him $1.5 million, which he was to bury on his property and draw from as the Order needed cash. One hundred thousand dollars was given to Dan Bauer, who was to spend it on high-technology research. A few of Bauer's contacts within the scientific community around eastern Washington had told him that for the right amount of money—and a guarantee that they could relocate to another part of the globe—they would look into developing laser weapons and thought-control techniques for the Silent Brotherhood. This research was to be called the "Reliance Project," but it never did have much more than a name. The fate of the $100,000 was a mystery to just about everyone.

Power in the group had been subdivided. Mathews became the coordinator, as opposed to the outright leader, of future missions. Pierce departed to form his cell, Parmenter looked into surveillance for the next robbery, and Duey was to indoctrinate new recruits. Each member of the Silent Brotherhood was given complex coded phone numbers to use when placing calls to the Boise message center, to be run by David Lane and Jean Craig. (Since Lane's stomach troubles that evening in Denver, the rest of the Order had decided to keep him away from high-stress missions.) Bob Merki was busy printing false Costa Rican driver's licenses in case the men had to flee the United States. Randall Rader was setting up his paramilitary camp near Priest River, Idaho. He needed firearms, tents, uniforms, and four-wheel-drive vehicles.

Bill Soderquist had been found in Salinas and Mathews devoted some attention to soothing his paranoia, explaining that first-robbery jitters were natural, to be expected, but it was time to leave his girlfriend, come back to Metaline Falls, and help the Order move forward. Soderquist complied, facing trouble on his return. The brotherhood had learned of the young man's recent transgressions: He'd blown some Order money on an expensive tape deck (it was a long ride from Salinas to northeastern Washington, and he'd needed road music); he'd spent other funds on cocaine; he'd told his girl about the Ukiah job. Mathews had always looked upon his younger friend with indulgence but others weren't so lenient. Richard Scutari, the group's head of security, thought that, according to the rules he had once laid down, Soderquist should be executed for spilling to his girlfriend. In fact both lovers should be killed. Mathews considered this option and also sending Soderquist on a suicide mission (what had happened to Earl Turner in *The Turner Diaries*—he'd dropped a nuclear weapon on the Pentagon and died in the process). In the end, Soderquist was fined two thousand dollars for getting lost after the Ukiah heist, docked another thousand dollars for spending money on his car, and his ten-thousand-dollar salary was withheld until the end of 1984. If he survived the probationary period, the money would be his. When he needed cash, he was to go to Richard Kemp and "Hammer" would dole some out. Kemp was as good at following orders as Soderquist was not.

In August the men went on another spree, buying a $10,000 truck, a Chevy Celebrity, and a new Camaro. In Las Vegas Randy Duey purchased a Honda Accord and in Spokane he bought a $549 television set and a $474 videocassette recorder. Scutari got a Cutlass sedan. The group bought 110 acres for Rader's military camp near Priest River, Idaho, and 160 acres in Missouri for a similar purpose. They bought mobile homes, guns and ammunition, computer equipment. Andrew Barnhill, who had worked at a Sears store in Missoula before joining the Order, bought a ski condominium in Montana for $15,000 cash. Rader and Loff had started a new business, Mountain Man Supply Company, whose sole reason for existence was outfitting this growing band of Aryan Warriors.

In August at a Holiday Inn near the San Francisco airport, Parmenter, Pierce, Scutari, and another newcomer, Ardie McBrearty, met with their two friends from the local Brinks company, Charles Ostrout and Ron King. The Order now wanted to rob the main Brinks vault itself, in San Francisco, where the take, the employees assured them, would not be less than $30 million. Merki was creating fake Brinks IDs for those who would participate in the robbery. King and Ostrout would divulge the inside information. Surveillance of the building was under way. Strategy sessions continued but the Brotherhood was no longer as focused as in the past. Money had scattered them; and so had fear. Denver Parmenter took his wife to the East Coast for a brief vacation in September. Bruce Pierce, his cell members, and their families were living in the rugged mountains of central Idaho, near Salmon, but were preparing to move again. Even that terrain was no longer safe. After police had recovered the gun Mathews left behind in the Brinks armored car at Ukiah, they traced it to Andrew Barnhill, who had purchased it the previous April in Missoula. On the fourth of August, just sixteen days after the robbery, the FBI came to Barnhill's residence in Laclede, Idaho. He was gone, on the run, but in his home the agents found diagrams of the holdup, latex gloves, red bandannas, telephone numbers, and weapons, all of which had been used in the crime. At his residence the FBI also found Aryan Nations literature. Agents planned to visit Hayden Lake soon and pose some difficult questions.

In early fall the Order decided the Brinks vault was too risky a target. Perhaps at the San Francisco airport they could rob a plane carrying Brinks money. Perhaps they should try the Ukiah route again. Nothing was congealing, except Rader's camp at Priest River. He was teaching foot soldiers like Bill Soderquist about endurance hiking, shooting, and reading a compass. While receiving the training, the men wore boots, German camouflage uniforms, backpacks, and guns. They needed an isolated refuge and planned to build shelters and other facilities at the camp in preparation for the approaching cold weather. If no new missions came to fruition, they could hide in the woods and survive—if there was time. August and September had evaporated. October was well under way and still nothing had been constructed to protect the Silent Brotherhood from a Northwest winter.

While they waited and hoped, police located the vehicles abandoned after the Ukiah robbery and found Richard Kemp's fingerprints inside the van left in Sparks, Nevada. The vehicles' previous owners were questioned and gave descriptions of the men who had purchased the van, pickups, and car. With this information, federal agents were able to track the movements of some of the thieves to northern California motels. From there the FBI began tracing calls made at nearby pay phones. Law-enforcement agencies were making progress. They knew that a number of recent crimes in the Northwest were somehow related, they saw a pattern in much of the surrounding activity, and had reason to believe the whole scheme was affiliated with a political cause. They were getting close but needed a break, a clue to the pattern, a piece of luck—and there it was.

On October 2, Tom Martinez decided not to join the Order and go underground. He also chose not to serve time on a three-count indictment for passing counterfeit money. In exchange for a suspended sentence, he told the Secret Service everything he knew. When the astounded agents had finished listening to him unravel the tale, they called in the FBI, the Bureau of Alcohol, Tobacco and Firearms, the Internal Revenue Service, and police officials throughout the West. Martinez knew the danger in his confession; he would not be surprised when in the future the Aryan Nation Liberty Net computer issued a call on its bulletin board for him to be found and killed. Before cooperating with the FBI he asked them for funds to live on while helping them capture Bob Mathews. The deal was struck—the government provided him with $379 a week for expenses plus other benefits. The entire package came to more than $26,000.

Martinez was regularly in communication with Mathews, who was still trying to persuade his friend to come to Washington State and be welcomed into the Order. In time Martinez would go west, but under circumstances quite different from those Mathews had in mind. Even after reaching his decision, Martinez appeared to have mixed feelings, and took little pleasure in anticipating what lay ahead.

"I'll tell you why I did it," he confessed to the *Philadelphia Daily News*. "I got a conscience. I thought if it was only for me, I'd run. But I got them to think of, my wife and kids . . . and people were going to die."

# 24

## "THIS IS WAR!"

Near 10 A.M. on the eighteenth of October, three FBI agents drove onto Gary Yarbrough's property in a Forest Service truck. Nothing identified them as law-enforcement officers of the United States government and they had no search warrant. Yarbrough's rented land on Pack River Road, about ten miles north of Sandpoint, Idaho, was well marked with "No Trespassing" signs, but the agents ignored these warnings. Three weeks earlier the FBI had discovered a Sandpoint storage locker rented by Yarbrough, and inside it they found a gun owned by Andrew Barnhill. (By September, scores of special agents from all over the nation were in Idaho and Washington, combing the area and pursuing the leads that were growing daily; the number of agents would eventually reach several hundred.) Agent James Wixon steered the truck through a gate and pulled to a stop in front of Yarbrough's house. The agents opened the doors and stepped outside.

It was Yarbrough's twenty-ninth birthday. From a stand of trees by his home he watched the truck, and as the men emerged from the cab he ran out of the forest, extending both arms and firing a handgun.

"It seemed," Special Agent Michael Johnston has recalled, "that we were looking right down the muzzle."

No one was hit. The agents jumped into the truck and sped away, back to the Sandpoint Police Department, where they began a complicated attempt to get a search warrant from a U.S. magistrate in Boise. Twelve hours later they returned to Yarbrough's home with the document, and as they drove onto his land this time, he sprinted from the front yard into darkness. Hiding in a ditch near the house, he waited and observed as the agents spoke to his wife, Betty, and young daughters, one of whom was connected to a kidney machine. The agents canvassed the entire residence, from one room to the next, before going upstairs and bending low to get through a doorway leading into a small space. Crossing the threshold, they came eye-to-eye with a three-foot-high portrait of Adolf Hitler, surrounded by black crepe paper and candles. In other parts of the house they found neo-Nazi literature, instructions for how the Order was to operate, code names for everyone in the group, two 12-gauge shotguns, a bolt-action rifle, a .45-caliber Colt pistol, five semiautomatic rifles, a Winchester .22-caliber rifle, a .308-caliber MAC-10 machine pistol with a silencer, a hundred sticks of dynamite, one and a half pounds of C-4 plastic explosives, grenades, night-vision scopes, more than six thousand rounds of ammunition, bandoliers loaded with .308-caliber ammunition, four loaded crossbows, 110 blasting caps, police scanners, and booby traps. They found one other gun, a .45-caliber MAC-10 machine pistol (and silencer) that would be sent to Washington, D.C., for examination by ballistics experts. After extensive testing, they determined it was the gun Andrew Barnhill had purchased from

Randall Rader in May for five hundred dollars, the one given to Bruce Pierce for target practice near Troy, Montana, the one that killed Alan Berg.

Yarbrough escaped that evening, and news of his adventure quickly reached Bob Mathews, who called a meeting at the paramilitary camp by Priest River. He gave a fiery speech, talked of going to Yarbrough's home and trying to retrieve whatever weapons or Order documents were still there. With difficulty, his cohorts dissuaded him from such a plan. Mathews's temper had never been long; it was contracting, and as it did his rhetoric became looser and more bombastic: He would take on the feds, battle them with gunfire, he didn't care how many there were, he would bring ZOG to its knees. (The Order's catchall term for the enemy was now the Zionist Occupational Government, or ZOG.) His cry, accompanied by a Nazi salute, was "Hail Victory!" and he said it often. He would do what Arthur Kirk, a confederate in spirit, had just done in Nebraska. Kirk, a hopelessly in-debt farmer, had become attracted to the ideas of Rick Elliott of the *Primrose and Cattlemen's Gazette* and decided he could simply ignore his crippling financial obligations. On October 23, 1984, when the sheriff's deputies of Hall County, Nebraska, showed up at his farm to serve Kirk with legal papers for a Grand Island bank, he pointed a pistol at one of the lawmen and told him to leave. That evening, the sheriff's department obtained a warrant for Kirk's arrest, asked a SWAT team to join them as they executed it, and went back to the farm. During an attempt to negotiate via the telephone, Kirk started yelling at a police sergeant: "Goddamn fucking Jews! They destroyed everything I ever worked for. I've worked my ass off for forty-nine goddamn years and I've got nothing to show for it. By God, I ain't putting up with their bullshit now. I'm tired, and I've had it and I'm not the only goddamn one—I'll tell you that."

Kirk ran from his house carrying a long-barreled .357 Magnum pistol and an automatic rifle. A trooper said he saw Kirk open fire. When fire was returned, Kirk's life was over, but his martyrdom had just begun.

At October's end, Mathews and the others concluded that the Order could not survive unless it was broken into half a dozen separate cells, each with a distinct mission. One would travel the country and recruit from the followers of Louis Beam, Glenn Miller, Bob Miles, and William Pierce. Another would run the training camp, another would handle intelligence, another assassinations, and another security. Mathews referred to himself as "National Command." In that role he advised Randy Duey to go to the Syrian embassy in Washington, D.C., and solicit support from that country. Surely they would align themselves with the Order against worldwide Jewry. The trip was never made.

As the autumn progressed and the FBI intensified its investigation, some members of the Silent Brotherhood sent wives and girlfriends into area graveyards to come up with new names of dead babies, so they could obtain more birth certificates and false identification. In Boise Bob and Sharon Merki were packing their belongings, preparing to leave their residence and take their printing press with them. On October 25, Bob Merki and Frank Silva, a Klansman from California who had lately become involved with the Order, stopped at an intersection red light in Boise, jumped from the van they were riding in, and leaped into a car driven by Sharon Merki. For six days the FBI had been following the two men, convinced they would not get away—but they did. In the abandoned van, agents found a map of Denver, two typewriters that had been employed in making phony Costa Rican driver's licenses, a printer that produced fake ten-dollar bills, and a number of clippings from Denver's *Rocky Mountain News*, stories about the slaying of Alan Berg. The FBI had let their quarry escape, and frustration was starting to rise.

By mid-November the weather had turned chilly and only a few men were still living at Priest River. The paramilitary outpost was cold, and it was snowing. Only months before, the Bruders Schweigen had held grand visions of a well-equipped winter hideout with warm, finished buildings and other modern conveniences. Now they were sleeping in tents and had no plumbing. Their only hope was to send Rader back to Missouri, where the Order had purchased other land, and move the operation east. They buried weapons and broke camp.

While they scattered, other members of the group were renting houses in Oregon and western Washington with the intention of moving the Order away from the Metaline Falls area. Frank Silva took a place in Brightwood, Oregon, and Randy Duey, the Merkis, and Ian Stewart (Sharon Merki's son) rented three houses near the town of Greenbank on Whidbey Island, a long stretch of woods fifty miles north and west of Seattle. Word went out from the message center that these "safe houses" were ready to be occupied, and several of the troops began the move west. They brought along guns and piles of money left over from Ukiah. They were happy to have departed eastern Washington altogether, and felt a sense of collective relief. If they got wind of the FBI coming to Whidbey Island, they would take their cash, their fake Costa Rican IDs, and go south for a good long respite from trouble.

The FBI had told Tom Martinez to set up a meeting with Bob Mathews, and he did so, arranging it for the twenty-fourth of November at a Portland hotel. Martinez flew into the city and was greeted at the airport by Mathews and Gary Yarbrough. FBI agents were skulking nearby, and when Mathews thought he detected one, he drew and pointed a pistol. No one responded so he put the gun away, left the airport with his companions, and drove toward the hotel destination. On the ride he was certain they were being followed; in the backseat, Yarbrough attached a silencer to a machine gun. Mathews changed his mind and drove to another Portland hotel, the Capri, where he and Yarbrough took a room next to Martinez. That night Mathews used all his powers of persuasion in an effort to bring Martinez into the Bruders Schweigen. Hadn't they been good to him? Hadn't they helped him buy a videocassette recorder and a new lawn mower and let him dream of remodeling his home with money they had given him? Martinez hedged and stalled, trying not to reveal that he was in a quiet frenzy, terrified. He needed to get away from the two men for a few minutes so he could fulfill his orders and contact the FBI. Finally, he said he was going out to find a lady of the evening. On the street he noticed a car behind him, following, its lights blinking, but he didn't know if it was the FBI or an associate of Mathews. He kept walking. At a hamburger stand, he stopped and an FBI agent jumped out of the car. Martinez pleaded with him not to try to capture Mathews and Yarbrough until he was out of the hotel and back at the airport. When he had extracted this promise he went back to the Capri and attempted to sleep.

The phone rang early in the morning, an agent telling Martinez to stay in his room and do nothing. Down the hall, in Room 42, Mathews stepped from the front door at 7:45, then pulled back inside. He stayed in the room for almost an hour, while one of the FBI agents, Arthur Hensel, alerted a local SWAT team to stand by. At a few minutes to 9:00, he emerged again and a shot was fired, shattering glass in the motel manager's office and injuring him. The fugitive ran from the room, and agents Hensel and Kenneth Lovin chased him, Mathews disappearing in the yard of a nearby apartment complex. A slow step at a time, the two FBI men approached the yard, and then Hensel entered it alone, while Lovin covered him.

"Look out, Art!" Lovin yelled, spotting Mathews behind a concrete pillar, fifteen yards away.

Hensel glanced at Mathews, who was aiming a pistol at his eyes. The agent fell onto his back and lifted his legs into the air, his only defense at such close range. Mathews fired once, hitting him in the left shin bone, then put a bullet into the toes of his left foot. Hensel fired back a pistol and Lovin a shotgun, one report hitting Mathews in the hand. He turned and ran from the yard, quickly lost in the streets of Portland.

During the shoot-out, Yarbrough had dropped from the second-story window of Room 42. He landed on his feet but was instantly circled by FBI agents, who grabbed him as he let forth a stream of obscenities. Being in custody made him brash. Unlike most Order members, Yarbrough had been arrested before. The threat of long-term incarceration wouldn't break down an old con like him. It was the inexperienced ones, he was certain, the Silent Brotherhood had to worry about.

Before long Yarbrough was holding a press conference from his jail cell. He enjoyed provoking readers of newspapers. In 1983, while clutching his daughter and speaking with *The Seattle Times*, he said the little girl, Autumn, would one day be a marksman, "firing bullets into the heads of kikes." From his cell in December 1984, he spoke with reporters about the Berg murder weapon being found in his house and denied assassinating the Denver talk-show host.

"I know nothing about Alan Berg," he said, "except that he was a Jew."

Who murdered him? the redhead was asked.

"God," Yarbrough said.

Several members of the Denver Police Department traveled to Boise, where he was being held, to ask him about the Berg matter. He refused to talk with them and kicked at the prison door separating him from the detectives, saying they "were out to do the dirty work of the Jews."

After Yarbrough's arrest FBI agents thoroughly searched Room 42 of the hotel, locating more Order documents, ammunition, artifacts, and thirty thousand dollars cash. Down the hall they also discovered Tom Martinez, hiding in his room and keeping still, exactly as he had been told to do. He had heard the gunfire beyond his door and was aching to know what had occurred. When the agents told him, he was furious; the FBI had broken its promise not to start the siege until he was out of the Capri and on his way home. (He immediately called his wife in Philadelphia and told her to take the children from their apartment, leave everything else behind, and never return to the address.) The feds were furious in return, though not at Tom Martinez. They were upset with themselves, embarrassed. While they were glad to have Yarbrough in handcuffs, they knew Mathews was the leader of the Order, the catalyst, the personality who brought the group into being and made it function. He was the man they wanted, yet he had escaped again, and in the process had shot and wounded one of their own. FBI agents, particularly a score of them, were not supposed to let fugitives run free. It would not happen again, not to the Federal Bureau of Investigation, no matter how many agents it took. It should never have happened this time, the special agents understood, but they were all certain of one thing. It would not happen again.

After fleeing the hotel, Mathews hitchhiked a ride to the house Frank Silva was renting in Brightwood, Oregon. Mathews's hand was bleeding but medical care would wait. He believed the FBI was hard behind him and he was right. Agents traced him to Silva's home and to a drugstore where bandages were purchased for the damaged hand, but by the time the FBI reached the pharmacy, Mathews was on his way to Whidbey Island and the three safe houses there. On the island, fired by the pain in his hand, enraged at what had happened to Gary Yarbrough, Mathews took his most ambitious action to date. No longer content to fight a few FBI agents or rob armored cars, aware that he was being pursued by the most determined band of detectives in the nation, Bob Mathews gave free reign to his imagination and proclaimed in writing what had been roiling inside of him for years. Earl Turner would have been proud of his document:

### DECLARATION OF WAR
*November 25, 1984*

It is now a dark and dismal time in the history of our race. All about us lie the green graves of our sires, yet, in a land once ours, we have become a people dispossessed.

By the millions, those not of our blood violate our borders and mock our claim to sovereignty. Yet our people react only with lethargy.

A great sickness has overcome us. Why do our people do nothing? What madness is this? Has the cancer of racial masochism consumed our very will to exist?

While we allow Mexicans by the legions to invade our soil, we murder our babies in equal numbers. Were the men of the Alamo only a myth? Whether by force of arms or force of the groin, the result of this invasion is the same. Yet our people do not resist.

Our heroes and our culture have been insulted and degraded. The mongrel hordes clamor to sever us from our inheritance. Yet our people do not care.

Throughout this land our children are being coerced into accepting non-whites for their idols, their companions, and worst of all their mates. A course which is taking us straight into oblivion. Yet our people do not see.

Not by accident but by design these terrible things have come to pass. It is self-evident to all who have eyes to see that an evil shadow has fallen across our once fair land. Evidence abounds that a certain vile, alien people have taken control over our country.

How is it that a parasite has gained dominion over its host? Instead of being vigilant, our fathers have slept. What are we to do? How bleak these aliens have made our childrens future.

All about us the land is dying. Our cities swarm with dusky hordes. The water is rancid and the air is rank. Our farms are being seized by usurious leeches and our people are being forced off the land. The capitalists and communists pick gleefully at our bones while the vile hook-nosed masters of usury orchestrate our destruction. What is to become of our children in a land such as this? Yet still our people sleep!

Everyday the rich tighten the chains that lay heavy upon our people. How pitiful the white working class has become. Where is the brave Aryan yeoman so quick to smite the tyrant's hand?

They close the factories, the mills, the mines, and ship our jobs overseas. Yet our people do not awaken.

They send an army of agents into our midst to steal from our pockets and enforce their rule. Our forefathers under King George knew freedom more than we. Yet still, still our people sleep!

To those who awaken, the reality is grim. John Singer [a polygamist in Utah, who shot it out with police because he insisted on educating his children himself] awoke. Concerned over the rampant drugs, homosexuality, and miscegenation in public schools he tried to teach his children at home. He was a stout Aryan yeoman who loved his family dearly. Government agents shot him in the back.

Gordon Kahl awoke. After four decades of submission to the tyranny of the IRS he tried to resist. He was a stout Aryan yeoman who loved his family dearly. Government agents shot him in the back.

Arthur L. Kirk awoke. For three generations his family farmed the land the usurious banker was trying to steal. Kinsman Kirk tried to resist. He was a stout Aryan yeoman who loved his family dearly. Government agents shot him in the back.

To these three kinsmen we say: "Rise, rise from your graves white brothers! Rise and join us! We go to avenge your deaths. The Aryan yeomanry is awakening. A long forgotten wind is starting to blow. Do you hear the approaching thunder? It is that of the awakened Saxon. War is upon the land. The tyrant's blow will flow."

By ones and by twos, by scores and by legions we will drive the enemy into the sea. Through our blood and God's will, the land promised to our fathers of old will become the land of our children to be.

We will resign ourselves no more to be ruled by a government based on mobacracy. We, from this day forward declare that we no longer consider the regime in Washington to be a valid and lawful representative of all Aryans who refuse to submit to the coercion and subtle tyranny placed upon us by Tel Aviv and their lackeys in Washington. We recognize that the mass of our people have been put into a lobotomized, lethargic state of blind obedience and we will not take part anymore in collective racial suicide!

We hereby declare ourselves to be a free and sovereign people. We claim a territorial imperative which will consist of the entire North American continent north of Mexico.

As soldiers of the Aryan Resistance Movement (ARM) we will conduct ourselves in accordance with the Geneva Convention.

We now close this Declaration with an open letter to Congress and our signatures confirming our intent to do battle. Let friend and foe alike be made aware. This is war!

## OPEN LETTER TO THE U.S. CONGRESS

All of you together are not solely responsible for what has happened to America, but each of you, without exception, is partly responsible. And the day will come when each of you will be called to account for that responsibility.

The day will come when your complicity in the betrayal of the 55,000 Americans who were sacrificed in Vietnam will be called to account. Whether you were a "hawk" or a "dove" will not carry much weight then. All that will matter is that you played politics while they were dying. All we will ask you is why you failed in your responsibility to them and to America, why you failed to use the full power of your office to expose the treason of your colleagues.

The day will come when your subservience to the anti-American "Israel Lobby" will be called to account. Your votes to strip American arsenals so that Zionists can hold on to stolen land; your acquiescence in a policy which has turned all our Arab friends into enemies, seriously jeopardized our oil lifeline, and bankrupted our national economy—those things are inexcusable. And no plea that you "had to do it," that the Jewish pressure on you was too great to resist, will acquit you.

The day will come—if America survives—when you will pay dearly for having weakened America and strengthened our communist enemies all over the world. And don't try to tell us that Henry Kissinger is the one to blame for that! You confirmed Kissinger's appointment knowing full well what his policies were. You went along with Kissinger. You could have stopped him any time you wanted to.

And it was you who allowed the Soviet Union to overtake America on the seas, to whittle down our lead in missiles, to build its military might while ours dwindled. It was you who bought votes by taking money from our defense budget and spending it on "welfare" and "pork barrel" projects. It was you who caved in to the demand of the media liberals that we scrap military superiority and settle for "parity" with the reds. That treason will cost us millions of lives one day, and so do not think that we will spare yours.

The day will come when, above all else, you will pay for betraying your race. Most of you will say that you are against the forced racial busing of school children, that you are against the Black terror which stalks the streets of our cities, that you are against the "reverse discrimination" which takes jobs away from Whites and gives them to Blacks, that you are against the flooding of America with illegal immigrants, because you know all these things are unpopular.

But you brought every one of these plagues down on our heads. You passed the "civil rights" laws which gave us busing in the first place, and then you refused repeatedly to specifically outlaw this monstrous crime against our children. It was your scramble for Black votes and your cowardice in the face of the controlled news media which allowed our cities to become crime-infested jungles. You set up the requirements that employers had to meet racial quotas. And you passed the immigration laws which started the flood of non-White immigrants into America—a flood which is now out of control.

We hold you responsible for all these things; for every White child terrorized in a racially-mixed school, for every White person murdered in one of our urban jungles, for every White woman raped by one of the arrogant "equals" roaming our streets, for every White family hungry and desperate because a White worker's job was given to a Black. Each day the list grows longer, but the day will come when the whole score will be settled and you will pay for every one of these debts in full.

Don't try to explain to us that you voted right some of the time, that government is a game of give and take, and that you had to vote for the bad laws in order to get others to vote for good laws. All we care about is that you have collectively ruined America and put our whole race in jeopardy.

We know what America used to be and what it could be today. And we can see what it has become instead—and you presided over that transformation. We placed our trust in you, we gave you the responsibility for our future, and you betrayed us.

You know how to lie smoothly and convincingly, how to talk out of both sides of your mouth at the same time, how to switch sides without blinking an eye, but when the American people finally rise up in righteous wrath and demand justice, none of your trickery and deceit will save you.

You may wave the flag then, but we will remember that when 55,000 young Americans were being butchered in Vietnam because the American government imposed suicidal "Rules of Engagement" on them which gave the enemy all the advantages, you did little or nothing.

You knew what was happening, and you did not shout it from the rooftops. You knew that out [sic] fighting men were being betrayed, and you did not attack the betrayers for all you were worth. You did not disrupt the councils of reason. You chose not to make a nuisance of yourself, to shout down the traitors on the floor of the House or the Senate, to give them no quarter. You remained a party to the treason, because you chose not to fight it so uncompromisingly that the chief traitors would have had either to back down or to expel you from the Congress.

Whether you were an instigator of the treason or whether you just went along for the ride will make little difference to us. We will not listen to your explanation that you were really on our side all the time. . . . We will only remember that you could have stopped what has happened to America, and, for whatever reason, you did not.

No, when the Day comes, we will not ask whether you swung to the right or whether you swung to the left; we will simply swing you by the neck. . . .

With these things said, let the battle begin.

We, the following, being of sound mind and under no duress, do hereby sign this document of our own free will, stating forthrightly and without fear that we declare ourselves to be in a full and unrelenting state of war with those forces seeking and consciously promoting the destruction of our faith and our race.

Therefore, for blood, soil and honor, for the future of our children, and for our King, Jesus Christ, we commit ourselves to battle. Amen.

The document was signed in bold handwriting by Mathews, Pierce, Duey, Scutari, Evans, Bob and Sharon Merki, Silva, and Ian Stewart. Mathews's intention was to send copies of the Declaration to members of the U.S. Congress, but he never did. For two weeks after writing it, he fulminated against his enemies and Tom Martinez calling repeatedly for his head, while others in the Silent Brotherhood gathered on the island. Randy Duey was living in one house near Greenbank, Bob and Sharon Merki, along with Ian Stewart, were in another half a mile away. Mathews was in the third residence on Smuggler's Cove, near the western shore, a small wood-frame home surrounded by foliage and located at the end of a two-hundred-yard driveway off an island road. Behind the house was a steep seventy-foot drop to the beach, a poor place from which to jump.

As November became December on the island, it was apparent to most of those present that the FBI knew of their whereabouts and would soon arrive. Besides the multitude of other leads the government had put together, in mid-November three young men previously associated with the Aryan Nations church robbed a bank in Grays Harbor, Washington, of $7,152 and were soon arrested. Two of them, Kelly Carner and Erik Maki, cooperated with the authorities and told what they knew of the violent organization that had spun off from Richard Butler's church. The third young man, Eugene Kinerk, who had formerly done janitorial and security work at Butler's compound, would fully testify a few months later, with catastrophic consequences.

Bob Mathews was undisturbed by the notion of an invasion of FBI agents. While others prepared to leave the island and fan out across the United States in a southern and easterly direction, he wrote a letter to the small weekly newspaper in Newport, Washington. In the past he had sent missives to *The Newport Miner* and was now intent upon getting certain things committed to paper before taking care of any further business (he went on record that the only reason he hadn't shot and killed FBI agent Arthur Hensel was that when Mathews sighted down the barrel, he saw Hensel's handsome white face and was compelled to lower the gun and fire at his ankles). Mathews's comrades could try to escape the island, but he had stopped running. He was ready to stand and fight. Lately he had taken to quoting poems to his followers, and one in particular would be passed along to other Order members and memorized by David Lane:

> *Give your soul to God and pick up your gun*
> *It's time to deal in lead*
> *We are the legions of the damned*
> *The army of the already dead*

In his letter to *The Newport Miner* Mathews told how he began his political career as a tax resister in Arizona, how he read extensively in European history and gradually developed the belief that the white race was headed for oblivion. His adopted son, Clint, would be "a stranger in his own land, a blond-haired blue-eyed Aryan in a country populated mainly by Mexicans, mulattoes, blacks and Asians." Mathews went on to acknowledge his role in the Portland shoot-out and once more stated that if Tom Martinez was found "we will remove his head from his body. . . . It is logical to assume that my days on this planet are rapidly drawing to a close. Even so, I have no fear. For the reality of life is death. I have made the ultimate sacrifice to secure the future for my children. . . . As always, for blood, soil, honor, for faith and for race."

By the third of December the FBI had come to Greenbank and taken up residence in the home of Bill and Winetta DeLapp, who lived only yards from the house rented by the Merkis. Winetta DeLapp offered the agents her home but later said if she hadn't they would have occupied it anyway. As they moved in, first two agents and then four, scattering guns on tables, chairs, and the floor, the DeLapps continued to live in the house as normally as possible. Other FBI personnel flew over Greenbank and took aerial photos of Mathews's place on Smuggler's Cove. On Tuesday and Wednesday, December 4 and 5, the agents started making arrangements for those living in the fifteen other waterfront homes to leave the area. The Silent Brotherhood was ignorant of the specific plans for a siege but knew the FBI was closing in, and as the weekend drew near the members began slipping away before the feds were ready to act. By Friday morning one hundred agents were on the island, many in camouflage gear with blackened faces, plus a score of local law-enforcement troops. This would not be another Portland. The feds believed that as many as seventeen people were hiding with Mathews in the house on Smuggler's Cove, in addition to those holed up in the other two residences. If combat came, they were prepared.

At 3 A.M. Friday morning, Bill DeLapp was still briefing the agents on how to approach the homes by land. When dawn broke a navy helicopter flew toward the Merkis' from offshore. The Coast Guard had shut down the shipping lanes in Puget Sound and Admiralty Inlet, backing up an outgoing Alaska state ferry and three Canadian military vessels, and air traffic below 2,500 feet was suspended over the island. As the helicopter hovered near the residence, naval recruits on board trained machine guns on the house and one seaman gave orders to the Merkis through a bullhorn—"Surrender now." On the ground, FBI agents stuck rifles out the window of the DeLapps' place, another form of persuasion. Inside, the Merkis were frantically burning Order documents and stashing money in crannies of the home or flushing it down the toilet.

The FBI had also encircled Randy Duey's house and told him to give up. For a time he resisted the notion, but at 7:45 A.M. he ran from the back door wielding an Uzi in one hand and a semi-automatic handgun in the other. Agents rushed him but he let himself be arrested peacefully, quickly turning over the loaded weapons. At 11:45 A.M. the Merkis came out of their house without incident, and by early evening Ian Stewart, who had been in the third house with Mathews, had done the same. When nabbed, the twenty-four-year-old had $40,000 in his possession. Two of the homes were now empty and from the Merkis' residence the FBI had recovered two rifles, a 12-gauge shotgun, a sword, a 9mm handgun, ammunition, two female wigs, fake moustaches, a padded bra, and $11,920 in cash. Following Stewart's arrest, the feds didn't know how many fugitives were left inside the house on Smuggler's Cove, or if Mathews was holding hostages. They tried to talk with him through the bullhorn, to negotiate his surrender, to determine the conditions in the home, but by late evening nothing had been accomplished, except the discovery of some island hospitality. Warren Caveness, the owner of the Greenbank general store, knew of the situation down the road and kept his business open all night long to serve the needs of the law-enforcement troops. As the hours passed toward morning, FBI agents came from the nearby woods, where they had been hiding, and gathered around the house. They were cold but they could wait. No one would escape this time.

The Merkis spent several hours trying to coax Mathews from

the house, but couldn't. At home in Metaline Falls, Mathews's wife, Debbie, learned of the siege and made an attempt to contact the FBI and speak with her husband. The authorities denied her wish. His brother, John, tried to reach him and failed. His girlfriend, Zillah Craig, was also informed of the situation, but too late. Electricity into the house had been cut off; the only information coming into the residence would be through the FBI. By Saturday morning, the agents were convinced that only Mathews was in the house, and this set off another effort at negotiation, FBI spokesmen shouting at him through a bullhorn. The fugitive showed no signs of cooperating. Like Adolf Hitler in his Berlin bunker at the end of World War II, Mathews had carefully orchestrated his exit, but he wasn't as passive as his hero. Bob Mathews would take no quiet poison or his own life. Ensnared by federal agents, abandoned by his brothers in the Order, his hand mangled and throbbing, he alone would fulfill the pledge he had created for the Bruders Schweigen at its inception: to fight and not be taken alive. There was no place left in his country for a man like himself. He would not belong, not accept, not surrender. He opened fire with an automatic weapon.

By late morning, the FBI had lofted tear gas into the home, and when that produced nothing but more gunfire they issued an ultimatum on the bullhorn—give up or they were coming in. He refused to walk out into the chilly gray afternoon, into the dampness and residue of tear gas hanging above the house. A SWAT team prepared for entry, along with a German shepherd named Oman. The dog went in first, barking and whimpering, and soon came out unharmed. The SWAT team was next, at 3 P.M., advancing into the smoke-filled first floor, where they were suddenly met by automatic gunfire from upstairs, bullets through the walls and through the ceiling, just missing one of the SWAT members. The team returned fire before retreating outside. Mathews appeared to have unlimited guns and ammunition on the second floor. It was too dangerous to take him by charging the stairs. One man was holding one hundred at bay.

By nightfall Saturday, nearly thirty-six hours had passed since the FBI made its initial move toward the three houses. Agents were tired, cold, and frustrated. The press had assembled nearby, reporting each possibility of a change, posing difficult questions to the feds: When was he going to give up? Why was this taking so long? Were they going to use more force? The agents did not want to go through another night in a standoff. He was still firing guns at them. What if, in the darkness, he somehow managed to escape again? The answer to that one was simple—FBI heads would roll.

The agents conferred, made their decision, and at a few minutes past 6 P.M., a helicopter flew over the house and dropped white phosphorous illumination flares on the roof. The structure ignited, flames shooting a hundred feet in the air. Explosions poured from the house—the sound of detonations, of automatic weapons fire from the second story, of Mathews blazing away. As the conflagration spread he kept his finger on the trigger, firing again and again, bullets ripping through the burning walls and over the heads of agents on the ground. For a long time the reports spewed into the night, hitting trees and splitting the black air. Then the darkness was still.

In the morning, when the house was charred rubble, agents advanced on it and found the remains of a body. To the layman it would have looked like little more than one left foot—the rest was beyond recognition, except for a medallion engraved with the words BRUDERS SCHWEIGEN around the fragment of neck. Some time later, dental records determined it was, in fact, Robert Jay Mathews, age thirty-one, who was found on the burned-out floor. He had perished of smoke inhalation, a form of death the chief medical examiner of King County, Washington, who performed the autopsy, labeled a homicide. No sooner had the fire been extinguished than rumors began on the far right that Mathews had not been given an adequate chance to surrender; he had, said his political allies, been murdered. Martyrdom was assured.

The FBI was sensitive on the issue of his death. In the days after the siege, the authorities were asked incessantly if there had been alternatives to dropping flares on the house. The response was always terse: The capture of Mathews and the search for the rest of his gang were part of a massive ongoing federal investigation and all questions on the matter would one day be resolved in court. They didn't have to answer to anyone and made a point of avoiding it. They had done their job, gotten their man. By the end of 1984 one thing was quite clear: The federal government took the Order seriously and wanted it squashed. On occasion FBI agents and police made jokes about being considered part of—or under the control of—a Jewish conspiracy, but when the law-enforcement machinery was set in motion to crush the Silent Brotherhood, the laughing stopped.

"Our message to them is simple," one assistant U.S. Attorney, called in to deal with the legal issues surrounding those arrested on Whidbey Island, said in private. "You fuck with the ZOG and we'll cut your balls off."

Soon there was talk of a memorial service for Bob Mathews to be held April 20, 1985, Hitler's birthday. Radical right tributes abounded for the dead man: He had shaped the Order, crystallized a lot of free-floating white anger across the nation, given it a political framework, led a small group of people to commit nearly seventy crimes, and conceived of plans to rid the Northwest of minorities and blow up Washington's Boundary Dam, which supplies nearly half of Seattle's power.

"He was a man of the highest idealism and moral character," the Reverend Richard Butler told the *San Francisco Examiner*. "He exhibited a willingness and courage to die for his beliefs. . . . It encourages me because it shows there are still some patriotic young men left in the country."

"I will not have my husband's name besmirched after his death," Debbie Mathews read from a statement written for the media. "It is easy and convenient to accuse a dead man of crimes because he cannot stand up and defend himself. I know in my heart that he would never have committed the robberies that the paid informant said he did. My husband and Gordon Kahl were guilty only of self-defense. Yet they were both murdered because they were brave enough to stand up and fight for God, truth and their race. Their deaths will not be forgotten."

Then, deviating from the text, she said, "He loved Clint more than anything. He did it for him."

Not everyone in Mathews's family shared his wife's views.

"I'm not so sure he didn't want to die," John Mathews, his brother, told the *Seattle Post-Intelligencer*. "If there's anybody we hold hatred for, it's the neo-Nazis. I love my brother but I was totally against what he was doing."

News of Mathews's death reached William Pierce, author of *The Turner Diaries*, two days after the fire. When asked his reaction to what had become of his disciple, Pierce said, "It's foolish to think in terms of opposing social or racial trends by violent or illegal means."

# 25

## *A QUIET DEATH,*
## *A LOUD GRAVE*

Tom Martinez had known Bill Soderquist from their time together in the National Alliance. On December 12, four days after the death of Bob Mathews, Soderquist was awakened in his home in Salinas, California, by a loud knock at the door. Before he could find his clothes, his living room was full of FBI agents asking him questions and telling him to get dressed. Since Gary Yarbrough's arrest nearly three weeks earlier, law-enforcement officials had gotten from him about what they had anticipated—nothing. They got the same from the other Brotherhood member in their grasp, Randy Duey. Agents quickly sized up Soderquist, and guessed that if offered a plea bargain he might tell them all sorts of interesting things. The deal they put forward was extraordinary and revealed just how much the FBI wanted to round up the rest of the Order and be done with them. Soderquist had taken part in enough criminal acts to be faced with, if convicted, 130 years in a federal penitentiary. His government gave him a choice. If he would tell them everything he knew, he would be free, immune from any type of criminal prosecution. If he took the deal, his only worry would be execution by one of his former colleagues on the extreme right. The government would even help him avoid that possibility by placing him in their witness-protection program and providing the resources necessary to establish a new identity in a new location. Soderquist thought about the offer for several hours; his loyalty had always been to Bob Mathews and to not much more. The decision the young man reached did not send him to jail.

On Whidbey Island, in the house rented by Randy Duey, agents found a letter addressed to Denver Parmenter, in a Seaside, Oregon, motel. The eighteenth of December was Parmenter's last day on the lam. For a while, sitting behind bars, he kept still, kept his oath to the Silent Brotherhood. But as he stayed in a Portland jail during the holiday season, missing his family and getting completely away from the Order for the first time in nearly a year, getting away also from the taste of alcohol, which had accompanied him throughout much of his adult life, he began to think about some things he had recently done. He started reading the Bible— all of the chapters and verses, not just those singled out for emphasis by Richard Butler at his Aryan Nations church. He had never tried that before. Initially, he was appointed a lawyer who was female and Jewish. Parmenter angrily refused to have any contact with her and asked for a replacement. As he sat in the cell a little longer, he began to think about that and to feel bad because he had hurt her feelings. When he asked her to come back and be his attorney, she said yes. By that time he knew what he was going to do next. The government would not present him with the kind of deal they had given Soderquist, but for a confession they would let him plead guilty to just one count of a federal indictment, which carried a sentence of twenty years, with a chance at parole in eight. When he accepted this offer, one of his main concerns was not simply what life would be like in a penitentiary but whether he would get to serve his sentence at all. How would the large black and Hispanic populations in prison feel about accepting an avowed Aryan Warrior? Would they try to kill him? He would not be alone in wondering about such things.

In the first week of January, informants told the FBI that Aryan Nations associates were going to kill Oregon senator Robert Packwood. He was given round-the-clock protection and the prophecy was not fulfilled. That same week Richard Kemp and Andrew Barnhill were arrested at a poker game in Kalispell, Montana, where the ante for sitting at the table was five thousand dollars. For some time Barnhill had been telling people that he was a professional poker player, a useful line when buying a condominium with cash. The night of his arrest his companion was a fifteen-year-old girl from Cincinnati.

Neither Kemp nor Barnhill pleaded guilty, nor did Jean Craig, taken into custody in Boise in mid-January. James Dye, the Vietnam veteran from Philadelphia who had witnessed the murder of Walter West from behind a bush, was grabbed by the FBI in a suburb of Spokane. At his home were guns, $5,600 in $20 bills, and a picture of Adolf Hitler. He would take a plea, then go into the Idaho woods three or four times with authorities in an effort to locate West's body. The grave never was found. On January 30, Charles Ostrout, the Brinks employee who provided inside information for the Ukiah heist, was placed under arrest. His fellow worker, Ron King, would soon be picked up and charged with plotting to rob the San Francisco Brinks vault of $30 million. Both men pleaded guilty. Toward January's end, the FBI came to Ken Loff's northeastern Washington farm to arrest the owner and dig around his barn for the $1.5 million he had buried there for Bob Mathews. The money was long since dispersed, but the FBI's arrival left no doubt in Loff's mind about one thing: Those confessing to the authorities were telling the truth; the feds had known exactly where to start turning over the earth. Loff agreed to talk and work with the FBI—place a few phone calls—to help find those who remained at large; in time he would get a mere five-year sentence and the prosecution team would recommend he be treated with great leniency. Loff was not only helpful but quite well informed. David Lane had told him about driving the getaway car at the Berg murder; Mathews and Scutari had told him about being at the scene as lookouts; Bruce Pierce had told him how the gun jammed after the thirteenth round, so only that many bullets reached Berg's body. Pierce had dwelled on this fact—the number thirteen held some obscure religious significance to him, or perhaps he thought of it as unlucky. Pierce told Loff that when he shot the talk-show host, "Berg didn't make a sound. He just fell to the ground." Lane also mentioned to Loff that shooting Alan Berg may have been a bad idea after all, because it had brought the dead man so much attention and turned him into a martyr, perhaps a hero.

After the confessions of Parmenter and Loff regarding the Berg murder, the FBI intensified its search for the three remaining figures who were suspected of the killing: Lane, Pierce, and Scutari. During January and February, as the investigation spread across the nation to include forty law-enforcement agencies in sixty cities and eighteen states, a grand jury in Seattle began listening to testimony from those who had struck plea bargains with the government. Late in February Eugene Kinerk traveled from his cell in Boise's Ada County Jail, where he was in custody for the past November's bank robbery in Grays Harbor, Washington, to testify. Hardly a key witness for the prosecution, Kinerk had spent considerable time at the Aryan Nations compound and was acquainted with several members of the Silent Brotherhood. After testifying in Seattle, he returned to his cell and hung himself with a torn bed sheet. The suicide note said he was afraid of what "they" would do to him since he had decided to confess. "I cooperated," he added, "to hurt those who will kill." Kinerk's death, like West's, Berg's, and Mathews's, was the fourth connected to the Order, but not the last.

On March 1, when Randall Rader came to Washington from Missouri to pick up his belongings, the FBI grabbed him in Spokane. He pleaded guilty, was very cooperative, and eventually received a suspended sentence. By late March, fifteen of the twenty-five core members of the group had been rounded up, but the three Berg suspects were still at large. Richard Scutari had been reported seen in Dallas in March and then vanished, David Lane continued in deep hiding, and Bruce Pierce had become the most wanted man in the West, although his range of travel was by no means limited to that part of the United States. He had guns, cars, trucks, an airplane, and was determined to exhaust them all. He had dyed his hair with something resembling yellow glue, and was considering plastic surgery for his face.

Pierce had often left the FBI cursing its bad timing and luck. Near Labor Day of 1984, the feds missed him by a few days in Troy, Montana (then missed him again when he returned to Troy and they were still searching the area). In the fall, he had been in western Colorado, near Grand Junction and Whitewater, but by the time agents conducted a manhunt there, he was gone. The day before the FBI laid siege to the homes the Order had rented on Whidbey Island, Pierce had driven off in a three-car caravan. In January 1985, he was spotted in Utah, where, the FBI heard, he had been to a dentist and had all his upper teeth removed; if he went down like Mathews, they would never identify him with such ease. In mid-February the FBI arrested his brother, Gregory, in Belen, New Mexico, and hoped that Bruce would turn up in the same town. Forty-five minutes before the authorities came to his ex-residence in Belen, he had deserted the place for good. Later that month he and his wife, Julie, stopped for a week in their mobile home in El Paso, Texas, where Pierce had bought an ultralight airplane for $3,400 cash. Under the name of Michael Schmidt, he was storing the craft at the Aero West Airport Hangar in El Paso, renting a space in a trailer park, and taking flying lessons on the outskirts of town. When the FBI came to the hangar they found a tape recorder, telephone books, a Bruders Schweigen medallion, and a grenade rocket, but Pierce had moved on. With Julie and their three children, he drove east in a recreation vehicle, the FBI quickly picking up his trail. The agents were at long last getting nearer their goal, and when Pierce halted at a campground by Stone Mountain, Georgia, they were ready to bait the snare.

On March 20, Elizabeth Ware, the manager of AAA Answering Service in Rossville, Georgia, received a call from Pierce (who used a known alias) asking her to accept delivery of a letter for him. The elderly widow said she didn't perform that function, but he continued to phone and restate his request. Simultaneously, FBI agents working the small towns of northwestern Georgia for clues, contacted Mrs. Ware and told her to accept the letter if the man using that alias called again. On Tuesday, March 26, the letter arrived and by then scores of lawmen—special agents, the Rossville Police Department, the Georgia Bureau of Investigation, the U.S. Marshals Service—were in or around Rossville. That evening Ware's neighbors were told to stay in their houses and be alert. Some officers were posted on the fourth floor of a bank across the street from Mrs. Ware's and others were in her white-frame home.

At 7:40 P.M. Pierce's van came to a stop at the curb outside and the tall young man—thinner now from his months of running, no longer as handsome under his yellow hair and scraggly beard—walked to Mrs. Ware's back door. She let him in and he followed as she went for the letter. Standing in the middle of her living room, he was absently staring at the wall when every door around him opened and armed men rushed forward, knocking him to the floor. Pierce had two pistols tucked into his pants and a derringer in his pocket, but he never made a motion toward any of them.

"They put a machine gun in his face," one Rossville policeman said later, "and he didn't have much choice."

Weapons experts were called in to examine his van. They used a long-distance rope to jimmy its door, fearing if they tried to open it in regular fashion this would trigger a bomb. They didn't find such a device but did uncover a loaded crossbow, chemical explosives, a tear-gas grenade, an automatic rifle with a silencer, a semi-automatic pistol, several fragmentation grenades, a pipe bomb, nine sticks of dynamite and two books: *Assassination: Theory and Practice* and *The Hit Man*. On March 27 Pierce's wife, driving a pickup and accompanied by her three children, was arrested in Jasper, Alabama, twenty miles north of Birmingham. Her vehicle contained an assortment of explosives, automatic weapons, hand grenades, and seven thousand dollars cash. Despite this arsenal, the FBI considered her innocent and set her free.

In Seattle, where a grand jury was sitting and preparing to hand down an indictment, the government's chief prosecuting attorney, Gene Wilson, received the news about Pierce with relief. "There is great joy in Fedville today," he said. "We've been looking for him for a long time."

One of Pierce's first acts as a prisoner was to ask to be deported; the authorities said no. Denver police went to Atlanta to question him about Alan Berg but, like Gary Yarbrough, he wouldn't talk with them. The young man hadn't been so reticent with the FBI. Months later, when he had a court-appointed lawyer and was more attuned to life inside the legal system, he would say that he had been drugged right after his arrest and a confession was forced from him. In fact he was simply exhausted from running, frightened, and spilled his tale, admitting his participation in the January 1984 robbery of a Spokane bank; in two armored-car holdups, in Seattle and at Ukiah; and acknowledging his use of nine aliases, including "Joseph Shelby," the name on a registration card at Denver's Motel 6 for the nights of June 16, 17, and 18, 1984. That was all they would get from Bruce Pierce. Or almost all. From the moment he was taken into custody in Georgia he made a practice of titillating the authorities by just about pleading guilty to their charges—and then pulling back. Each time he changed his mind for the same reason: He wanted nothing to do with the Berg killing. First-degree murder in Colorado could mean the death penalty. He didn't even want to think about that.

When the talk-show host's name had been brought up to other Order members it elicited a response. Yarbrough said that God shot Alan Berg; Mathews told any number of people that the radio personality had gotten what he deserved; David Lane wondered aloud to Ken Loff if the execution of Berg had been a mistake. Bruce Pierce said nothing. He seemed to have no opinion on the matter. He didn't appear worried or glad. In the past he had told those in the Silent Brotherhood that Berg fell as if the carpet had been pulled out from under him and that the man died quietly, not even making a sound. Those remarks revealed only how distant the event was to Pierce, as though he expected a man shot in the head and chest with an automatic pistol at a range of five feet—a man with thirty-four wounds and holes—to stand up and talk.

Like Pierce, David Lane had been ricocheting around the country for much of the past year: Denver, Washington State, Philadelphia, Denver, Boise, Denver, the southeastern seaboard. In recent months he had been on his own and trying his hand at the art of minimalist survival. In Denver, he had once learned how to get along cheaply, eating at McDonald's and stretching a dime, but then he had at least been surrounded by the diversions of a city. On little money one could stay amused. Since early March he had been living by himself in a clapboard shack in the rolling farmland near Charity, Virginia, a town of one hundred by the Blue Ridge Mountains, close to the North Carolina line. The dwelling had no electricity or plumbing. An adjacent tree had a tire swing hanging from a branch, for recreation. No glass was in the structure's windows, the front door was propped open by a wooden plank, and the back door didn't exist. Furnishings were two mattresses, a wood stove, a cookstove, and a kerosene lamp. At night the late-winter air was cold. He had knives, ammunition, and a copy of Hitler's *Mein Kampf*. He had a computer printout of people in the United States who would harbor fugitives like himself. For comfort he had a sleeping bag and a half-gallon jar of moonshine.

The shack's owner, Keith Atkins, had met Lane at a rally sponsored by Glenn Miller, the leader of the Carolina Knights of the Ku Klux Klan. In return for staying in the building, Lane helped tend Atkin's cattle, dug a spring, and did a few repairs on the house. He also wrote. During his career as a radical he had turned out a number of articles on his beliefs, and privately had composed love poems to white women—Aryan Princesses. Lane was driven to think about things, and at the abandoned country house he had plenty of time for musing and outlining how the revolution should be carried on. He knew the FBI was hunting him and when they found him he could die. What he put on paper on those chill March afternoons and evenings, sitting alone with his jug and pen in the poorly lit shed that rose from the earth at a cockeyed angle, resembled a last testament:

## BRUDERS SCHWEIGEN
### PART I  PURPOSE

This is a short manual explaining the purpose, structure, and membership of the Bruders Schweigen. . . . We are realists, recognizing that under the current one man one vote democratic system, we are outnumbered a hundred to one, not only on this continent, but worldwide by a coalition of blacks, browns, yellows, liberals, communists, queers, race-mixing religious zealots, race-traitors, preachers, teachers and judges. All of these are under the total control or influence of organized jewry, and all of them desire nothing more fervently than the extermination of any White man so courageous as to make a public statement advocating the continued existence of his Race . . . We have but one pure and holy cause and that is to continue the existence of the images of the Gods on this earth. We believe with all our hearts that the Race of men from whom sprang the Magna Charta, the constitution of America, the law, the technology, the medicine, all the creations of what is called Western civilization is the highest work of the Creator, and if we are mongrelized then the earth shall drift eternally thru the ether, devoid of higher life. . . . Our Race is our Nation, we love no other. Our concern is not political, religious, or economic systems for these too have been used to divide and destroy us. These things evolve and can be returned to their original form, but our Race which now faces near certain extinction cannot be brought back once it is mixed and destroyed. . . . Bob Mathews, the founder of the Bruders Schweigen and the bravest most noble man it has been my privilege to know was fond of the Norse sagas and their fatalism. His two favorites which he never grew tired of repeating were the following.

*"Fearlessness is better than a faint heart for the length of my life and the date of my death were fated long ago."*

---

*"Cattle die, Kinsmen die, I too will die, the only thing I know that does not die is the fame of dead men's deeds."*

PART II MEMBERSHIP & STRUCTURE . . .

A properly equipped unit will carry no less than two 308 caliber semi autos, two 223 caliber assault rifles, two 12 gauge riot guns with double oo buck, six handguns, preferably 9 mm with extra clips, and whatever special weapons the action might dictate. . . . Do not underestimate the value of diversionary tactics before your primary action. Porno theatres and bookstores are full of filth showing homo-sexuals and niggers doing vile acts with white women. A large bomb planted in one of these places not only creates an excellent diversion but it serves the will of our God. In the larger cities the majority of pimps are negros [sic] and they prefer white whores as they bring better prices. Most of them push drugs also and they often have large amounts of cash on their persons, in their cars, or at their homes. Most of them also serve as drivers to deliver the girls for their "Dates." You can arrainge [sic] a "date" at a cheap apartment and capture the pimp when he arrives. After he sees the whore lose her head and he has lost a few body parts, he will gladly tell you where the cash is. After that, let your conscience be your guide. When on the road or staying at motels do not be seen in groups larger than two or three in order not to draw attention. When in public do not discuss "company" business. Learn to chatter about typical goy garbage such as the local nigger basketball star. You must learn to become two entirely different persons. Sometimes you are sheep and then you change to a wolf. Until you can sit at a table or in a bar with a beautiful white woman and her nigger boyfriend or husband and convince them you are overflowing with brotherly love and affection you are not yet a completed agent of the White Underground. When with a reassuring smile, establishment patter and a friendly pat on the back, you are able to convince them to take you into their confidence, perhaps even invite you into their home, then you are in a position to engage in a little affirmative action of your own. Again, let your conscience be your guide. It is recommended that no kinsman be put in combat situations i.e. raise the sword against ZOG until he has planted his seed in the belly of a woman. The same for kinswomen. If possible they should bear the child of at least one warrior before putting their own life on the line. This was the practice of the Spartans. The genes of those who possess the courage to fight ZOG are too valuable to squander. If there is life beyond this one, for each individual, is a question pondered by man thru all history and one which we can only truly answer after our death. However there are two kinds of life after death we can be sure of. One is thru the fame of our deeds, the other is thru genetic memory passed on to our children thru our pure seedline. You must reproduce or the images of the Aryan Warrior Gods will forever disappear. . . .

Telephones: like it or not you will have to use them for much if not most of your communications. They are POISON POISON POISON, yet they are unavoidable. If the following rules are followed ABSOLUTELY, you will probably be OK. If you disobey them you are a dead duck. Firstly, no long distance calls between members from their own phones. The first thing ZOG does when he becomes suspicious is get all your phone records for the last 10 years. Then he puts bugs and tracers on your phone and everyone you called. If necessary then he puts bugs and tracers on the phones of all those who your friends have called. In this way they soon have a giant net in which they can cross reference and determine who knows who. For this reason all sensitive communication must be *from* a pay phone and often *from* a pay phone *to* a pay phone. . . . From time to time, those who plunder the treasuries of ZOG will find themselves in possession of large amounts of the currency of the realm. . . . In the time honored tradition of warfare, by those who are oppressed, you have a right to a large portion of the spoils of war. Just do not lose sight of the reason we took up the sword and that is to provide a future for White children. . . . Do not buy a $15,000 chariot that draws the attention of ZOG. Rather buy a six hundred dollar chariot, then spend $300 here and five hundred on a paint job, $400 on an interior and three hundred on tires. Soon she will have the finest classic in town and ZOG will be none the wiser. Do not neglect to set some aside also, for the White man does not have the widows pension that ZOG gives the wives of his hired killers. As for those young warriors who have no mate, even we old timers remember the urges of our youth. If you indulge certain comforts and pleasures of the flesh your Viking ancestors watch with hearty approval as they Drink, Brawl, and Wench their way through Valhallah. Just beware, for booze lubricates the lips and every young warrior wishes to brag to the fair young damsels. . . . Thirdly, Prisoners of War. It is up to each unit leader to prepare himself and every member for this possibility. Name Rank and Serial number is all a POW gives the enemy. So it has always been and so it must be. I don't know how long we have preached about keeping your mouth shut if captured yet still someone turns weak and blabbers like a baby. You had better realize before you ever take up the sword against ZOG that if you are captured you will either be executed or live in a ZOG prison till ZOG collapses. If you cannot make the decision before you join that your lips are sealed, then don't raise the sword for then it is too late. If you do not understand how desperate the situation is, if you do not understand the truth of the last line of our motto "We are the army of the already dead" then get out now, but if you get in then seal your lips. As for the rest of the unit, if a member is captured, assume he has talked. Even if he is loyal, ZOG is already drugging POWs and soon there will be torture also. After the Genocide treaty we can expect to be exported to Israel for torture, trial and execution. . . .

The requirements for membership in the Bruders Schweigen are simple. You must look White, act White and fight White. You must believe with your entire being that there is no other issue of importance at this time than to provide a future for White children. You must raise the sword against ZOG. We have by necessity been light on details and heavy on philosophy in this manual but such is necessary when in an occupied country. If you should elect to join our holy cause then you have accepted the highest calling ever bestowed on man. May the God of your understanding protect and guide you thru the perilous times ahead. May the immortal spirit of Robert Jay Mathews and the spirits of all the White heros [sic] of ages past give you strength and inspiration. For Blood, Soil, and Honor with loyal faith in the resurrection of our people.

THE BRUDERS SCHWEIGEN
*David Lane*

On Friday, the twenty-ninth of March, three days after the arrest of Bruce Pierce, Ken Loff called Lane, while the FBI tapped in. During their conversation, Lane said, "When I go, I'm gonna go just like Bobby [Mathews], I think, unless they catch me unawares, only I'm not gonna be as nice to the federal dogs."

Before hanging up, Loff asked Lane to phone him tomorrow, and the call was arranged for a certain time and place. The next morning Lane was in Winston-Salem, North Carolina, where he had come with Keith Atkins and Clyde Jones, another acquaintance, to get supplies at the Winn Dixie supermarket. His two companions stayed at the pickup while Lane, wearing a T-shirt and blue jeans, went into the store. When he emerged, six FBI agents met him on the way to the truck. Unarmed, he offered no resistance, and in the first moments of being captured he set the tone for his behavior for many months to come. He acted relieved.

Earlier photographs of David Lane show a tall, upright man with a pleasant but intense face. By the time of his arrest only the intensity remained. He was slumped, as if something had snapped in his back, his eyes were sunken, and he looked terribly strained (not unlike the way Adolf Hitler's doctor, Ernst Günther Schenck, a nutritionist for the Nazi army in 1945, described the Führer in his last days: "His spine was hunched, his shoulder blades protruded from his bent back, and he collapsed his shoulders like a turtle. He seemed to be carrying a mountain on his shoulders. His eyes, glaring at me painfully, were blood-shot, and the drooping black sacs under the eyes betrayed fatigue and sleeplessness. Suddenly, it hit me like a hammer stroke. I was looking at the eyes of death"). Lane told those who reported his arrest that he felt as if he had aged twenty years while on the run. Indeed, he looked closer to sixty than forty-six. Despite his appearance, he seemed in remarkably good spirits. To the press he dropped one-liners about his poverty—he had been arrested holding fifty cents—about how much he needed soap and toothpaste, and about how well he got along with black inmates in the jail. They had a helluva time, he said, playing cards. He bragged that the Order had thrown a serious scare into the FBI, repeated that Bob Mathews was the greatest white man in history, and went on at some length about his alliterative politics. The purse and the press, or the media and the money, were behind everything in the United States, he declared, and all under the control of Jews.

When another subject was broached, his upbeat mood fell. It came as a shock to Lane that many in the Bruders Schweigen had already closed such swift and convenient deals with the federal government. The Silent Brotherhood had turned out to be anything but silent; a number of those who had never been arrested before first wept in their cells and then talked. Lane had thought them made of sterner stuff, and groused openly about their lack of commitment and backbone. Their flipping over for the FBI appeared to hurt and disturb him more than being incarcerated.

Then Lane himself began to consider a plea bargain. In return for his testimony about the Berg murder, he wanted the Denver authorities to guarantee him a sentence of no more than six years. The local district attorney, Norm Early, rejected the offer as far too lenient, and this rekindled Lane's revolutionary fervor. He regarded himself as a POW now, locked in the oppressor's den, paying his radical dues. He got himself a lawyer, Thomas Keith, who had successfully defended the nine KKK and neo-Nazi members accused of shooting to death five communist sympathizers in the Greensboro anti-Klan rally in 1979. One of those acquitted in that trial, Roland Wayne Wood, showed up at Lane's first court hearing in Winston-Salem wearing a green T-shirt. It read: I'D RATHER BE KILLING COMMUNISTS.

Lane contended he was innocent; he hadn't dealt in counterfeit or stolen money and knew nothing whatsoever about the murder of Alan Berg. Yet he did have an opinion on the dead man, one he had voiced in the past and one he brought up again to reporters who had traveled all the way from Denver to Idaho, to Georgia, and now to North Carolina, to ask questions of those who allegedly knew something about the demise of Berg. The Denver press was so thick at these locations it disrupted and angered the FBI and other law-enforcement officials working on the investigation. It got so bad that the feds told the Denver police to stay home if they were going to bring along that irrepressible, loud-mouthed pack of journalists. Leaked details can ruin a trial or prejudice a jury. Denver police complained about the reporters, and vice versa, and the whole affair kept the topic of the dead talk-show host as alive and heated in the spring of 1985 as it had been on June 19, 1984. All of this colored David Lane's opinion of what had happened to the former radio personality at KOA. Berg, he told the press, was a far more difficult enemy in the grave than he had ever been alive. People just wouldn't shut up about him.

# 26

---

# "IT'S OVER NOW"

---

On April 4, the FBI arrived at Ardie McBrearty's home in Gentry, Arkansas, with the idea of capturing him and the $100,000 he had received from the Ukiah job. His wife, Marlene, was appalled at the notion of armed federal agents bursting into her home, but she quickly recovered and told the boys to sit down and relax. No mere criminal charges against her husband were going to keep her from showing a little Ozark hospitality. Ardie didn't take it so well.

Most Order members, when nabbed by the FBI, became either defiant or nervous or quiet or showed some pride in the fact that they had given the feds a long hard run. They were revolutionaries, after all, and had expected to be chased across the land and hunted with guns. McBrearty was indignant, disgusted by the whole notion of having these authorities come to his home. He knew nothing whatsoever about the politics of that gang up in Washington or any of the crimes they may have committed. They were a group of tax resisters, he'd been told, who had given him $100,000 in case they got arrested during a tax protest and needed bail money or a legal expert. He was an old tax protester himself and claimed some knowledge of the law. The Order had taken him on as a kind of free-lance financial consultant, he indicated, and he was happy to have the work.

One could see by looking at his wounded expression that it really annoyed him to be arrested like this. A man was supposed to be able to live his own way in America, or at least in Arkansas. When they locked McBrearty up, the first thing he did was lose some weight, and then some more, until he'd lost fifty pounds. He complained about several ailments, his heart especially, and Marlene said that neither she nor Ardie would see ten more years. Sitting in jail in Pierce County, Washington, thirty miles south of Seattle, where all the Order prisoners were being funneled, McBrearty demanded a kosher diet. He would not touch pork, shellfish, goose, or duck. As one of God's Chosen People, he had a right to eat the food his religion dictated. The jail disagreed, adding to his sense of persecution.

By mid-April, when the indictment in Seattle was finally unsealed, only five of the twenty-three people named in the document were still at large. No one knew where Richard Scutari was, but David Tate, Thomas Bentley, Frank Silva, and Randall Evans were all believed to be in the Ozark region, perhaps at the compound of the Covenant, Sword and Arm of the Lord. While the FBI gathered nearby and prepared for another siege, half a continent away in Seattle, lawyers, journalists, and any number of legal minds perused the 21-count, 93-page indictment, which would eventually be superseded by a 124-pager. The Order had committed 176 acts of what the federal government was calling a conspiracy to violate the RICO Act; after conspiring, they had committed 67 crimes.

The 1970 Racketeer Influenced and Corrupt Organizations statute had been designed to prosecute organized-crime outfits—"enterprises" whose goal was to make money. To come under the RICO umbrella an enterprise had to be engaged in not one but a pattern of racketeering activities: robbery, arson, murder, wire fraud, loan sharking. Count 14 of the indictment read: "On or about June 18, 1984, in Denver, Colorado, Bruce Carroll Pierce, Richard Scutari, David Eden Lane, Jean Margaret Craig and Robert Jay Mathews did then and there unlawfully and feloniously . . . cause the death of Alan Berg contrary to" the laws of Colorado. This count, however, did not represent a charge of first-degree murder. RICO is a federal statute, and murder, in most cases, is a state crime (in Idaho, the law describing a death like Walter West's says that such a killing is a result of "an abandoned and malignant heart"). A RICO conviction would not mean that the group had specifically murdered Alan Berg or Walter West, but only that the Order had engaged in a pattern of racketeering. Most important, to be convicted on RICO charges, the accused must be found guilty of two separate criminal acts. If any of the defendants were culpable only, for example, in the Berg or the West matter, he or she could go free.

Instantly there were attorneys—some of whom had been appointed to represent Order members—denouncing the RICO indictment. The Silent Brotherhood, they reasoned, was not a longstanding crime family or an enterprise created for profit. The Order's real goal was something other than making money. The defendants deserved to be tried separately on specific criminal charges. Lumping them all together as racist or religious fanatics, went this argument, would make convicting the whole group a good deal easier. "If you have everyone in the same boat," said one Order sympathizer, "then you only have to sink one ship."

The government, which felt no particular need to explain its legal strategy, found many appealing things in the RICO Act. First, it swung a wide net, allowing them to accuse twenty-four people (Charles Ostrout was charged separately, in California), plus those who avoided being named in the indictment because they had already pleaded guilty. Second, it meant one long, expensive trial, as opposed to perhaps a dozen. Third, each count in the indictment carried a twenty-year sentence and a $25,000 fine; the government felt it could put the core of the Order behind bars for several decades. Finally, if convicted under the statute, the Silent Brotherhood would have to turn over all the assets it had accumulated to the federal government. Thus far the FBI had seized a ski condominium in Montana, 160 acres in Missouri, 110 acres in Idaho, 150 weapons, thirty-nine motor vehicles, one boat, two ultralight aircraft, a Harley-Davidson motorcycle, and $429,696 in cash. From Bruce Pierce alone the feds had recovered property in Texas, New Mexico, Georgia, Montana, Oregon, Washington, Idaho, Virginia, Pennsylvania, North Carolina, and Alabama. When arrested he had $30,132 in cash, two computers, a printer, a color television, a microwave oven, two Honda motorcycles, a ham radio, and a $3,000 Rottweiler dog. Other Order property would one day be found, but more than half of the stolen $4 million never did turn up.

While defense attorneys made plans to file motions against the RICO charges, and prosecutors got ready for a June 17 trial date, law-enforcement officers continued the hunt. On Monday, April 15, as the lengthy indictment was being read in a Seattle courtroom, a Missouri state trooper, Jimmie Linegar, was stopping traffic near Ridgedale, in the Ozarks, for routine license checks. In early afternoon he waved a brown Chevrolet van with Nevada plates to the side of the road. The driver had an Oregon license, and the thirty-one-year-old officer had a faint suspicion. Leaving the van for a few moments to make a call into his office, he ran the license number through the National Crime Information Center computer and discovered the vehicle belonged to "Matthew Mark Samuels," wanted on an illegal-weapons charge in Oregon. It was a known alias of David Tate. Linegar was well armed and wearing a bulletproof vest, but he knew how dangerous those associated with the group could be. He made another call. Several minutes later a second trooper, Allen Hines, arrived to assist Linegar. When Tate saw him, the twenty-two-year-old jumped from the van and opened fire with a submachine gun, hitting Linegar four times and Hines three. As Tate ran toward the woods, Hines returned the fire but didn't graze him. The young man disappeared into the foliage and Hines, who had been hit in the shoulder, arms, and hip, radioed for help. He attempted to give Linegar cardiopulmonary resuscitation but the effort was futile. Jimmie Linegar died at a nearby hospital.

The search for Tate in southwestern Missouri and northwestern Arkansas began immediately, totally. Killing a trooper was all the initiative the state police needed. The next morning they rode shotgun on school buses, gazing out into the rocky, densely forested landscape for Tate, who looked too young to shave. Officers stopped trains and passed through every car but didn't see the fugitive. They went home to home in the mountain cabins around Branson, Missouri, and they set up roadblocks throughout the area. Fishermen were urged to avoid the countryside. Homes and businesses locked their doors twenty-four hours each day. Tate's abandoned van had contained hand grenades, six machine guns, tools for making gun parts, dynamite, other firearms, and a pint whiskey bottle full of nitroglycerine; no one doubted he could kill again. Two hundred lawmen conducted the search. After three days, when they had found nothing of substance, another hundred joined them. National Guard helicopters scoured the wilderness from above. Tate was proving to be far more elusive than Frank Silva, arrested near Gentry, Arkansas, on the sixteenth of April and jailed without bond in Fort Smith. Predictably, his vehicle had been stocked with automatic weapons, hand grenades, and dynamite.

The first lead came when Tate pilfered cookies and soda pop from a truck parked at a rock quarry east of Branson. The search intensified around Three Brothers, Arkansas, an area where Pretty Boy Floyd and Jesse James had once hid while running from the law. Nearby, at the Covenant, Sword and Arm of the Lord compound, the FBI and a state SWAT team had arrived, encircled the camp, and were demanding the surrender of its leader, Jim Ellison, the self-proclaimed "King of the Ozarks." Ellison was being charged with conspiring to possess and manufacture fully automatic weapons, a violation of federal statutes. Roadblocks were set up around the camp to stop the possibility of David Tate's sneaking in (if he wasn't inside already). The FBI wanted not only Ellison and Tate but other Order fugitives believed sheltered in the compound. In full combat regalia, standing at the CSA perimeter, the feds waited, attempting to negotiate. Sixty men, women, and children—many were armed—waited inside the camp as a day passed, then another, with Ellison trying to decide whether to surrender or fight.

On Saturday, April 20, the sixth day of the manhunt, a citizen of Forsyth, Missouri, spotted a young man hiding behind some bushes in the city park. He recognized David Tate from photographs and called the police. When they came, the fugitive, like Pierce and Lane before him, offered no resistance. He was picked up within twenty miles of where he had shot Linegar and was taken to the small Forsyth jail. A crowd of townspeople gathered outside the prison and began to shout: "Kill him! Kill him! Kill him!" Tate was eventually convicted of first-degree murder in Missouri and given a life sentence, with no chance for parole.

The morning after his arrest, which was the third day of the ongoing siege at CSA, the FBI advanced slowly on the compound, wary of triggering land mines or other buried explosives. The camp was surrounded on three sides by Bull Shoals Lake. Several agents paddled across the water toward the compound, as those within its boundaries retreated farther, until Ellison and his followers were behind a barbed-wire-fence enclosure. At Whidbey Island the FBI had shown that combat was one of their options, and they were equally willing to exercise it in the Ozarks. Preparations were made to evacuate the women and children on the other side of the fence.

On Monday, April 22, Jim Ellison gave up peacefully, saying God had told him to do so. The CSA leader added that he wanted to answer the charges against him, because they were untrue (in time he pleaded guilty to conspiracy and illegal possession of firearms). With considerable relief, the FBI moved into the compound and seized computer equipment, ammunition, grenades, Nazi writings, a small bomb factory, automatic weapons, and thirty gallons of cyanide. They also picked up Randall Evans and Tom Bentley, who were hiding near the camp and went into custody without a fight. Within days other arrests occurred, but they were of tangential figures, not named in the April 15 indictment. Several months later, Eldon "Bud" Cutler, an associate of Richard Butler at Aryan Nations, was nabbed in Idaho on a murder-for-hire charge: He'd offered an undercover FBI agent $1,800 to behead Tom Martinez. Cutler got twelve years.

By April's end, with the exception of Richard Scutari, the Order was in prison or being transferred west toward Seattle (all told, the government arrested sixty right-wing militants during its 1984–85 investigation). The roundup was so vast and the legal proceedings so complex, most qualified observers felt the Order's June 17 trial date would never be kept. A huge number of motions were on file and had to be considered. As summer approached, the government offered plea bargains to many of those arrested in return for their testimony against the Bruders Schweigen. Nearly half of the defendants turned over, increasing the bitterness of those who would not. Bruce Pierce hadn't turned, but word filtered back to the Pierce County Jail, where the defendants were being held, that he had confessed to several crimes to the FBI. His reputation as an Aryan Warrior fell hard and fast. Inside the jail, the other defendants looked to Frank Silva to assume a leadership role and recruit new members. He obliged; he was under thirty and had already been a Grand Cyclops in the Ku Klux Klan.

Less than a year before, the group had been exhilarated by guns and money, pursuing their own shortcut toward the American Dream. Sitting in prison, life slowed down. They turned pale without sunshine, lost weight, and a number of them became quiet or slack-jawed, as if they wished they had never heard of Bob Mathews. They learned to kill time, to wait, to relive those days when it seemed as if the revolution had wind in its sails and they would conquer. While they waited, employees at the federal courthouse in Seattle, the site of the upcoming trial, processed the growing number of affidavits, volume upon volume, being generated daily by the lawsuit.

"What's that case about?" a visitor to the clerk's office asked one afternoon when he saw the mounting documents.

"Oh," the secretary said, shrugging and smiling. "Last year a group of boys in Idaho had some fun in the woods. But it's over now."

# 27

---

# *A SMUDGE ON HISTORY*

---

The day after the initial scheduled opening of the trial—it had been moved from June 17 to September 9—was the first anniversary of Berg's death. Denver's reaction on June 18, 1985, was nearly as surprising as the one immediately following the assassination. Flowers arrived on the steps of his townhouse. Onlookers drove past the Adams Street residence to stare. Television and radio stations held lengthy memorials, and away from the media people talked about the dead man and his impact. It had, if anything, deepened in the community in the twelve months of his absence. On KOA, the audience heard tributes from his friends, ex-wife, listeners, co-workers, and from

Berg himself. Speaking of him, some people burst into tears, others into laughter. A number of callers wanted the suspects brought to Colorado, tried, and executed. Many who phoned the station imitated Berg's voice and sounded strangely like him, giving way to an outpouring of joy and grief.

Seattle, a far wing of the country, was a good setting for the RICO trial. Several of the crimes had taken place in the city: an armored-car heist in March, another in April, and the bombing of the Embassy theater, only a handful of blocks from the federal courthouse and the chambers of the Honorable Walter McGovern; when the trial began, the Embassy was featuring *Nasty Girls*. Seattle is a quixotic town, full of young people with backpacks, drunken bums and Indians, expensive shops on Fifth Avenue, a frenetic bay, a cosmopolitan feel for its size, and many transients who have drifted west across the nation until they ran out of land and took up residence on the city's streets. At dawn one sees them rising from concrete mattresses to start a long day of panhandling. By the waterfront, Orientals hawk vegetables, flowers, fish, lobsters, and huge salmon banked on tubs of ice. Potential Jack Londons fill the sidewalks with faraway looks in the eye. They might be writing novels or planning to jump a freighter to Alaska.

Rain comes early most autumn mornings. Near the bay railroad bells clang and mingle with the horns of ships gliding through the fog. Gulls cry and float past new office buildings, flying reflections in the glass. Brakes squeal at red lights at the foot of steep hills. Seattle remains bohemian, romantic. One can imagine Bob Mathews, Gary Yarbrough, Bruce Pierce, Randy Duey, and Denver Parmenter eyeing these streets and plotting to murder the Baron de Rothschild at the Four Seasons Olympic hotel. One can dream in Seattle, with all those tugs and freighters and passenger ships just out the window, saying someone is escaping, leaving, moving on to another life. These men could drift and dream too, bigger and bigger, tired of waiting for change, annoyed at history, anxious for something more. In Seattle it isn't so difficult to imagine rewriting your own life, or even the life of your people. And if that fails, ships are always coming and going, echoing in the harbor, departing for something fresh, gliding without resistance, and you can ride the next one to the water's end.

At the largest trial of a white-supremacy group in American history, security was beyond tight. If any of the Order's sympathizers were considering springing the defendants, the federal government wanted them to know precisely what they were up against. The U.S. Marshals Service sent more than a score of officers to Seattle for the assignment, which would last nearly four months. Each morning at 5 A.M. the marshals rousted the prisoners from the Pierce County Jail, put them in armored vehicles, drove them the thirty miles to Seattle, taking a different route as often as possible, and slipped them into a side door of the courthouse, while other marshals stood guard, flashing large black guns. At any given moment during the legal proceedings eighteen armed marshals were in the courtroom and four were standing in the adjoining hall. The defendants' chairs had been bolted to the floor to prevent them from being thrown. Metal detectors outside the chambers were touchy enough to pick up the nails in one's shoes or a pacemaker in the heart. Machine guns were hidden in the courtroom, in case of a riot. Armed guards controlled every movement into and out of the courtroom with grave seriousness, and a defendant did not go to the restroom without a marshal at his side. The accused were constantly handcuffed, except when court was in session. The only chance for trouble was when a marshal, exhausted from rising at 3 A.M. for another's day work, dozed off during testimony. But then the defendants sometimes fell asleep too.

At considerable expense Judge McGovern's courtroom had been rearranged to accommodate the eleven defendants, their eleven lawyers, the six government attorneys, a few FBI agents, and the plethora of U.S. marshals in the room at all times. The trial began on September 9 with the effort to select a jury, a more complicated affair than usual. Defense attorneys could reject up to twenty jurors on the grounds of prejudice. The case had received extensive publicity in the Seattle area and the beliefs of the Order were, their attorneys knew, going to be abhorrent to many people. After apologizing at length to the huge jury pool assembled on the ninth, and explaining that these were abnormal circumstances, Judge McGovern said he had to ask them their views on school busing, interracial marriage, and other political issues, and if any of them were Jewish. Some were, and in time they were sent home. So were the blacks, the Orientals, those with traces of foreign accents, and anyone else who appeared to deviate from a standard of white, middle-aged-or-older, Gentile, and poorly informed on the case. If one showed glimpses of having read or thought about the Order, he or she was dismissed. Even some white middle-aged Gentiles couldn't qualify. The judge asked one potential juror how he would feel if he learned that the defendants believed the Holocaust had never occurred. The man said he would find that unacceptable. What reason, Judge McGovern asked, did he have for feeling that way?

"I can think of six million reasons," the man said, before going home.

After three days—His Honor was not one to waste time—a jury was seated. It was comprised of nine white women and six white men; three of these fifteen were alternates, but no one among them knew who they were, keeping all of them alert for the duration of the trial. Judge McGovern also allowed jurors the option of taking notes, an unorthodox move. From the opening session, McGovern made it clear this was his courtroom and he could behave in it exactly as he wanted. A handsome, quick-witted man in his sixties, the judge combined good cheer and a withering tongue. He had a wonderful grandfatherly smile and each morning he traded jokes with the jury. He appeared gentle and understanding—for a while. If an attorney was having a problem formulating a question, the judge brushed him aside and posed it himself. If a lawyer was squandering time, McGovern frowned at him, and if that didn't work he interrupted and gave him a good scolding. He wore his emotions on his robe. The scuttlebutt in Seattle's legal community was that he was an extremely competent benchmaster and one should not be surprised if he were the next appointment to the

United States Supreme Court. He was, said lawyers who had worked in front of him, utterly fair during a trial, but at sentencing he could be harsh.

The prosecuting attorneys, who came from Seattle, San Francisco, and Idaho, were for the most part a jovial and confident bunch. They had a case and they knew it. Their head man, David Eugene Wilson of Seattle, was a tall balding fellow with broad shoulders, a strong jaw, and spaces between his teeth. He had the air of one who likes nothing better than putting criminals behind bars, and knows how to do that. When he spoke, Judge McGovern listened.

The defense attorneys were tanned, their clients sallow; by and large these lawyers were subdued. Appointed by the court to represent the clients, some of them conveyed a hint of distaste for the job ahead. Defending an outright murderer or rapist—especially one with an insanity plea—might be preferable to arguing the merits of an unrepentant neo-Nazi. Since being arrested, most of the defendants had professed a greater commitment to an all-white Christian nation than ever before; they ballyhooed what was now being called "the 10 percent solution"—taking the five states of Washington, Idaho, Oregon, Montana, and Wyoming, which make up roughly 10 percent of the American mainland, and purging them of blacks, Jews, and other minorities. In their opening statements the defense attorneys emphasized that the Order's political and religious beliefs were not on trial, and the defendants were guilty of nothing by having extreme racial or biblical views. Still, the hearts of several lawyers appeared to be elsewhere. Bruce Pierce and Randy Duey were in the front row of defendants, and throughout the trial Pierce whispered to his companion. On occasion he spoke above a whisper. His attorney, Mike Ruark, looked disturbed and embarrassed by this behavior, but also helpless. Pierce was as willful as ever—one could see it in the blankness of his eyes and the way he held his strangely delicate hands. Ruark had filed motions to have his client examined in depth by a psychiatrist, claiming that Pierce's mother had experienced schizophrenic episodes and Pierce himself was subject to blackouts in which he did things beyond his control. Little came of the requests.

While Pierce jabbered, Gary Yarbrough leaned back and closed his eyelids, as if meditating or snoozing. His prominent head, small eyes, and big red beard made him resemble a visionary nineteenth-century Russian writer. Jean Craig looked heavy and morose, like a farmwoman who has lost her farm. Richard Kemp had on a new gray suit and perfectly coiffed dark hair, but they couldn't hide his six-foot-seven awkwardness and shy discomfort. At twenty-one, he looked astonishingly young and innocent, innocent in a way that goes beyond the verdict of a courtroom. One of the original defendants, Tom Bentley, pleaded guilty after the first day of testimony. He had no stomach for the long ordeal. He was aging and all the blood seemed to have drained from beneath his skin, leaving him chalky and with an air of permanent fright. He looked in need of an iron lung. He got seven and a half years for his plea.

Frank Silva, the former Grand Cyclops from California, was represented by James Trujillo. Some Chicano attorneys might have rejected the opportunity to defend an avowed white separatist—the Order now insisting they were separatist and not supremacist—but Trujillo was color-blind. Before the jury, he spoke of Silva's plight with incisiveness and passion. He portrayed the diminutive fellow as a wronged man who had been arrested only to satisfy the government's desire to jail everyone on the far right. Silva, Trujillo contended, had done little but handle a few phone calls for the group, and this was after the major crimes had been committed (each defense lawyer, it soon became apparent, conceded that some of the other defendants had done all sorts of terrible things but not his own client, who didn't even know the others' code names).

Andrew Barnhill's lawyer was Anthony Savage, a rotund bearded man who walked slowly and spoke softly and could be likened to a prickly bear. Locally he was known as an attorney who defended those accused of the worst crimes—crimes that can lead to the death penalty—and sometimes he won. His name was perfect. He pursued his job with a savage interest. He used the law—its reason and its elasticity—to do everything in his power to help his client, regardless of what the defendant had done. Without question he was the best defense attorney in the courtroom and commanded the obvious respect of Judge McGovern. One of the longstanding complaints of Order members—David Lane in particular—was that blacks and other minority citizens were guaranteed free legal help. The Silent Brotherhood railed against a system that provided justice only for the very poor and the very rich. Average white men, they said, had no such good fortune. Andrew Barnhill, an average white man by every indication, had been appointed a lawyer who gave him the kind of counsel that money can't buy.

Lane's attorney was Brian Phillips, a meticulously dressed, well-spoken man with prematurely gray hair and the demeanor of a bright schoolboy. He rarely missed an opportunity to go into the restroom, during recesses, and smoke. Like the other lawyers, he allowed no one to interview his client; the theory was that if the defendants spelled out their ideas in public, they would be condemned for holding them. This was possibly a false assumption. A number of Order members were bright and articulate. Some were engaging and some were disturbingly intelligent.

Lane genuinely appeared to appreciate his attorney's good mind, and he seemed quite intrigued by what was going on around him. He watched the trial with a touch of pride, as if his group were, finally, after all the rhetoric and waiting, making a mark on history. Someone was paying attention to them. It was costing the U.S. government a lot of time and money to attempt to put them away, and every day, through the papers and other news media (or "Jews media," as Lane called it), the Silent Brotherhood was getting more public exposure. At the trial's opening, *Newsweek* magazine was present, *The Atlanta Constitution*, AP, *The New York Times*, UPI, the *Baltimore Sun*, TV and cable networks, papers from Portland and Spokane, the Denver media en masse, the *Chicago Tribune*, and a bevy of local reporters. Lane's expression indicated that this was a far more meaningful fate than writing for defunct periodicals or hustling dollar bills on a golf course.

Ardie McBrearty was the only defendant without a court-appointed attorney, the only one to take the witness stand. According to his wife, Marlene, she had to sell a bag of silver from their home in Arkansas to pay for his lawyer. Even that wasn't enough. Marlene had come to Seattle for the length of the trial and was looking for a job as a waitress, working nights, because she insisted on sitting in court every day. She saw herself as a goodwill ambassador, and with her husky voice, her smile, and her bright dresses with plunging necklines, she charmed more people than she baffled. Part preacher, part steady Christian wife, part hardscrabble woman—she looked like a country-and-western singer who had once touched bottom. Her worn, friendly face, her wavy black hair, and her patter all suggested Arkansas. She always seemed to have a Bible in one hand and a cigarette in the other.

"I opened the door and a gun was pointed right at me," she told a group of listeners one day, describing her husband's arrest. "I don't like guns. I got shot in the stomach eight years ago and I don't like 'em. Ardie knows that. We don't even keep one on the place, except for a BB gun." She took a long drag. "I made coffee for the FBI and we drank it in the living room."

Her repertoire in the courtroom was broad and deep. She blew kisses to McBrearty. She said the whole trial was in "the hands of the Lord." She instantly befriended every black reporter covering the case and was seen walking arm in arm with one of them through the halls of justice. She got one's attention and tried hard to keep it. Marlene said things like, "My husband may be a defendant but he *damned* sure isn't a guilty one," and the way she said it made one wish she were telling the truth. She flashed pictures of her Filipino grandchildren to everyone in sight, talked of what a fine young man her stepson was and what a law-abiding family he'd come from. The stepson himself, Marine Sergeant Danny Stokes, testified that Ardie McBrearty wasn't a racist and had readily accepted his marriage to a Filipino woman. One time McBrearty "sat me down and verbally thumped me on the head and told me to get along with that fine young lady," Stokes told the court.

McBrearty, for his part, had done what any thoughtful, tax-protesting, right-wing Christian might have done under the circumstances. He went out and got himself a brash Jewish lawyer. Neil Halprin, facing suspension from his practice in Montana on a legal technicality, was more than willing to come to Seattle and defend McBrearty. He needed the work, and had been involved in tax-resister cases in the past. He was fearless. On occasion he talked of his mother and said she was the only one among his Jewish family and friends who had criticized him for defending Ardie McBrearty against the United States of America. Did she protest on religious grounds? he was asked.

"No, no," he said. "It's not that. She just thinks that the government is always right."

Halprin, a cheerful young man with eyes that were usually asquint, was having a wonderful time in Seattle. As he paced around the lectern from which the attorneys posed questions to witnesses, he resembled a stand-up comedian. He asked former members of the Silent Brotherhood who testified on behalf of the government why they didn't like Jews. He asked them if they like Jews better now that they had struck plea bargains with the government; if they wanted to kill him, since he was Jewish; if it bothered them to use Uzis (Israeli-made machine guns) in their war on ZOG; if Jews were God's Chosen People; if they could learn to like him, because he was Jewish. He talked about the size of his nose and asked a witness if Richard Scutari's Mediterranean nose was bigger or smaller than his Jewish proboscis. Halprin was funny, outrageous, and at times a little reminiscent of Alan Berg. Watching him work, David Lane couldn't help but smile and even chuckle. Lane seemed to admire his guts, his refusal to be what others expected him to be, his joy in being different. Judge McGovern wasn't quite as amused. When Halprin would commence an impenetrable line of questioning, which went on and on and led nowhere, His Honor would sigh and pick the lint off his robe. When the robe was clean, he would lean forward from the bench and growl, "Let's get on with it, Mr. Halprin."

As the trial progressed, Ardie McBrearty looked more and more worried. He took great exception to being addressed by Peter Robinson, a government attorney, as the "Professor"—his alleged code name in the Order. And he became very upset when Robinson listed on a large sheet of white paper the six illegal things McBrearty was charged with doing; the first letter of each charge, read top to bottom on the paper, spelled GUILTY. This maneuver caused his attorney to throw a legal document and ask for a mistrial. During Halprin's long-winded performances, McBrearty stared up at him in dismay. He needed a lawyer, not a nightclub routine.

One reporter asked Halprin if he wasn't a little concerned about the neo-Nazi movement in America.

"I don't take it seriously," he said. "If I did and if I thought there were a lot of these guys running around the country, then I might worry about it."

He didn't take Bruce Pierce seriously?

"Bruce Pierce is psychotic," he shot back uncomfortably. "If ever there was a man who should enter a plea of not guilty by reason of insanity, it is Bruce Pierce."

The government called 290 witnesses (the trial's total was 370) and presented more than 1,500 pieces of evidence. The proceedings lasted 113 days. The most important witness for the United States was Denver Parmenter, on the stand for 6 days. He told the court he had been unstable for most of his adult life, and that the Order had given him self-worth "as a person who was fighting for my race." On reflection, he said, "I failed to recognize my own short-comings and lack of discipline." He stated that he did not dislike Jews or other minorities, denounced the Order's beliefs, and apologized for what he'd done. If he was acting, as some defense lawyers later accused, he had talent.

Like most of those who pleaded out, Parmenter faced twenty years in a federal penitentiary, although the government recommended him for early release. He told the court he no longer feared being killed by black or Hispanic inmates and incarceration was different from what he'd anticipated. He got along fine with the other prisoners. At times during his six days of testimony, when he became weary of talking, or when Tony Savage bore down on him in order to catch him in an inconsistency, or when Neil Halprin made it seem that he would never stop asking bizarre questions during cross-examination, Parmenter dropped his head and raised his hands in front of him. He was praying.

The defendant most visibly affected by Parmenter's testimony was Randy Duey. The two men had together ventured to the Aryan Nations compound in 1981, together joined the Silent Brotherhood, together committed crimes in 1984, and sworn the oaths of eternal loyalty. Once, while Parmenter was on the witness stand, Duey turned utterly pale and began whispering to his lawyer, Fred Leatherman. The attorney jumped up and requested that His Honor interrupt the proceedings briefly, so his client could visit the restroom. Judge McGovern said fine, Duey left with the guards, and soon came back looking much better. On press row the speculation was that he had vomited.

Tom Martinez also took the stand and shunned ideas he had once embraced. Defense attorneys badly wanted him to come across as a liar or a turncoat, and they did all they could to make this happen, but failed. Like all the government witnesses who were no longer espousing the party line (twelve former Order members testified against their old brethren), Martinez sounded almost noble decrying the Silent Brotherhood. He told the court, "The Klan, the National Alliance, the Order, all those groups have a lot of hate. They accuse the Jews of everything from fruit flies to airplane crashes. . . . It just isn't right. . . . I just realized I wasn't cut out for this sort of thing. I love my wife and kids too much to go around hating people."

Bob Merki told the jury that industrialist Armand Hammer and New York senator Jacob Javits, were, according to plans revealed to him by Colonel Francis "Bud" Farrell, to be killed in the future. When Ken Loff was asked why he became involved in the Silent Brotherhood, he gazed at the defense attorney posing the question and said, "You ever see a million and a half dollars? It does something to you." Randall Rader testified that even though he had trained people in the Order the techniques of self-defense and killing, he still believed in God.

"How do you think God feels about your activities?" Neil Halprin wanted to know.

"He's pretty aggravated," Rader said.

He added that he was drawn to the Order because he was poor and Bob Mathews offered him money, but his feelings about the group had begun to change after the murder of Alan Berg. Killing a total stranger in cold blood did not set well with him. As with Parmenter and Tom Martinez, Rader's trip to the witness stand was something he seemed to have been looking forward to for a long time.

Bill Soderquist, who had been granted total immunity, was unpunished and unrepentant. On the witness stand, this young, mentally gifted mind from Salinas, California, was surrounded by a beard and dark glasses. He appeared nervous in the courtroom; disguising his face was no doubt a good idea. He told the jury everything he knew and implicated nearly everyone on trial in a number of serious crimes. The defendants glared up at him, trying to penetrate his sunglasses and trying not to hiss. Soderquist was not only more than willing to send his ex-cohorts to jail; he was, so he testified, still a thoroughly committed neo-Nazi. He told the court that the Holocaust "is definitely overexaggerated" and there had been no "concerted effort to exterminate Jews during World War II." From his perspective, Jews continued to be the enemy.

"Did you see the pictures of the death camps where the women and children were waiting to die?" Mike Ruark asked him. (Ruark, Bruce Pierce's attorney, seemed to vent the anger and frustration he felt toward his own client on Bill Soderquist.)

"I saw what purports to be pictures of that," the witness said.

"Purports? The S.S. took those pictures," Ruark said. "Were the six million who died in the gas chambers—were their deaths the results of brave individual acts of Aryan Warriors?"

"I don't believe the premise exists."

"Mr. Soderquist, do you have any grasp of reality? You have so much experience ignoring the facts and manipulating the evidence, that you have no idea what the truth is anymore, do you?"

"No. I don't think that's true."

When asked if David Rockefeller was Jewish, as the Order seemed to believe, Soderquist said, "From what I've read, yes."

The judge listened with fascination and indulgence to Soderquist's remarks, until the witness implied that he—U.S. District Judge Walter T. McGovern—was part of ZOG, and under the control of Jews. His Honor sneered and rolled his eyes.

Steve Moen, the attorney for Richard Kemp, asked Soderquist

some pointed questions: Did it bother him that he was free while his friend, young Mr. Kemp, along with Randy Duey, was accused of killing Walter West? Did it bother him that he and Mr. Kemp faced very different futures?

"Yes," the witness said, but quickly explained that Kemp made up his own mind about the actions he took in the Order.

"It does trouble you?" Moen asked.

"Yes," Soderquist said, offering nothing more.

Kemp looked too bewildered to open his mouth.

A local Nazi, carrying a big red notebook, attended the trial for several days. He bore an eerie likeness to Adolf Hitler. Five Orthodox Jews appeared one morning and drew stares and grins from the defendants. They quickly left and never came back. Federal agents learned of a plan by Order sympathizers to blow up a fuel tanker on the street outside the courthouse. During the resulting chaos, a squad of guerrillas would charge the courtroom and free those on trial. The idea was never developed. The only violence that occurred was between a U.S. marshal and an FBI agent, when the fed, called to testify, tried to push his way past the marshal and met resistance. One visitor to the courthouse press room distributed a leaflet claiming that the Order was part of a Central Intelligence Agency plot and Bob Mathews was Jewish. He went upstairs to the seventh-floor chambers, sat through brief testimony, and on his way out gave the defendants a Nazi salute.

During the four-month-long ordeal, a Vietnam veteran, Gino Casanova, fasted for fifty-one days near Seattle, in an effort to bring attention to the missing-in-action troops left in Southeast Asia. After much publicity and many requests from Casanova, President Reagan finally called him and said he would consider what could be done for the MIAs. In Colorado, a farmer smashed the walls of his bank when he drove his tractor into the front of the building. In Iowa, Dale Burr, another farmer under extreme financial pressure, killed his neighbor, his banker, his wife, and himself.

A month into the proceedings, the government devoted a week to the slaying of Alan Berg. Although the defendants were not on trial for murder, the prosecution made the talk-show host's death the focal point of their case. The Order had declared a Holy War against American Jewry and one Jew had died in battle. The other crimes—robbery, counterfeiting, transportation of stolen property—could have been committed by anyone, but not the assassination. It was the logical result of the Brotherhood's ideology—and the most emotionally charged issue in the courtroom. When Berg's *60 Minutes* appearance was viewed by the jurors, several of them couldn't help but laugh at the man's mad energy and humor. When a videotape of the murder scene was shown, there were silence and tears (David Lane watched it with absorption but Bruce Pierce didn't seem that interested). In his closing remarks to the jury, chief prosecuting attorney Gene Wilson snapped his fingers, and when he tried to speak his voice cracked: "Bruce Pierce in no more time than that snuffed out Alan Berg's life. . . . They showed their friends the newspaper stories about the killing as part of what they had done. Everybody is happy. Everybody is joking. Everybody is proud. After all, they managed to kill him, even though Berg was armed with a lit cigarette."

After three and a half months of testimony and argument, the final jury of eight women and four men went into deliberation. Their instructions for reaching a verdict on the ten separate defendants were contained in a sixty-two-page manual, which took Judge McGovern several hours to read and explain to them. Two weeks later they emerged with a decision—all ten defendants were guilty of racketeering and conspiring to racketeer. Bruce Pierce, Randy Duey, Gary Yarbrough, and Richard Kemp were convicted for a variety of other crimes in the western district of Washington, although Yarbrough was exonerated in the bombing of Seattle's Embassy theater. On February 6, 1986, Pierce got one hundred years, Duey a hundred, Yarbrough sixty, Kemp sixty, and Andrew Barnhill forty. The next day David Lane, Jean Craig, Frank Silva, Randall Evans, and Ardie McBrearty got forty years apiece. Judge McGovern had given the defendants, who would be sent to federal penitentiaries across the United States, the maximum sentences available, but all would become eligible for parole in ten years.

The trial cost an estimated $3 million, and expenses for the FBI investigation that preceded it were put at a similar figure. Assistant U.S. Attorney Gene Wilson said the case was the most satisfying legal victory of his career. Tony Savage told reporters the defendants had gotten a fair trial, and other defense attorneys indicated they would appeal. Judge McGovern acknowledged that presiding over the case had been the most difficult chore of his twenty-seven years on the bench. While in deliberation, several jurors said they had discussed their fears of retribution from right-wing activists, if they convicted the members of the Order. They found them guilty anyway.

Following the verdict in Seattle, there was much talk of a murder trial in Denver. The local district attorney, Norm Early, often spoke of the possibility, but also mentioned the problems attached to it. Bob Mathews had told many people about the killing but he was dead; his words were not admissible in a courtroom. Under Colorado law each defendant in a murder case was entitled to a separate trial, and the rules of what evidence could be admitted were complex and tricky. At least three trials—for Lane, Pierce, and Jean Craig—would have to be held, and the cost, Early said, would exceed the $6 million in his annual budget. He would be forced to go to the city council and ask for more funds, just to complete this one lawsuit. What if he got the money and then lost the case? He had no witnesses, no confessions, nothing but circumstantial evidence. What if a skillful defense attorney convinced a jury of Denver radio listeners that Berg had provoked the killers?

If Richard Scutari was ever taken into custody, Early indicated, his office might consider plea-bargaining with him in order to convict Bruce Pierce and David Lane of first-degree murder, with a possible sentence of death. But the DA did not want to offer leniency to either Lane or Pierce to convict one or the other. Both men, Early felt, were equally culpable. In March 1986, Scutari was arrested in San Antonio, Texas, where he had been living and working in an auto-repair shop for nearly six months. In late April he pleaded guilty to the federal RICO charges and on June 5, he received a sixty-year sentence. The Denver authorities hoped to bargain with him in exchange for his confession against Lane and Pierce, but he refused to talk with them out of a sense of personal loyalty and fear. Immediately, and accompanied by outrage and protest both within and beyond the legal community, the district attorney announced that the Alan Berg case was closed in Denver. For the foreseeable future, the murder has been dropped.

As Randall Evans was being led from the Seattle courtroom after the final day of the federal trial, he told those assembled that "Christ is King!" Randy Duey, from Pierce County Jail, proclaimed that the Lord would get them out of prison and away from the black and Hispanic cons. Bruce Pierce said he hoped to bring glory to God, adding that it wasn't a matter of *whether* something would happen to spring them from incarceration—an earthquake or a parting of the penitentiary doors—but only a question of *when* the miracle would occur. Gary Yarbrough promised to spend his time behind bars recruiting new members to the Order's philosophy. Watching the trial unfold from Hayden Lake, the Reverend Richard Butler told the press that the verdict would have no effect on his church or Aryan Nations. "The word of God goes on," he declared.

"There were no surprises, no emotional things of one type or another," David Lane said of the trial's outcome. "It was simply a fact, but there is only one true judge, history, and there is nothing we can do about it. If your system can't stand us, be rid of us. We will ask to be exiled or deported to any white nation that will have us and let us live among our own kind, and we will never darken the shores of this continent again."

*EPITAPH*

———

# VOICES, LIVING
# AND DEAD

"Meeting him for the first time was like seeing an eight-piece band come through the door playing out of tune."
  —*Bob Palmer, Denver's KCNC-TV*

"He did a whole show once on which way to roll your toilet paper—over or under. People responded for hours. Some got so angry they hung up."
  —*A caller*

"One day he said he was gay and it shook up the whole town. TV stations came out to interview him. The next day he said that in the dictionary *gay* means having an exuberant personality."
  —*A caller*

"He got me through a divorce and my sister through a stillborn baby. Just by listening to his show."
—*A caller*

"The highest compliment is when someone who hates me, can't stand me, goes in and patronizes a sponsor of my show. They're saying, 'I don't like Alan or what he stands for, but I believe him.' The beauty of talk radio is that you're paid to tell the truth. I can think of almost no other profession where that's true."
—*Alan Berg*

"His mind was like carbonated water."
—*Judith Berg*

## ALAN

*My Friend, Lover, Mentor, Partner*
　*was murdered*
*Gunned down in the street*

*I heard, sighed, cried, died*
　*a little inside*

*They called from near and far*
　*for a comment, to detect emotion,*
*extract a notion*

*I could not sleep, constantly weeped*
　*and felt no feeling in my body*

*I cried his name, talked to him, asked*
　*him why he had to die. I told him*
*stop kidding around—get up—get*
　*off the ground*

*He laughed, red hair streaked, cigarette*
　*in hand and said—*
*They love me, I'm a Star.*

　　—Audrey Oliver, paramour

"He was like a magician, always trying to conjure up the demons, always saying bad people were waiting out there to get him. They finally showed up, just like he said they would."
—*A listener*

"The guy was just obnoxious. Just obnoxious."
—*A listener*

"After John Lennon was killed, he said the Beatles were overrated. He said that just to make people mad at him."
—*Ev Wren*

"Don't say to me what you think you're supposed to say. Don't tell me, 'I think gays are all right,' because most people don't think gays are all right. It's the new era—you can't dislike blacks, you can't dislike Jews. Baloney. You can dislike anything you like in this world. Most people are racist, most people are prejudiced about one of many things. . . . Even people who do things together are isolated because they don't get to say the things they really want to say."
—*Alan Berg*

"He died for our sins."
—*KOA talk-show host Ken Hamblin*

"He wasn't a martyr for any cause, unless it was committing suicide."
—*A listener*

"Apparently talk-show host Alan Berg angered the wrong person once too often. . . . Among those 200,000 [listeners] were many, many people he would insult in typical obnoxious Jew fashion. The favorite victims of his arrogant and rude remarks were the American Nazi Party and others who shared their common dream of a white, clean and wholesome America."
—*Glenn Miller, in* The Confederate Leader

"He just said the wrong things to the wrong people too many times. They got tired of it and solved the problem. You don't have to agree with them to understand what happened."
—*A listener*

"Talk radio is like Russian roulette. When you push that button,
you never know what will happen."
—*Alan Berg*

"He looked at the dark side, the ugliness, in himself and wanted
others to look at it in themselves. That makes folks uncomfortable."
—*A listener*

Elderly woman caller: "I changed the spelling of my name and
    didn't have any trouble gettin' Social Security. My birth certif-
    icate had my named spelled differently."
Berg: "Wonderful. Do you have any view on lesbian priests?"
EWC: "Uh, no."
Berg: "Any view on masturbation?"
EWC: "No."
Berg: "Just let it be?"
EWC: "Just let it all hang out."
Berg: "Do you believe in a statute, like in Arizona, where they say
    that if you get an erection in your pants it's a felony or misde-
    meanor?"
EWC: "Well, I, I, I'm not really interested in that. If they wanna
    do it, let 'em do it."
Berg: "Can you imagine being arrested for something that might
    happen in a totally uncontrolled situation? A man is walking
    down the street and he suddenly gets an erection. Can you imag-
    ine him being hauled into jail?"
EWC: "That's ridiculous."
Berg: "Isn't it? Hah!"
EWC: "But this name business. I didn't have a bit of trouble gettin'
    Social Security."
Berg: "Fine. Good for you."

"I adored him. I've never been so close to a man. I was watching
a comedy show on HBO when a friend called and said, 'Alan's
been shot.' I said, 'Oh, shit.' I got chills. I got dizzy. I didn't sleep
a wink that night. I went into my bathroom and just cut loose. . . .
I would have done anything to make him happy."
—*Ev Wren*

"I remember the last time I talked with him. He called me in '77 or so and asked me if I wanted to see his new car. I said, 'What the hell have you got now?' He said, 'I've got a Bricklin.' We met and he showed it to me. It was made in America. A horrible bust. Junk. Alan drove it a few times and it began falling apart. Had a helluva time. He couldn't get a door fixed. Typical of Alan. Never bought anything that made any sense."
—*Bob McWilliams, former boss at KGMC*

"I didn't know I was a bad dresser until I heard him talk on the radio."
—*A listener*

"He'd come into the restaurant two or three times a week and one time I said, 'You're such a beautiful person and you get on the radio and you're such an asshole. Why do you do that?' He said, 'That's my shtick.' I don't think I really bought that answer but I don't know what the answer was. I'd hear him tear someone apart on the radio and I'd think, That's not you. But it must have been because he wasn't that good of an actor."
—*Tom Wilscam, Denver restaurateur*

"Whether in between the two sides of Alan Berg there was a 'real' Alan Berg I would love to have known. I wasn't through with him, with trying to figure him out, with understanding what drove and motivated him. Before I had a chance to make those final decisions, he was gone."
—*KOA general manager Lee Larsen*

"Could a healthier person have played that public role? No. A 'healthier' person would have been so introspective and reflective that those things would be automatic censors on what they said and did. A nice little dose of craziness made him what he was. After being around him, you felt dull."
—*Dr. Kathy Morral,*
*Denver forensic psychiatrist*
*and guest on Berg's show*

"Had he been healthy, he'd have been a great lawyer and we would have had kids. But he was very neurotic and very enticing."
—*Judith Berg*

"I'm not half of what I should be. I could have accomplished so much more in my life if I had not been so caught up in neurotic behavior."
—*Alan Berg*

"It was karmic. You can't put out that much bad karma without it coming back."
—*A listener*

"To my dying day, I will hate the sonsabitches that took him away from us."
—*San Diego media personality Laurence Gross*

"My first thought was that I couldn't believe anyone could hate him that much. Disagree, dislike, but not kill him. My second thought was that he always wondered if there was a God. He said we had to wait until the evidence was in. I thought, Now you know, Alan, now you know."
—*KOA producer Anath White*

"The killers made him a very serious person. It's like, Hitler created Israel. Did you know there is now a memorial forest in Israel for Berg?"
—*A listener*

"At the memorial service someone said, 'If Alan were still alive, he'd be defending the person who killed him. He'd be taking the role of the underdog.' I know what they meant."
—*Tom Wilscam*

"In his mind no two ideas were mutually exclusive."
—*A listener*

"He couldn't take yes for an answer."
—*A listener*

"He was morally outraged without being morally superior."
—*A listener*

"He had something beyond the courage of his convictions. He had the courage of his perceptions."
—*A listener*

"The worst call is, 'I agree with everything you say.' They aren't thinking when they say that. I don't agree with myself all the time, so how can they?"
—*Alan Berg*

"If he could have had all those little parts of himself acting in a well way—but it was too overwhelming and you become tired. So you do the best you can, which is to become very angry and very funny."
—*Judith Berg*

"On the air, he presented this image of a person who didn't care about what others thought of him. He cared desperately about what others thought of him."
—*KOA talk-show therapist*
*Dr. Andrea Van Steenhouse*

"He always knew he could perform mentally, and with words, but not sexually. There were always doubts. That must be why he often told people he had trouble in that area."
—*Judith Berg*

"Alan was a pathological liar and he didn't know what to do about that. He put his head in my lap and cried about it. He was okay well. He didn't need all these other things, but he thought he did, to be interesting. God knows he was interesting enough without any of the lies."
—*Judith Berg*

"Judy has described him in some sense as a pathological liar. But in terms of his feelings about life and people and issues, he was very honest and connected to the truth. So much so that someone couldn't stand it and killed him. They didn't like what he had to say, because the truth hurts."
—*Doatsy Peifer, a friend*

"Free speech isn't free at all. It's a very expensive commodity."
—*Frank Oliver, Chicago attorney and friend*

"He said that fat women who wore tight pants deserved the death penalty."
—*Ev Wren*

"He would pull a nationally well-known name out of the Denver phone book, like Jesse Jackson, and say he would be on the show tomorrow. Then he would call up Denver's Jesse Jackson and put him on the air."
—*A listener*

"If you have the chance to be on [the radio], why not enjoy it? It's all going to end one day. There's nobody who ever entertained who didn't finally have his career one day cut short. It's gonna happen to me."
—*Alan Berg, December 15, 1983*

"I've gone back and forth. I've admired him and hated his methods. But he had an impact on people, and that's why we call people important, not because they were good or bad. He made people think about who he was and what he was doing."
—*A listener*

"As opposed to somebody who does good—or who creates things—Alan brought things out in people. They would call him and a part of them that was unacceptable was getting out. They could never have acted that way otherwise but it was all right with him on the air. He had an enormous impact on people. That was his gift."
—*Dr. Andrea Van Steenhouse*

"Sitting in the radio booth doing my show, one thing leads to another and I get a roll going and I hear him talking to me and then it ends and I think, Jesus, this guy had more of an effect on my life than I ever realized. Sometimes, he possesses me."
—*Ken Hamblin*

Elderly woman caller: "I expect you to hang up on me. You are the great humanitarian who makes people miserable three hundred and sixty-five days a year."

Berg: "It shows what masochists people are, when you look at what I've done in talk radio. If people have such a need to listen all the time, they must have an enormous need to be masochistic. Why are you listening now?"

EWC: "I'm listening . . ."

Berg: "Why? If I make people miserable three hundred and sixty-five days a year, you must have a need to be miserable. Also, considering that I'm not on the air three hundred and sixty-five days a year, you don't count well."

EWC: "That's right."

Berg: "Unless you play tapes of my show on the weekend to make yourself further miserable. If you really think I am such a terrible broadcaster, you really are a masochist. I don't stay tuned to anything I don't like. You really have a problem."

EWC: "I do, I do. I agree with that."

Berg: "Now, maybe we can find a cure for you. Would you like the name of a doctor? Would you like to come to my Common Sense Counseling Program?"

EWC: "No, I don't think so."

Berg: "Perhaps I could help you through this grief you're experiencing."

EWC: "I'm not experiencing grief."

Berg: "What is the point you're making—that I bring grief to people? Why do you listen to me?"

EWC: "I don't, Alan, I don't."

Berg: "Oh, darling, I don't think you've missed a show I've done for the last seven years I've been in the business. You're always there and you always know what I've done. It's an amazing thing for a lady who says, 'God, you make me miserable.' "

EWC: "I'm waiting for a certain program to come on."

Berg: "Well, why turn here? There are thirty-four other radio stations in this town. Why turn here if I make you miserable?"

EWC: "You don't make me miserable."

Berg: "You realize what a hypocrite you're making of yourself?"

EWC: "I feel sorry for you."

Berg: "You made an utter fool of yourself. You have no credibility. You *dig* what I do. You have a need. Unfortunately, you have no sense of humor. And that's why you can't ever enjoy this show. And that's why you're a loser, as are all people who

313

have no sense of humor. And you are categorically one of them. Bye!"

"Our view is that you don't give groups like the neo-Nazis or a Colonel Mohr access to speak on the radio, as Berg did. You don't give them the chance to spread their poison. They're outside the pale. Basically, I couldn't stand Alan Berg."
*—A spokesperson for*
*the American Jewish Committee*

"In the recent past, hard-core fundamentalist thinking has affected all religions. The Christians, the Jews, the Moslems, the Sikhs. It can set the stage for all kinds of actions. If God tells you to do something, how can it be wrong?"
*—Don Jacobson, Denver lawyer and former head of*
*the Colorado Zionist Federation*

"I really resented it when he went to Israel. At the time I was in the Allied Jewish Federation in Denver and when that organization sponsored him, I told them, 'This guy has no feeling—other than an occasional corned-beef sandwich—for anything Jewish.' When you get to Israel, regardless of what you are, you are at a lot of religious places and you will have feelings. Alan was a stone. Maybe he was like his father, and anti-Semitic."
*—Allan Lackner, fraternity brother of Berg's*
*and best man at his wedding*

"Norma and I were together when we learned who had killed Alan. We started to laugh. We said, 'Of all things. Alan being killed because he was a Jew.' The most un-Jewish Jew imaginable."
*—Ruth Berg, his mother*

"I can't absorb it. I think he's still out there in Denver doing his thing on the radio."
*—Norma Sacks, his sister*

"His head was shaped like a question mark."
*—Judith Berg*

"It's ironic that a man who lived a life that was whimsical and fantastical should be killed by a group of people living out *The Turner Diaries*. A fantasy group killing a fantasy man."
*—Beth Ames*

"It was the most logical way his life could have wound up."
—*Norma Sacks*

"It doesn't surprise me that they killed that bombastic, vitriolic human being but it does surprise me that they killed that gentle, melancholy man."
—*Beth Ames*

"In the movie *Bambi*, during the forest fire, the mother deer says to the fawn, 'Run, Bambi, run!' Those words are on his headstone. They summarize his whole life. He was always running."
—*Norma Sacks*

"I'm an outlet for frustration. I'm a focal point for them to dislike something other than what they, in fact, dislike. . . . It's always someone else's fault, not theirs. I've never seen so many victims in my life and I end up being the victim." He laughs. "I take all this heat and I'm a nice person."
—*Alan Berg*

"We did fashion shows around Denver and guys would show up and want to fight him, until they saw him. Then they would say, 'This isn't the person I was dreaming about punching out.' Alan wasn't big enough, tough enough physically, to do what he did. To walk that talk, as cons say. He lived like he had an invisible force around him."
—*Judy Wegener, former Denver talk-show host*

"They killed the mockingbird."
—*Peter Boyles*

"He called his show the last neighborhood, the one location left in an increasingly mechanized society where people could find someone to listen, but in truth it seemed as if the person most in need of the neighbor was Alan Berg himself. . . . Who could Alan Berg have become? This is . . . the real tantalizing, frustrating question, never to be resolved even if the technical criminal matter is clarified in full. Some will miss Alan Berg as he was; others will not. All should miss what he—what any talented person cut down before his time—could have become."
—*Obituary, Denver's* INTERMOUNTAIN JEWISH NEWS

"Alan knew about David Lane. He talked about him and was afraid of him. He honestly felt that if his demise came, it would be at gunpoint with David Lane."
—*Judith Berg*

"Lane crapped his pants. That shows you what a novice he was. Or that he liked Alan Berg."
—*A listener*

"Isn't it strange that he felt it necessary to update his insurance policies in 1984?"
—*Judith Berg*

"If you challenge people's beliefs, it's like pulling the rug out from under them."
—*Alan Berg*

"He went down so fast it was like someone pulled the carpet out from under him."
—*Bruce Pierce*

"Berg was always ashamed because he knew he wasn't one of God's Chosen People."
—*A listener*

"Maybe he was, after all."
—*A listener*

# II
—

# *IMAGES, MOVING*
# *AND STATIC*

—

Early in the summer of 1985, the Denver Police Department had a series of pictures on display in one of their downtown offices. Most depicted the Aryan Nations compound in northern Idaho and several members of that group, but the largest was of Alan Berg, dead, naked, lying flat on a table at the morgue. Pale-skinned and so thin as to appear frail, his body had an aura of blue. His hair was longish, in an unmodern or perhaps Roman, way, bulletholes had left gashes in his side, his arms were slightly spread, and his face was recognizable despite the thirteen rounds delivered at close range. He looked better than one would have expected and yet, there was something very dis-

—

turbing about him, beyond the fact that he was dead and had obviously been murdered. He didn't look like Alan Berg. He looked like . . . had he been vertical as opposed to horizontal, had his hair been darker and he somewhat younger, had he been wearing thorns on his head, he would have resembled scores of medieval paintings of Christ on the Cross. The image was alarming enough to make one turn away.

Later that summer, Warren McKinzie was walking in Denver's Washington Park on a warm Sunday afternoon, a day with the right mixture of sunshine and breeze. Young women on bicycles glided past him, their hair reflecting the sunlight, and he stared after them with his dark searching eyes. His muscular arms and beard added to his air of seriousness. McKinzie has an undertone of spirituality that comes out with time and probing. It could be his lapsed Mormonism or his past flirtation with the Ku Klux Klan and Aryan Nations or his sense that there should be more than brilliant Sunday afternoons with bicycles and women flying past.

From time to time he blinked, a kind of denial.

"I can't imagine him being locked up," he said. "Dave loved moving around, being free."

He walked along a path, leaves overhead catching and returning the light. Rain had fallen not long before and the smell was still in the park, on the earth and grass, an odor of freshness. In the distance were more bicycles, children jumping and tumbling, ducks on a body of water near a boathouse, a collage of light and warmth and motion.

"It doesn't add up to what he was like," McKinzie said, shaking his head. "I can't imagine being stupid enough to kill Alan Berg and then to keep the gun around. The first thing I would do is get rid of the gun. Wouldn't you? You've *got* to get rid of the gun."

Judith Berg sat in a station wagon in front of 1445 Adams Street, the engine running, her foot on the accelerator as she stared at the townhouse. From the street, holes were visible in the garage door, four of them, pockmarks in the wood. In the year since the death, she had never driven down Adams or walked past the address or gazed at the front of the building. There was no traffic in mid-afternoon and the summer air was heavy and quiet and gray, adding to the silence of the street.

She whimpered, and raced the engine. She barely nodded her head, backed the car up, drove forward, almost aiming it toward the garage door, changed her mind, brought the station wagon to a stop nearer the curb than before. Her lips trembled as she stared at the concrete driveway. Gripping the steering wheel, she craned her neck to glance up toward the third-floor apartment.

"He was the only person I could trust," she said. "Couldn't trust anyone else. Ever."

Tears ran down her face and she clutched the wheel tighter.

"I just wish I'd been with him when he came back home. I don't want to know what I learned afterwards about people. How they think, how they felt about him, how they felt all along. He fought so hard for everything, like a maniac. He was so goddamn opinionated. In spite of all the illness, all the problems, his brain went on. It got better and better. He fought all his life to be as well as he was. Maybe he wasn't where he wanted to be. I know he wasn't. But so many things were in the way. He had more guts and more fight and more moral fiber than anyone, regardless of what people said. He had the greatest hands, always moving, with the blood pouring through them. When he talked, his temples—you could see the veins."

She brushed at the tears, raced the engine harder, gave an exhausted sigh.

"He just wouldn't give up. He just wouldn't shut up!"

She put the vehicle in gear and backed along the street, wiping at her cheeks.

"If I could just hear one more word. I can't listen to the tapes. I can't. One more live word."

Judith changed gears and drove north on Adams Street, reaching Colfax Avenue and turning right, slipping into the afternoon traffic. She was no longer crying and when she spoke again, of the number of cars surrounding her, the voice was softer and not trembling and she was caught up in the flow of automobiles, weaving in and around the others as she traveled east on the busy thoroughfare. A strange calm, a dull gray one, matching the summer afternoon, filled the interior of the station wagon.

Driving straight for two or three hours she would have reached the empty open plains of eastern Colorado and then the more barren stretches of western Kansas, hundreds and hundreds of square miles of farmland and pasture, of lightly populated territory that had once been within reach. On a June afternoon farmers are in the fields, harvesting wheat or planting a summer crop or cultivating one already in the ground. Modern combines and tractors have radios to warn of bad weather, to entertain and keep away the loneliness of riding for hours over dust. One ceaseless questioning voice could make a thousand deserted acres seem crowded, like a roomful of chatter and ideas, and move an indignant farmer to drive his implement home fast, run into the kitchen, grab the receiver, and make an impassioned apologetic telephone call. The atmosphere is less charged since the murder. This afternoon the heavy summer air might bring rain or just the stillness that settles above the countryside but doesn't split any clouds.